FIRST THOUGHTS

A Psychoanalytic Perspective on Beginnings

Jayne Hankinson

PHOENIX
PUBLISHING HOUSE
firing the mind

First published in 2022 by
Phoenix Publishing House Ltd
62 Bucknell Road
Bicester
Oxfordshire OX26 2DS

British Library Cataloguing in Publication Data

A C.I.P. for this book is available from the British Library

Paperback ISBN-13: 978-1-912691-26-5

Typeset by Medlar Publishing Solutions Pvt Ltd, India

www.firingthemind.com

For
J^3R

Contents

Part II
Engagement with the phenomenon

Part III
Reappraisal

Part IV
Reformulation

A tribute to Chris Mawson

This space, normally occupied by a foreword, has become a tribute to Chris Mawson who died in November 2020. He had very generously agreed to write the foreword for this book, and had just started before he very suddenly died. He had written in the notes section of his phone the following:

> ***Foreword to* First Thoughts**
> *A famous student of ancient forms of the art of unarmed combat once advised that we should try to take in what is useful, discard what is not and to add what is uniquely your own—wise and challenging advice in learning any art. I found this book to be expressing in a language that is very much her own, Jayne Hankinson's ...*

I am intrigued to think about what else he might have written, but his note certainly fits with my hope that readers see this book as an attempt to discover my own thoughts and realisations through combining my experience with the learning of others. He had been deeply acquainted with my ideas and had constantly encouraged me to "write a book", and as such, there would have been no better person for me to ask to write its foreword. I think it is very apt to include here, instead, a tribute to him.

I first came across Chris when he was giving some seminars on Bion almost nine years ago. I had looked forward to these seminars as I was keen to learn more about a Bion that had become enigmatic in my mind. Chris's enthusiasm for Bion and his manner of leading the seminar stood out from a growing awareness of the enormity of Bion's legacy. These seminars took place before *The Complete Works of W. R. Bion* had been published, and Chris was generous in sharing with us some of Bion's original writing, and also the details of how he had laboured alone over the editing for more than a decade. I remember feeling awe, not so much about Bion's writing, but for the application and dedication Chris had demonstrated in completing such a mammoth task. These were qualities that impressed me about Chris over and over again in the years since that first meeting. It was also during these seminars that I learned he lived and worked very close to where I lived.

My contributions during these seminars had been positively taken up by Chris and, to my mind, I felt that, perhaps, he had overestimated my capacity and understanding. This feeling pervaded my experience of Chris to the extent that when I was looking for a supervisor I decided that I would not approach him—I felt I could not live up to what I felt his expectations to be. However, finding a supervisor that would work logistically (these were pre-Zoom times!), as I lived outside London, and who would fit in with my psychoanalytic thinking, proved to be harder than I imagined. I was eventually left with little choice but to approach Chris, and he graciously accepted.

During the first year or so of meeting weekly for supervision, any thought that Chris might have had an overinflated view of me dissipated. I was left with a feeling that my work did in fact constantly disappoint him, and I struggled with my confidence. What began to emerge, though, was the awareness that Chris was very fair. He could equally both praise and criticise with sincerity and passion, and I also began to appreciate his capacity and excitement in just "following a thought".

This coincided with my growing personal interest in beginnings and belonging. I had already written, for myself, Chapters Nine and Ten in Part II, and had begun to develop further thoughts about Adam and Eve. I was beginning to think in terms of an Adam psychology and an Eve psychology and this came into a supervision one day. Chris encouraged me to talk more about it and we were soon immersed within a shared space of thinking and fascination. We began to meet twice a week, once for supervision and another just to talk about life, philosophy, psychoanalysis, and the universe—and this continued right up until his death.

These meetings were at one and the same time microscopic, macroscopic, and megascopic in that they followed wherever our thoughts took us, one moment looking within atoms and the next moment the whole universe; one moment looking at psychoanalytic theory, the next looking at *Doctor Who*. He took every thought seriously and was able to call upon a huge encyclopaedic knowledge of Bion, Klein, Freud, philosophy, literature, and more in his associations wherever our discussions took us. He constantly amazed me by even being able to know the pages within a text from where his quote had come from.

I greatly enjoyed these meetings, and he both challenged and encouraged me to take my thinking even further; and often, I think, I challenged him to take his thinking further too. I feel very privileged to have had this opportunity to "just talk" with someone who had an obvious excitement and passion for thinking, and who took my thinking seriously.

Over time, Chris moved out of the realm of being my supervisor, or mentor, to being my friend. He was supportive through some personal difficulties, as was I to him when difficulties came his way. I met Donna, his partner, and he talked about her and his children and grandson with enormous love and pride. It was evident that he was entering a very creative and happy phase of his life, and it is a great sadness to me that this future was only partially realised.

My last conversation with him was a phone call at the beginning of a half-term break that he was taking. He'd had an urge to call me as he had been reading the draft that I'd sent him of my book. He said that he had to let me know that he was really enjoying it and had had to number the pages as he had been taking notes as he was reading. True to form, my immediate reaction was to think about all the things I felt were wrong about the book, and I started to tell him the list of problems with it. This had been a repeated experience with him over the years, but, this time, when I started to do this, I stopped and simply said, "Thank you," and accepted what he was telling me. I was greatly moved and appreciative that he had taken the time to call me. We had a few email exchanges in the following days, one of which was about the foreword, but he died before we were able to meet again.

Chris' death has left a big hole in my life, and I am aware of the even greater loss for Donna and his family. He was thoughtful, caring, sensitive, full of excitement and passion for thinking, challenging, encouraging, and much more—and this book would not have been written without him.

Part I

Dissatisfaction

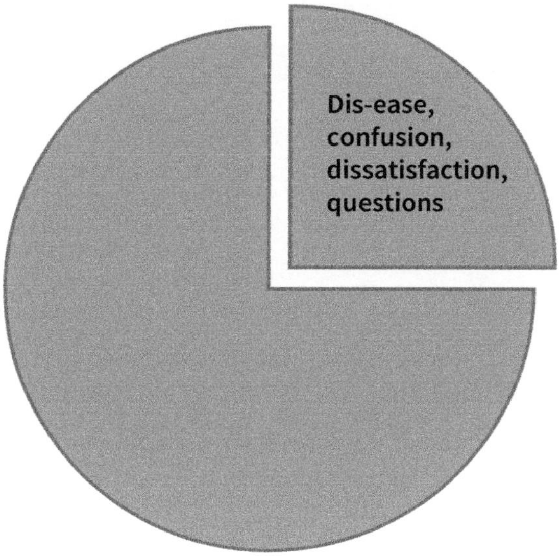

Setting the scene, or the first quarter of my hermeneutic loop

Wisdom is to discern the true rhythm of things; joy is to move, to dance to that rhythm.

—Old Russian proverb

CHAPTER 1

My beginning

This book has come about from my long-standing struggle to find my own path and identity, both within my professional life as a psychoanalyst, and my personal life. As such, the starting point from which this struggle has taken place is important to consider.

The ignition that started the process was my experience during training, and, in particular, a confusion about belonging. It resulted in an attempt, more than eight years ago, to "discover" a beginning that sufficiently satisfied several aspects of myself—my "hats" of psychoanalysis, science, childhood, and, above all, being female. This attempt is included in Part II. As, at this time, I had already developed an interest in creation myths, beginnings, and forms of belonging, my attempt cannot be said to be uninfluenced by this interest, but I can say that I approached it with a freedom of discovery and that I let it take its own path. The place I arrived at in the course of my experiment was the story of Adam and Eve. The impact of this exercise has been fermenting ever since, and I found myself starting to think of Adam and Eve not as separate mythological beings, but as modes of being that exist in dynamic tension within *all* minds, male and female. Initially it was a useful way of understanding certain personal difficulties, but it soon spread to be a useful way of thinking about my patients. Over the next few years, this thinking developed and deepened and has resulted in this book.

This is a deeply personal book. The concepts and discoveries I arrive at come from something within, and, as such, they "belong" to me. They are, mostly, not new; but what might be considered different is the frame I am attempting to set them in. I cannot treat each concept I arrive at during this personal struggle with a literary search and citations; I would get lost and the book would become something else entirely. I have obviously done so with themes I've arrived at through research, but I haven't done so with themes I've gained insight into as a result of my own endeavours and struggles. These I feel I have "ownership" of, even though many have owned them before me. If you like, these parts come from what I have begun to consider as an "Eve" aspect of me, and thoughts, concepts, or words that come from Eve are different from those that come from Adam. They have been smelt, tasted, seen, heard, and felt—discovered at a visceral level, not learnt by a sophisticated Adam aspect of mind.

Freud in *Moses and Monotheism* (1939a) talks about "a victory of intellectuality over sensuality" (p. 114). Here, I am advocating a "right to be" for sensuality (in that it is based upon the perceptual and feeling-aware realm) and the status of everything that emanates from this part of the mind to be "owned" by the discoverer. As W. R. Bion (1967) says in *Second Thoughts*:

> [A]ny psychoanalyst must find his own way and come upon well-known and well-established theories through experiences of his own realizations. It is clear that the realization which approximates to a theory he has learned will be unique, and may therefore appear to be so different from the theoretical formulation that he cannot recognise the bearing of the one upon the other. By contrast he will force a theory to fit a realization because it is difficult for an inexperienced analyst to tolerate doubt ... There can be no harm in errors of this kind: "original discoveries" of the already well-known, and "confirmation" where none would be found if clinical flair were mature. It becomes fatal to good analysis if premature application of a theory becomes a habit which places a screen between the psychoanalyst and the exercise of his intuition on fresh and therefore unknown material. (p. 169)

Bion recognised the difference between discovery through intuition and realisation, on the one hand, and the learning of a theory on the other; I am advocating for the status of "original discovery" to be valid. It is "original" to the particular thinker—it has been "thought" from experience—and therefore has a right to be "own[ed]" by that thinker, even if countless others have owned it before. Bion also states how important it is for this type of thinking to be available to the psychoanalyst—it is this thinking that changes a treatment into an authentic relational experience from which the patient can benefit.

When I stumbled into psychotherapy and analysis in my early thirties, I devoured everything I came across. I read books and papers from the first word to the last and then reached for the next one. I have understood this as being a very strong epistemophilic drive, but also a quest for meaning that felt urgent to me. From the realisations I come to in this book, I could say that my Adam mind was acting, and trying to take in something, which would give meaning to Eve.

The influences, occupations, and preoccupations in my preceding years had been an upbringing in a broken, working class family in South Wales, being a secondary school science teacher, and being a mother to my three very individual children. I mention this as this book is concerned with beginnings, and my starting point has been important in setting the scene for what I am now writing.

How I have perceived the world and myself, and the corresponding struggles with belonging, can all be traced in my thinking and searching for something that felt like the "truth". While recognising that one person's truth is not necessarily the same as another's, I was searching for something that could help me make sense of "me", as well as resonate with what I knew about the natural world. I needed it to correspond with both my sense of something inside and my perceptions of the world outside.

A memory from my childhood that had puzzled me for many reasons has also helped me understand that perhaps I was always going to be a psychoanalyst. This memory has been fundamental in how I have formulated the concepts in this book. When I was about eight years old, I had been taken by a friend and her father to a derelict house in a countryside setting. This ruinous and collapsed house had a big impact on me, and I vividly remember feeling that one day I would return to this site and build a house for myself to live in. I can understand this experience in many ways, but what confused me for many years was both why I had remembered it so vividly, and my inability, due to feeling overcome by shame, to talk about how I had felt. This memory, together with other aspects of my "beginning", began to have a life of its own in the sense of a need to find a structure from which I could orientate myself.

This personal quest was a big factor in my epistemophilic stage, and it persisted until probably halfway through my analytic training. This coincided with being established in my analysis too. I began to feel that while some aspects of theory resonated, others simply felt wrong. My quest still felt alive and kicking, but I was not so easily satisfied. In particular I was at first disturbed, but later fascinated by, the vehemence demonstrated by some of the adherents of any particular theory, and the oppositional nature of the various "clubs". How could this be and how could this fit with my initial view of psychoanalysis as a bastion of truth and tolerance? Surely to be an analyst was to be able to tolerate all truths, to continue growing and asking "why?" It occurred to me that the vehemence was due to the fact that each adherent was working from a position of *believing* their particular theory to be *the* truth, and considering the *other* theory to be either not upholding this truth, or a destabilising influence on it—that is, a threat to the "structure" of the belief.

This phenomenon was to become fundamentally intriguing and important to me. There seemed to be something overarching going on, something that perhaps was being enacted or having an influence in ways that were obscure and unconscious. Again, how could this be, when the actors in this enactment or drama were the analysts themselves? How can several theories and positions be accounted for, which arouse vehemence and outright denial between each other, and still all be thought of under the umbrella of the quest for the truth? There seemed to be something bigger, some frame which had yet to be named, something influencing those who were supposedly the freest of minds.

My thoughts during this time started to become preoccupied with beginnings. It began to feel very important what the particular beginning each individual structure of mind emanated from; or, more accurately, what particular phantasy of beginning could be discerned. I began to find out about the various creation myths that exist and discovered repeated themes and phantasies.

It started to become apparent that, in writing this book, I was engaging in what Reg Harris (2015) has called a "hermeneutic loop" (see Figure 1).

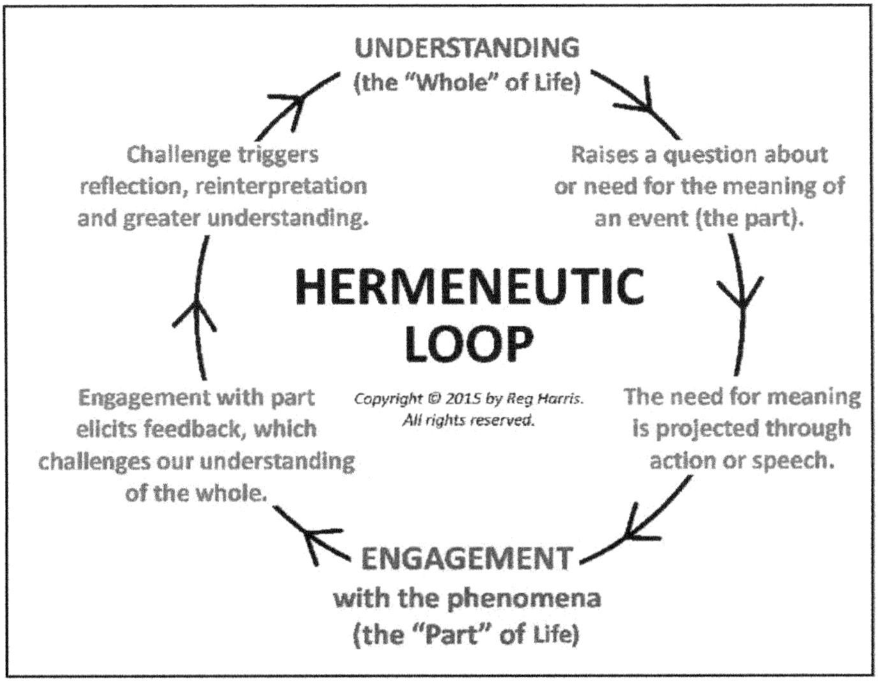

Figure 1. Reg Harris' hermeneutic loop

Hermeneutics is all about interpretations—how we interpret ourselves, the world we live in, and our position in it. As John D. Caputo (2018) writes:

> We move around within this interpretation without even appreciating that interpretation is going on, that the world in which we live, and we ourselves, have *already been interpreted.* When we arrive in the world, the interpretation of the world is already up and running … It is like the air we take for granted, something we do not notice unless it is cut off or fouled by some odour. It is given by simply being taken as *a given,* without … giving it a thought. Interpretation is always running in the background while our attention is taken up by what is going on in the foreground. So, the work of hermeneutics is to *work out* our "always and already being interpreted", to bring it to the forefront or the surface. (p. 35, italics in original)

Harris' hermeneutic loop seemed to be a process by which this attempt to bring the "givens" to the foreground of thought might be possible, whilst also being a dynamic and constant re-evaluation of the world as it is experienced. This book has evolved naturally into something which follows this process for me. I started off feeling unsettled and uncomfortable with the structures which were available. I then raised questions and had a need to find meaning and belonging, especially in relation to my training. This led to active self-exploration and research—I became engaged with the phenomenon. This engagement then elicited feedback which began to challenge my view of a larger structure, which led to a greater understanding of the position in which I found myself. This enabled me to have a deeper understanding of how I saw the "whole of life". I have adapted and personalised Harris' loop into one which follows my trajectory in writing this book (see Figure 2).

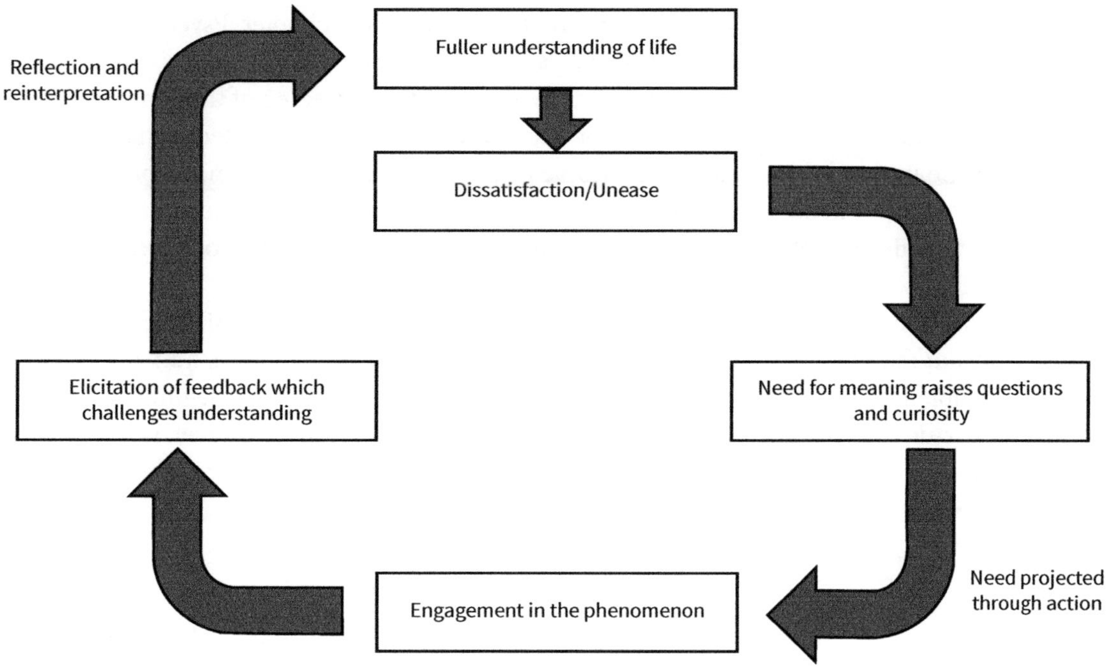

Figure 2. Adaptation of Harris' hermeneutic loop

In a way, this is no different to the processes which could have influenced the authors of many of the creation myths I am looking at. They would have felt the same dissatisfaction with the prevalent understanding, and would have had similar needs for structure and the assuaging of anxiety. I have noticed a difference between certain types of creation myth which allow for this hermeneutic loop process and those which do not.

There are many myths which do not allow for an evolution of knowledge—they are more like dead metaphors, used consciously and unconsciously to remain in a particular way of thinking and being. They exist to justify a particular *present*, rather than as structures to represent a search for the truth. From this perspective, they are more of a hermeneutically influenced straight line than a loop. The processes that initiated the straight line might be the same as those for a loop, but the result is stagnation rather than a fluid and evolving system.

My hermeneutic loop has resulted in a fuller understanding of life for me—a considerable claim, but nonetheless true. With regard to its use for others, a wish is for my loop, presented in this book, to encourage the creation of further hermeneutic loops.

The "straight line" creation myths, prevalent in all cultures, provide a perspective from which to understand developing states of mind and relationships to anxiety, fear, the unknown, and between male and female—but the wider frame they insinuate has not been addressed. An evolution of these myths, and the establishment of alternative myths which represent a fuller understanding, has not occurred; perhaps because of an important difference between written and oral myths, which I explore in more detail in the next chapter. Psychoanalysis can be caught up in the same disputes and in the same stagnation of thought that is inherent in these myths, and it is only by understanding a wider frame that a freeing of thought can occur. While the structure I arrive at will no doubt become redundant or outdated, it has served a purpose for me in that it has widened my frame of reference and enabled me to put words to aspects of my sense of being that were missing before. I would hope that in becoming aware of my process, a reader might question and discover what their own unconscious creation myth might be and also understand the importance of doing so.

In thinking about creation myths, religion also inevitably needs to be considered. While this book isn't *about* religion—I am trying to consider the "beginnings" of nature, humankind, and how we are able to "be" in the world—religion and its conception of the "beginning" form a point of departure for my exploration of Creation. What I have written, however, is primarily a musing; a freeing of thought and following it wherever it leads, and this is the approach I apply to religion too.

* * *

These "setting the scene" chapters in Part I will elaborate on various themes and ideas that I consider relevant to the understanding I arrive at, and which I will be referring to later. They follow the trajectory of my thinking, starting from the awareness of an unease:

- I begin by introducing creation myths, and explain how I use the word "myth", before looking at psychological developments that can be seen within them.
- I then move on to explore the themes of "presence and absence" with reference to Mendeleev and the periodic table. I had begun to see things as being "present" or "missing" in certain psychoanalytic theories, and was often confused as to how they could fit all together. Mendeleev's process demonstrated a hermeneutic loop as well as an ability to bear the unknown. His story shows the importance of curiosity and the need for a frame to be in place.

- In the next chapter, I look at the dispute between Augustine and Pelagius at the Council of Lod. This dispute was to do with the location of God—whether he was to be found outside, in a transcendent position, or located internally. I feel that the exploration of the enduring nature of this dispute might shed light on present-day battles within psychoanalysis.
- "The binding of Hans" focuses on a catastrophic state of mind that comes about when an outer, society-wide illusion meets the internal world and its perceptual apparatus. I represent this by looking at the story of *The Emperor's New Clothes*, and the philosophical trolley problem. These are important as they represent the dilemmas that arise when we come across any theory which is being used to represent reality. The event horizon—between the perceptual apparatus, an external, lived societal illusion, and an inner awareness of needs, wishes, and anxieties—is an enormously complex one. The individual "solution" to this dilemma inevitably involves the sacrifice of one or more of these essential factors. The pressure to join the prevailing creation myth is powerful, and resistance to it often means punishment and isolation.
- The next chapter explores the complexity behind the belief that *in the beginning was the Word*; or, more accurately, the difference between a belief in the "start" as a word, and a belief in the "start" as chaos. The awareness of the psychological importance of this difference began to be significant, especially with respect to the necessity of a structure which had a place for a maternal function.
- The final chapter discusses "circularity and straight lines". In becoming immersed in the themes of "beginnings", I looked deeper into Jewish mythology and became aware of Adam Kadmon. Chayyim Vital wrote about the teaching of Luria, and he highlighted the importance of "circles" and "straight lines" to their ideas in formulating the concept of Adam Kadmon. In this highly anatomical description of a beginning, several bodily and psychological functions can be identified. Among the rich symbolism is an acknowledgement of projection, introjection, container–contained, and interiors and exteriors. This shows the enduring nature of the theories within psychoanalysis, and suggests that these fundamental bodily themes have had a presence in the mind and a representation in thought since time began. Our response to them is a primary influence upon behaviour, character, and disturbance.

Part II is a conceptualisation of a fundamental beginning, and a working towards something more complex. It is highly speculative, and therefore depends upon the reader extending both a dramatic and a scientific licence to it. I also begin to investigate penetrative processes, magical structures, and the concept of wholeness.

Part III looks at the work of Sigmund Freud, Melanie Klein, Donald Winnicott, and Wilfred Bion with a view to formulating my understanding of what their particular creation myth or sense of beginning might be.

Part IV outlines my position following the process of writing this book. It is the "deeper understanding" that arises from engaging in my hermeneutic loop.

This book is a chronicle of my struggle and suffering with a question, and the eventual arrival of my truth. I do not wish to claim it as a definitive truth, but, rather, as a truth that has helped me.

I hope that in reading my musings, you will begin to question the nature of the "always and already being interpreted" beginning that influences your "being" and that this ignites the start of your own hermeneutic loop.

CHAPTER 2

Creation myths

The most important question anyone can ask is "what myth am I living?"

—Attributed to Carl Jung

In becoming interested in creation myths, I believe I was trying to make sense of something that seemed elusive and unrepresented. I then had a wish to find a story or structure that could "hold" this elusiveness, whilst also saying something important about what *was*. Myth has served this purpose for millennia. From the ancient Egyptians, who provide the world with the earliest known creation myths, to the present day, these myths have represented events, cycles of nature, and gender dynamics, and have had religious importance for more than 5,000 years.

Each myth can be shown to reveal a particular "solution" arrived at, at a particular time in history, which "answers" the psychological dilemmas regarding existence, being, and how man (Adam) sees himself in relation to woman (Eve), and other creatures. The solution or myth that is arrived at then serves as a "container" or structure which is drawn upon to allay fear and anxiety, and also to enable the person to become able to "be" in the world. Without this structure, "being" is impossible.

I am using the word "myth" here to try to draw a distinction between it and fact, documentary, fiction, fantasy, and so on. In using "myth", I am inferring something which has evolved primarily as a defence against primitive terrors, as well as a means of satisfying the need to express something relating to the unconscious "reality" (phantasy). In a way, the "reality" of the illusory experience is to be found within the myth.

Thus, a myth (for me) both represents and expresses states of mind, and incorporates the defences against awareness of these, and, at the same time, says something about the nature of the unconscious reality. Interestingly, more in its written form, it can also serve as a tool used to preserve the defensive structure, and to reinforce the hierarchies that are inevitably created. Once the myth has been created, it also serves as a "container"—something which provides a structure within which people can place themselves. This structure has the impact of reducing anxiety, and this function also serves to perpetuate the structure even though it may defy nature and reason. Hence, creation myths are held onto, even when they seem to be in direct opposition to nature and reality.

This way of defining myth is partly similar to Lévi-Strauss' statement (R. A. Segal, 1999) that myth is distinctive in not only expressing oppositions, which are equivalent to contradictions, but also in resolving them: "[T]he purpose of myth is to provide a logical model capable of overcoming a contradiction" (p. 46). He suggests that myth resolves a contradiction dialectically by providing either a mediating middle term, or an analogous but more easily resolved contradiction.

These myths can also be referred to as "origin myths", but I am going to use the term "creation myth" throughout this book. I am choosing to do this due to the meaning that the word "creation" conveys. The *OED* suggests that "origin" can mean "that from which anything originates, or is derived", a "source of being or existence", a "starting point". "Creation" can mean "the action or process of bringing something into existence", or, in relation to religion, "the bringing into existence of the world or the universe", especially when regarded as an act of God.

Given these myths are almost all concerned with the how, the why, and the when "life" and the universe were created, usually by an act of a God, the use of "creation" appears more accurate. For those myths which do not overtly have a "creating deity", but describe the bringing into existence of "something" via a *process,* the first definition of "creation" also applies.

"Origin", from the above definition, evokes a particular time and place which represents a fixed beginning with nothing before it. The word origin also lacks the dynamic nature which these myths embody, not only in the sense in which they were written—depicting a creative force bringing the universe and life into existence via some process—but also in the awareness of the science behind how things interact and come together to make complex forms and entities. Processes are involved. As a consequence of these insufficiencies, I prefer the term "creation myth".

Creation myths are found throughout the world and are stories which become part of humanity's collective development. They can be seen as attempts to explain natural phenomena, such as how the earth formed, but they also provide a rich insight into society, behaviour, and psychological forces. They have had a profound effect on ancient cultures, and, together with ritual, can be said to form the foundation of religious beliefs. They have influenced all forms of cultural expression, values, attitudes, and the mind.

The first stories were inevitably delivered through the medium of speech. Stories would have been shared, and served a purpose not only in explaining the unknown, but also in allaying fear. For instance, the people of ancient Egypt were dependent upon the Nile flooding every year to fertilise the ground. If the flood was too great or too little, the impact was severe.

The fears inherent in these situations would have been alleviated by a story, and in this way the cycle of nature could be passed down the generations.

These first oral myths would have evolved not only over time, but also from one telling to another. Each narrator might render a slightly different story to the one originally heard, as well as adding or omitting aspects according to their own knowledge, fears, and needs.

The evolving, mutating, shifting, and developing nature of these oral myths represents something of great importance. The myth is flexible and can incorporate new knowledge as well as adapt to each specific need. It is like a living and breathing entity which can not only learn, but is also gracious enough to be able to change its mind and adapt to a new situation.

The earliest known creation myths are those of the ancient Egyptians. These oral myths can be shown to be in existence from about 3000 BCE and earlier. The evidence of these myths is mainly art and tomb wall decorations, and interpretation of these shows that there were many differing stories of Creation featuring many differing gods and motifs. It wasn't until the Egyptians started to use writing more extensively during the Old Kingdom (*c.* 2686–2181 BCE) that the myths perhaps began to take on an enduring form.[1]

This progression—from the first perceptions of the natural world along with need and fear; to developing a language to begin to communicate; to an oral myth which holds knowledge and fear, but also serves as a container; and then to the written myth—has had, I believe, a profound impact on how we see ourselves and others.

I will expand on this to try to show how the movement away from the oral myth tradition towards the written myth could have the impact of stagnating development and forcing myth into directions which favour the formation of gods over the appreciation of nature and reality. I will also look at the contents of creation myths and show that the processes they are concerned with are dynamics between the genders, anatomy, projective and introjective forces, birth and death, and essentially "who" has the power to create, or who "owns" Creation.

Cosmology—the creation of the universe

Across Egyptian history, each major city during a particular era developed or adapted its own creation myth according to which particular god that city worshipped. These gods were originally local deities in these cities, before evolving and rising to prominence.

[1] As Regulski (2016) notes, by the beginning of the first dynasty (*c.* 3150 BCE), hieroglyphs were becoming more extensive; leading to the earliest known complete sentence in *c.* 2690 BCE. For the later Old Kingdom, (2686–2181 BCE), it has been estimated that only 1 per cent of the population possessed writing skills, almost entirely men, and the social setting in which writing emerged was dominated by the ideology of sacred power and performance of royal ritual.

Hermopolis (from the early Old Kingdom)

(*Hieroglyphic writing was being developed*)

The earliest known myth is that from Hermopolis (*c.* 3000 BCE and earlier) and is depicted in the hieroglyphic writing of the pyramid texts (Hart, 1990, p. 11). It is focused on the nature of the universe before the creation of the world. It suggested that in the beginning were the primeval waters which consisted of the Ogdoad, a set of eight gods. Each of the four male gods had a counterpart female goddess. Nu and his female Naunet represented the inert primeval water itself; Huh and Hauhet represented the water's infinite extent; Kek and Kauket personified the darkness present within it; and Amun and Amaunet represented its hidden and unknowable nature, in contrast to the tangible world of the living. These two groups of males and females eventually converged and interacted explosively. This burst of energy thrust up, out of the water, the primeval mound located at Hermopolis and the god Ra was born, who created all which came after (Allen, 2014, pp. 159–160; Hart, 1990, pp. 19–21).

Heliopolis (from the Old Kingdom)

(*Mummification was first used in* c. *2600* BCE *and writing on papyrus was growing*)

By *c.* 2600–2150 BCE, the prevailing creation myth in Heliopolis had shifted to include Atum, a deity closely associated with Ra, but who was said to have existed in the waters of Nu as an inert potential being alongside the Ogdoad. His name means "Lord of Totality" (Allen, 2014, p. 175). This myth suggested that Atum was a self-engendered god and the source of all the elements and forces in the world. He, through his own means, appeared on the mound and gave rise to the air god Shu and his sister Tefnut. The myth suggested that he was able to do this by using a "masturbatory" process and the "use of his hand". Other versions of the myth also suggested that he "sneezed" Shu out of his body and "spat" out Tefnut. The generation of Shu and Tefnut has been described as "when he was one and evolved into three" (Allen, 2014, p. 177). Shu and Tefnut then coupled to produce the earth god Geb and the sky goddess Nut. Geb and Nut then have children who represented the forces of life—Osiris, god of fertility and regeneration, Isis, goddess of motherhood, Set, god of chaos, and Nephthys, the female complement of Set. These nine gods were grouped together to form the Ennead and represented the process by which material life was made possible. The eight lesser gods, and all other things in the world, were ultimately seen as extensions of Atum (Allen, 2014, pp. 175–177).

Memphis (The Middle Kingdom)

Later, in Memphis (*c.* 1500 BCE), the god of craftsmen, Ptah had slowly gained importance and gathered powers (Allen, 2014, p. 205). The capacity of craftsmen to envisage a finished product and shape the raw materials to create that product was especially revered. Ptah was said to have created the world in a similar way to the craftsmen. As Allen (2014) notes, the "Shabaka Stone" text references the Heliopolitan creation account before continuing:

> But much older is Ptah, who enlivened all the Gods as well as their life-forces ... through this heart and through this tongue ... His Ennead is in his presence in teeth and lips, which are the seed and hands of Atum: for Atum's Ennead evolved from his seed and his fingers, but the Ennead is teeth and lips in this mouth that pronounced the identity of everything. (p. 205)

This was a retrospective claim to establish Ptah as having preceded the Heliopolis account, and focused on creation being in the realm of thought and words. The ideas developed perceptions within Ptah's heart (regarded by the Egyptians as the seat of thought) which were given "form" when he named them with his teeth and lips as a "pronouncement". By speaking these names, Ptah produced the gods and all other things. Ptah's creative thought and speech were believed to be the origin of the formation of Atum and the Ennead (Allen, 2014, pp. 204–206).

Thebes (The New Kingdom)

For the people of Thebes (*c.* 1500–750 BCE), Amun, a member of the Ogdoad of Hermopolis, was the hidden force behind all things. All the ideas of creation attributed to other gods became conflated within Amun, who transcended all other deities (who were thought of as immanent). In being "beyond the sky and deeper than the underworld" (Hart, 1990, p. 22), Thebans thought of Amun as the force which caused both the Ogdoad and the Ennead to form and, due to being transcendentally separate from the world, his true identity was hidden from the other (lesser) gods. At the same time, as he was the ultimate creator, all these other gods were merely aspects of Amun (Allen, 2014, pp. 222–223). Hart elaborates on this further, and says, "in the words of the Leiden hymn, Amun is 'too great to inquire into and too powerful to know'; the penalty for trying to get illicit information on his identity is expressly stated as instantaneous death" (p. 22).

* * *

It is my contention that, looking at these myths and their development over time, they can be seen to be directly influenced by the evolving means of communication, the awareness of science and thought, and by gender "disputes". The oral tradition was giving way to the written tradition as well as the representation of representation itself.

The observable shift in this progression—from a "primeval water" holding the essences of four male and four female deities who interact to form a mound from which Creation can occur; to Atum "creating" himself and then creating through masturbatory or bodily effluents; to genesis arriving through "thought" and the "word"; and finally to a transcendent "super god"—can also give an important insight into the development of the mind. The evolving means of symbol formation and representation has to be considered as a factor influencing the evolution of not only the myth but also the mind.

I don't think it is a coincidence that Atum arrived in the psyche of the myth narrators during a period when writing was becoming established in Egyptian culture, along with the expansion of scientific knowledge.

If I think of a time before words (in infancy, or prior to language), then the "containing function" is a maternal one. Looking at the great apes, the young spend a great deal of time during the first years clinging to the mother. Mother is the protective force and allays fears—even as adults, as Frans de Waal (2006) notes, male bonobos are known to seek their mother's protection when alarmed (although chimpanzees behave differently). A young primate not only learns from his mother's behaviour and responses to a wide range of experiences (dangerous, pleasurable, survival-based, climate, social, and so on) but is also able to internalise her capacity and use it as a structure from which he can also "be" in the world. When alarmed, the immediate container or relief of fear and anxiety is mother and her body. Later, when the infant is becoming independent, the container is that structure carried *within* the infant which "makes sense" of the world. This is what I am referring to as the personal creation myth needed by all who have managed to emerge from under their mother's care.

This time, before words, is nature-based and built on a sense of experiencing the world, learning, and "taking in" primarily the mother's capacity to allay fear. Females would have also been observed giving birth and being able to feed the young; therefore the act of creation, nurture, and making the world safe might seem to be capacities that "belong" to the female. In ancient societies or in the mind of an infant, these capacities, without awareness of the "science" behind them, might seem magical and enviable.

When communication became possible for hominids and words began to serve as symbols or representations of objects and experiences, the maternal containing function might have diminished in importance, in the minds of the male in particular. Now it was possible for the male to "teach" the young through *his* words. Instead of creation being "magically owned" by the female, the male could now "create" himself—he could create words which could appear to be a substitute container. He could name things and feel powerful—power to control as well as to impart knowledge. This use of the word as an external substitute container suggests that the actual containing process using the female body and mind can be bypassed.

In looking at a variety of myths from all over the world, I have been struck by the repeated references (some obvious, but others more subtle) to anatomy. It seems that myths evolved according to increasing knowledge of the internal body, and sometimes in direct opposition to that knowledge. Anatomy, the inside of bodies, the differences between the male and the female, and how life is created are some of the enduring mysteries which have perplexed humanity for millennia.

In the Hermopolis myth, the starting point is the primeval waters which hold the essences of the eight gods—the Ogdoad. Not only would the ancient Egyptians have had an intimate relationship with, and need of, the River Nile—it alone provided the fertile ground from which they could sustain themselves—but they also would have observed the waters released from the female body before birth. From this dual impression, the fertile Nile and the fertile water of the female body, their myth might be seen to represent something fertile and creative that emerges from the primeval waters. It also represents the idea that something explosive and energy-releasing needs to occur between male and female elements before creation can occur. This explosive energy might be considered the orgasm that accompanies sexual intercourse, or it might also represent the lightning strikes that bring the rain to flood the Nile. The myth is attempting to represent something that is experienced, as well as serving as a structure to make sense of the world. It also emphasises that Creation is brought about via the interaction between a male and female.

For the people of Heliopolis, things had changed. Writing was now more available and so the means of representation had shifted from an oral tradition, with art work, to an increasingly written one. I imagine that the awe and power associated with the transition from a time without words to words is similar to the transition from the oral to the written. If a movement away from "no words" to words had the impact of bringing the paternal function[2] into existence and reducing the importance of the maternal function,[3] then the movement from the oral to the written would further amplify this effect. The person who could use words would be able to name, create, contain, and control. The person who could write could not only take advantage of all that speaking conferred, but would also be able to set his words down for eternity. Eternal life was possible—the creation myth that was once flexible, alive, able to evolve and incorporate new knowledge, was now set down and imposed on generations as something that *is*. A structure of mind, or "solution" to fears, of a particular group of people in history, was now something deemed to be written in stone—an unchanging "truth" not able to evolve. This promise of an eternal life is, in reality, a dead, stagnant metaphor which quickly outgrows its usefulness. It is interesting that mummification was first used in this time too. Entombment of the mummified body to attempt to ensure a good afterlife was in fact ensuring an eternity of its inability to become incorporated into new life.

Atum, in Heliopolis, is now able to create "himself" without the intercourse that had a representation in Hermopolis. He creates through his own bodily secretions, and as a result the male is "owning" creation for himself. This movement from the earlier myths being based more or less in nature, to more magical and narcissistic methods can be seen throughout the world. It is the progression from the time without words to words, to the written form. It involves the birth of the paternal function, and the male feeling, as a potential outcome of this, that he can

---

[2] By "paternal function", I mean that "position", "thought", or "word" which can be utilised by both males and females alike, and is arrived at by a process of thinking originating from an external source (either a law, knowledge learnt, regulation, religion, taboo, etc.). It does not involve the penetrative process of curiosity.

[3] By "maternal function", I mean that "position", "thought", or "word" which can be utilised by both males and females alike, and is arrived at by a process of thinking originating from an internal source (awareness of experience, feeling, fear, anxiety, love, etc.) and the capacity to reduce anxiety. It involves the penetrative processes of being receptive to the tumult of the infant and "maternal" curiosity.

"own" creation for himself. For the authors of the Heliopolis myth, sperm and all things male have taken over creation. The myth has now evolved to serve another purpose—that of maintaining a favourable position for the male elements which wish to promulgate this new way of being.

For the people of Memphis and their worship of Ptah, the situation had shifted again. Ptah was the god of craftsmen, working with his hands to produce something. This recognition of the work inherent in creation seems to be an echo of the recognition of the work involved in the maternal function. The mother works with her hands and mind to hold and nurture the infant, resulting (when adequate) in the creation of an independent person whose "being" or "self" can exist in the world. However, what is worshipped in Memphis isn't the work itself, but the thought that comes before "naming". The nature of this thought could be considered to be maternal, in that a mother would be able to engender thoughts (and words) about her infant which can then give the infant a form and a self, however, in Memphis, this process seems to have become appropriated into the paternal function. This is able to be inferred due to the lack of "coupling" represented in the myth—things are brought into existence by Ptah's thought and words. The ethereal is given priority over the forces and elements of the material world—that is, thought is revered above manufacture—and thus the intangible creativity of man is prioritised over the physical creativity of woman.

Creation from the perspective of the maternal function always involves the process by which a "penetrated object" and a "penetrator" come together in equality to produce something. It can then not only mean the product of reproduction, but also the product which is created from a maternal function process—the giving of form to something that would otherwise remain formless—and the inner awareness of self.

This maternal function—a structuring and forming of the self of the infant—requires the penetrative acts of maternal curiosity and the ability to receive the tumult of the unformed inner world of the infant. What is then created is the thought, or idea, or form of what was previously unformed. This process can then be owned by the individual mind upon maturation. Words, thoughts, ideas, forms, and the sense of self and other are all products of this type of creation.

Creativity in the paternal function provides something different—constructions and interpretations more involved with the external and the gaze (not from the inside). This process can involve the use of imagination or ideas to create something from an external interpretative position, and is rooted in learning, external observation, and so on. It has occurred without the penetrative action necessary in the maternal creation. This type of creativity is that art which can accurately represent what is seen in the world, or interprets the world from an "uncoupled" perspective. Creativity from a maternal function perspective involves an awareness of an inner interpretative realisation. Of course, most creativity considered "great" would combine both positions.

The movement from a male and female coupling, to a male creation, and then to a thought and naming creation, shows the vagaries of gender dynamics, the evolution of a particular kind of narcissism, and the growing separation of man from nature.

The creation myth from Hermopolis seems to be serving the function of a structure which can incorporate knowledge, allow man to orientate himself within the universe, and allay fears. It is not overdetermined. This kind of myth is flexible and grows with knowledge and development. The myth that is in place in Heliopolis is different; it states that Atum has created himself and can create by himself. This says very clearly that man, in his ultimate form, does not need woman: creation is a male preserve. This myth is serving as a structure to justify a state of being for man, and comes about through envy and a wish to own creation for himself. It is as though man has felt the power inherent in words, naming, and writing and sees it as superhuman; he can be a god, own creation, and have eternal life. He is not only superior to woman, but can also justify seeing her as an object owned by him to give him pleasure.

The creation myth prevalent in Thebes has shifted again. The main god (or superhuman who has been thought into existence in order to "know" everything that is unknown, and is the source of creation) is Amun. Amun is a transcendent, omnipotent, and omniscient god, the one "true" god. As the myths are moving further away from real experience and knowledge, each mutation of an original oral myth can be thought of as coming about due to fear, envy, a need for power, and also a defence against awareness. The myths are structures which now justify a present which is reinforced by the myth's existence. If, in Heliopolis, someone might say, "But wait, creation cannot exist without coupling"—thus raising questions about the nature of the myth—a person in Thebes cannot do so, as the answer would be, "Amun knows everything and cannot be questioned."

Transcendence, omnipotence, and omniscience are the qualities that all gods will inevitably end up possessing once they have been "thought" into existence. Whether it is a god set up by an ancient tribespeople, or a personal response to, say, a reading of Freud, Klein, or Winnicott—one which takes their writing and words as doctrine—there is only one outcome. That is, the god, or words, or writing will eventually need to be thought of as transcendent, omniscient, and omnipotent.

If all gods who are thought into existence in this way have gone through this progression, and can be seen to be the end point of a story put in place to justify a particular state of mind, then the evolution of the stories can reveal the development of a male narcissism. By this I mean the narcissism which comes about from the Adam aspect of *all* minds. Although it may be more easily seen in males, it also exists in females.

Each story, from Heliopolis to Thebes, is striking in the reduction in importance of the female element. The omission of female functions and their appropriation by the omnipotent male shows what happens in this form of narcissism. All reminders of reality need to be eradicated, and the female position needs to be restricted. If the demiurge is unconditionally male, then even the female capacity to give birth and nurse the infant becomes something which can be denied. In this situation, the biggest threat to the structure of life that the creation myth is espousing is awareness of reality and nature, and the biggest source of this awareness is the female body itself.

If the female has lost her position as an equal partner in the creative act, as the body that nurtures and brings life into being, and as the source (that is, in being the penetrated object—the receiver of projections) of the maternal function (which gives form to the formless), then all of these qualities will need to find a place somewhere else. They are needed for life itself, and so need to be thought of as being somewhere else. Over time, every god will need to become omniscient, omnipotent, and transcendent to prevent challenge—and, once this occurs, the god will also need to appropriate the female aspects and maternal function, which are now stripped from the female. It is interesting that a similar progression can be seen in the Christian Bible between the Old and New Testaments, whereby the figure of Jesus can be said to take on the maternal function.

I have been trying to demonstrate a progression that I see in the evolution of creation myths. From the oral beginnings of something essential in providing structure, meaning, and an allaying of fear, to something which is used to preserve a way of being which serves a fearful, power-hungry, and envious aspect of mind.

This state of affairs leaves the female body and mind unchartered, as she is left unrepresented in the prevailing creation myth (or the personal structure that an individual unconsciously applies to life). She becomes the mysterious threat to the structure the male aspect of mind has created—the actual site of the primeval waters, chaos, and disorder that gods (in the myths) defend against. The very processes that might remind the male (Adam) of nature, and what he has done to the female (Eve), become abhorrent to him. If he were to go inside the female and see what is there, not only would his world structure crash down, but he would be fearful of seeing the damage he has done. It is interesting that the Christian Church actively prohibited the science of anatomy for almost 1,000 years and it was only around the early twelfth century that the science began to grow again.

In viewing woman only as an object of pleasure, man's penetration of her body becomes one which is without love, as it is without her equal involvement. He blinds himself to what might be inside, leaving him with only the outside to gaze at. Beauty, aesthetics, and his gaze become the meanings in life—all giving him a pleasure that is an appropriation of the joy that is only possible in equality. This pleasure is of the same order as his orgasm—sought to excite and gratify him from a position of feeling in power and being able to "own" his world. The true joy of connecting with nature and having pain received is a distant memory, or, if it is more available, is projected onto a god figure in order to maintain a position of superiority over the female.

While the creation myth at Hermopolis might be considered a story which can serve as a hermeneutic loop, the subsequent ones are more like a hermeneutic straight line, a dead structure, dictating, and serving to oppress any challenge. The only "growth" possible is to bolster its message, rather than evolve with new knowledge and awareness of reality.

These brief descriptions of the cosmic creation parts of the Egyptian myths show what I see as the evolution of monotheism, and also reveal the twisting and turning of the question "Who owns creation?", especially in man's relation to woman. The following section focuses on parts of creation myths which highlight how man came to be created.

"Let there be man …"

All of us labour in webs spun long before we were born.

—Attributed to William Faulkner

The Adam and Eve story has been thought to date from between 950 and 600 BCE. It provides the basis of the *how* and *when* man, creation, and the universe as we know it started according to Christianity and Judaism. The essence of it has been handed down for thousands of years. I believe that not only does it fundamentally say something important as to *how* we have become, that is, it elucidates aspects of psychic development; but it also becomes the source which almost justifies and preserves the dynamics inherent within it.[4]

Each generation, in handing down the myth, is stating that this is the way the world is, this is the way our minds work, this is the *when* we began—that is, when a deity started to "name" the universe. Even if a person considers themselves to be non-religious, I feel that this story is still deep in their minds, and that their unconscious is steeped in the symbolism and defensive strategies involved.

* * *

It appears to be a law that you cannot have a deep sympathy with both man and nature. Those qualities which bring you near to the one, estrange you from the other.

—Henry David Thoreau (1882, p. 317)

If we look at other creation myths from around the world, it can be seen that many of them are similar to the Adam and Eve myth—they often suggest, for instance, that there was a first entity, usually deemed to be male, who either named to create or magically created, and one of his creations was man, who is special to the creator. Woman is then created as a helper and mate to man. There is a move away from nature in these myths, as "magical" forces take precedence. Many myths adhere to this formulation, which suggests that the psychological forces at play are universal and thus are part of the developmental struggles of humans. This structure, however, is not the only one; there are other formulations of creation myths which try to represent a different potential beginning, and consequently allow more of nature.

---

[4] (An aside.) The Adam and Eve story is so imbued in our culture that I feel almost free to refer to it without referencing it. It is interesting that I notice two counter positions in my mind—the Adam aspect which would need to reference it from an Old Testament source, as a "learning", or academic experience; and the Eve aspect which does not need to, as the importance in this position is that of the story being told orally, settling into my mind and having a myriad of consequences. But, how would I reference it anyhow? What was the moment I first heard it? Do I prioritise the written account that I might have first read, or the oral account which I heard? Whichever and whenever this experience might have been, it inevitably sowed seeds in my conscious and unconscious mind as to how to structure the world, gender, and creation.

The myths can, therefore, broadly be categorised as being either based in nature with a relatively strong adherence to physical reality, or in the supernatural with a limited adherence to physical reality. It is perhaps not surprising that the tendency to be more supernatural is prevalent in all the major Western religions, while the nature-based creation myths tend to be found among ancient indigenous tribespeople. Noting this tendency led me to consider how I might approach thinking about each myth.

I thought it would be interesting to try to remove the magic from the myths, to treat them as stories that have arisen from a defensive state of mind which was utilising a magical structure as part of the defence. This would also serve as a way of preserving an advantageous hierarchy and a means of filling a void of understanding.

I also decided to note if each myth involved a coming together between a male and female, or not. This coupling is essential in all acts of creation in nature and its presence or absence in the myth seemed to be a strong indicator of whether the myth could be placed in a hermeneutic straight line or loop.

Another aspect I paid close attention to was whether the myth demonstrated an awareness of something having existed before the supernatural being and creation, or not. This aspect was important, as it was an indicator of a "negative capability",[5] or a tolerance of the unknown, being present in the minds of the people who created the myth—this would indicate, or not, an awareness of the relevance of the maternal function.

I also looked at the use of "naming" as the process of bringing things into creation, and the gender (if specified) of the creating deity. The emphasis on things having been created by a naming process has an inherent misogyny within it—denying a time before "the (paternal) word" and hence the importance of the maternal stage. It prioritises the creativity function of the paternal over the hard work of creation and formation of the maternal.

Finally, I looked at the character of the created man—what he was thought to be "made of"—and, in particular, whether he had been born with an "original sin" or not. This has an enormous impact in psychoanalytic theory and is the point of deviation for many of its opposing thoughts.

The following are brief summaries of a few of the myths that illustrate some of the points I have mentioned.

In **Raven the Creator**, an Eskimo creation myth, the starting point is the Raven who accidentally creates man, who emerges from a pea pod. Raven created the pea pod, but was surprised when man emerged from it. Raven, upon seeing the form of man, takes off the raven mask and reveals himself to be a man. Raven creates other creatures for man to have company by moulding them out of clay; each time magically placing life into the clay creatures by replacing

---

[5] Negative capability was first used by the poet John Keats (1899, p. 277) in a letter dated 1817 as a term to signify the endeavour to pursue a vision of artistic beauty even when it leads into intellectual confusion and uncertainty. W. R. Bion (1968–1969, p. 70) also used this term to represent a capacity to tolerate the pain of not knowing, rather than imposing a system from the prevailing wisdom of the day.

his mask and waving his wings over them. Raven eventually moulds woman out of clay and places life into her and tells man that she is his helper and his mate. "'She was very pretty,' said Man, and he was happy" (Hamilton, 1992, p. 7).

In this myth the actuality of man being born of woman is subverted. Man emerges with no work or pain from a pea pod. It does not suggest there was a time before the raven deity, but does suggest that all creatures and things are first thought about and created by the magical power of the Raven—except, that is, for man, who seems to be formed and created without thought, leaving Raven surprised. This myth has a deity who creates a special place for man, portrays woman as subject to man, subverts the actuality of observable facts of nature, and contains no acknowledgement of a time of chaos.

In **Phan Ku the Creator** from *c.* 600 BCE China, the starting point is a universe in the shape of a hen's egg. Within this egg was a mass called "'*no thing*' [and] inside *no thing* was something not yet born" (Hamilton, 1992, p. 21). This something was Phan Ku. When Phan Ku eventually formed and emerged from the egg he was the size of a giant and grew more every day. He set about carving and chiselling the world … first separating the sky from the earth … the light sky being *yang* and the heavy earth being *yin*. He chiselled out the rivers and valleys and formed the mountains. Only when Phan Ku died, after many thousands of years, was the world complete:

> Soil was formed from his body, rocks were made from his bones; rivers and seas from his blood. All plant life came from [his] hair … the wind and clouds are his breath. Rain from his sweat and from the fleas that lived in his hair came all humankind. The form of Phan Ku vanished in the making of the world. After he was gone, there was room then for pain, and that was how suffering came to human beings. (p. 23)

Here, the creator works to create the world; sweat is produced and things are made through hard activity and not magic. In its emphasis on a creation involving work over many thousands of years this myth is very different from others. It is not easy to place Phan Ku into a magical creator deity category; he does not "name" to create, he does not use obviously magical means, and he does not have an existence which persists after his creation. Also, in the emphasis of the "nothingness" before Phan Ku, this myth suggests that time did not start with Phan Ku and that there is another state of being other than that of creation. Implicit in this is also the awareness that this other state of being can be returned to—this is shown in how the form of Phan Ku becomes broken up and the particles of his form are used to create other entities; the *no thing* state being a necessary stage in between the existences of different entities. To me, this myth also has the vital awareness that *something* cannot be born from *no thing* without the *no thing* first being contained, that is, having a boundary, a point which delineates inside from outside, which is only possible after a maternal function act of containment. This myth is very different from most other myths I'm aware of, and seems to stay more with the knowledge of the natural order of things, rather than subverting them. But it does, nonetheless, leave out the essential coupling aspect between male and female elements which is the foundation of creation.

Another myth which emphasises an "empty" space beginning is the **Ta-aroa the Creator** myth from the Society Islands in French Polynesia. Ta-aroa lived in an egg-shaped shell which revolved in dark, empty space for a long time. He then broke out of the shell and, being alone, created Tu as his companion and helper in the work of creation. They created land, creatures, and eventually man, Ti-i. Next a woman was made, Hina; she was half god, half mortal. Hina had a face both in the front and back, was full of good, and made "hard things easy and hurt less painful" (Hamilton, 1992, p. 101). Ti-i was mean and liked to see others suffer. Because of Ti-i, unhappiness came to the universe, and gods started warring with each other and with man. Ta-aroa and Tu spoke curses to punish them: "'We curse the stars!' they said. And the stars blinked. / 'We curse the moon!' The moon faded and went out. / Hina thought to save the stars and the moon" (p. 102). They cursed the sea, but Hina saved the sea. Every curse was countered by Hina, but eventually they cursed mankind. Hina started to try to save them too, but Ti-i used magic to conjure them to death. "So it is that the Tahitians say it was the man [Ti-i] who caused people to lose eternal life" (p. 103).

This myth not only acknowledges nothingness as the beginning and the need for that nothingness to be contained, but also acknowledges the need for a coming together (after the initial creation of Tu) of a male and female figure before creation can occur. This myth also shows how the maternal function is important in transforming pain into something more tolerable.

The **Mawu-Lisa the Creators** myth from Benin is unusual as it begins with a female deity. It describes how Nanu Buluka, the Great Mother, created the world and then had twins, Mawu and Lisa. The Great Mother did nothing after this. Mawu was the female moon who had power over the night and Lisa was the male sun. When there was an eclipse—one of them being in the shadow of the other or another heavenly body—they came together and created children. Mawu and Lisa were the mother and father of all other gods (Hamilton, 1992, pp. 43–45).

Another myth which starts with a female deity is the **Divine Woman the Creator** myth from the Huron confederacy of Native Americans (Hamilton, 1992, pp. 61–63).

The **Apsu and Tiamat the Creators** myth from the Babylonian creation verse narrative "Enuma Elish" is considered to be the oldest written myth known. In it, Apsu and Tiamat are not only ancestors of the gods, but also symbolise the living, unformed matter of the world. The narrative takes its name from its first line, "when on high the heaven had not been named" (Hamilton, 1992, p. 85). During this time, when heaven had not been named, "[T]here was Apsu [male] the begetter, the fresh and sweet-water sea. And there was Tiamat [female], the salt-sea waters. They mingled as a single body and soul" (p. 79). They created the great gods, Lahmu and Lahamu, who went on to have more sons. These sons and brothers became unruly in the waters and Apsu and Tiamat grew frustrated. Apsu decided to destroy them in order to give Tiamat some peace, but Tiamat said "[T]heir ways are awful, these gods, but let us act kindly!" (p. 80). However Apsu still plotted to kill them, and upon realising this, one of the gods, Ea, tricked Apsu and killed him instead. Ea then had a son, Marduk, who was "perfect and to be praised as the most high god" (p. 80). Tiamat became restless and "moved and moved, day and night" (p. 81) due to the winds, and this upset all the other gods. The gods reproached Tiamat, said that she didn't love them, and blamed her for letting Apsu be killed. In response, she "who could fashion all things" (p. 81) gave birth to a monster serpent—Kingu—who was able to fight to avenge the death of Apsu. No god could withstand Tiamat and Kingu except Marduk who agreed to fight her as long as the other gods bestowed on him the power to create with words. Marduk defeated Tiamat and Kingu, and from the dead Tiamat created the heavens and earth. He then "spoke" into existence a creature and he named it man.

This myth, while emphasising a time before creation (when Apsu and Tiamat were together) does not pinpoint this as the beginning of creation. Rather, the myth develops the "naming" done by Marduk as the beginning of the creation of man. This myth seems to try to sustain the natural law but ends up with the primacy of the law of gods (man). The female element is destroyed and nature is overcome and thwarted by magic. Creation becomes something which doesn't need the coming together of something, but is done by "naming" and the "word". This evolution from something more in line with nature to magic and naming is similar to the evolution evident in the Egyptian cosmologies.

* * *

Obviously there are many more myths than those referred to here. The ones I have picked out illustrate some of the opposing themes present: for instance, there are those that acknowledge a time before the creative force, and those that suggest the creative force has always been present; those that emphasise a coming together of a female and male aspect as the start of creation, and those that suggest that start to be a deity; those that suggest "things" coming into being through work, and those that suggest creation occurring by magical or naming means.

The acknowledgement of a period of chaos or nothingness before creation is important. Those myths that do acknowledge it also seem to be aware of a need for that chaos to be contained in some way before creation can occur. This highlights the necessity of the maternal function which enables the vastness to become boundaried. This function—a containment, a maternal holding, a receptivity, an encapsulating of something which is felt to be chaotic, unordered, unruly, "too much", fretful, frenetic, painful, "on-the-precipice-of-something", tumultuous, and full of energy—is of vital importance in allowing two states of being to be felt, thereby enabling precursory thoughts to be thought and creation to occur.

Adam and Eve

Every time I thought about the Adam and Eve myth it didn't make sense to me, even when I tried to suspend my critical faculties and embrace it as a creation myth within the belief system of a religion. The disturbing aspect was the profound repudiation of nature within the story. I began to wonder about the psychological purpose of creation myths, especially Adam and Eve, as it has such an unquestioned existence in the minds of people. I started to feel that it might shed light on the "bigger frame" that I felt to be in existence.

After much thought and writing (set out in detail in Part II) I came to the position of seeing "Adam" and "Eve" as two different psychological ways of being that were anathema to each other when in isolation. Adam represents the aspect of our minds which creates external structures such as religions, theories, laws, and hierarchies in order to deal with pain, envy, fear, and death. Eve represents the aspect of our minds which bears pain, understands nature, and is aware of humans belonging to the natural world, like all creatures, and that we will die. The unequal interaction between these aspects also seemed to account for much of the misogyny, racism, and hierarchical systems which plague mankind. From this starting position of seeing Adam and Eve as representing something in opposition to each other, I later developed this into thinking of a primary Adam and Eve, and then a secondary Adam and Eve. I will elaborate on this later.

From this position, I wondered if we all are somehow "framed" by an unconscious creation myth that we organise ourselves from. One which influences how we see the world and how we structure ourselves in relation to it. I began to feel that when a theory is held on to, or treated as a religion, the theory tends to provide the thinker with a necessary structure with which they orientate themselves. That is, it is being used as a defensive creation by the Adam aspects of our minds and therefore other thinking (and Eve) is anathema to it. Adam and Eve have two discrete and opposing psychologies, one based on projection and the other introjection, which might account for the oppositional nature of some psychoanalytic theories. They each seemed to be trying to describe either the psychology of Adam or Eve. Whilst Eve is generally able to be aware of Adam, Adam is very threatened by the existence of Eve.

The ramifications of this are profound, and the basic question, "Which creation myth is a person unconsciously operating from?" began to feel important. If a person has an Adam-dominated mind, then their creation myth is one of an all-powerful and magical demiurge. If there is an awareness and valuing of Eve, then the creation myth in operation is more likely to be a natural, evolution-based one.

The eventual focus on the Adam and Eve myth arose primarily as it was where my musings led me, but in thinking about it later, it seemed apt as it is the "beginning" in most Western religions, and therefore does become the foundation from which the structure of our thinking and our lives, even if we are not overtly religious, emanates.

Concluding remarks

What a considered view of creation myths began to reveal was that all of these forces at play come together to create a story which serves to "hold" pain, anxieties, terrors, and envies in a way which seems to bring control, order, and power to certain positions within the consequential hierarchy. But what became clear was that this internal situation was also an external one—societies en masse were all cooperating in illusions which perpetuated the drama inherent in the myths. I also began to view the different psychoanalytic theories in this way too—

proponents of a particular theory were cooperating to perpetuate a certain creation myth, for all the reasons outlined above.

The factors that I have mentioned—the presence or absence of something within the structure, magical creations, naming, the consideration of whether "time" began with the "word", and so on—could also be parameters from which to look at psychoanalytic theories. The aspect of naming and whether creation begins with the "word" or "chaos" is especially applicable to how we can view the theory. The theory itself becomes the structure or creation myth which is being used as a frame to orientate the self, the patient, and where the "word" has originated from.

Throughout Part I, I look at these aspects using instances in history or myth which show that these issues have been enduring ones and are certainly not new to psychoanalysis. However, this realisation also brings with it the necessity to reframe psychoanalytic theories as being, in a way, modern-day creation myths, with all of the tensions, defences, and vagaries inherent in the establishment of the myths of old.

The next chapter looks at some of the processes inherent in "structures", especially with regard to the properties a structure might require to be an adequate container.

CHAPTER 3

Presence and absence

One of the biggest sources of dissatisfaction with psychoanalytic theory was the feeling that there was something fundamental missing or misrepresented in each version I came across. Each strand of thinking seemed to have elements which were represented (having a "presence"), such as envy and aggression within Kleinian thinking and the maternal provision within Winnicottian thinking, but there didn't seem to be a structure which held everything together. All these schools of thought either felt incomplete or at odds with each other.

There seemed to be something missing which would adequately inform me about aspects of myself, as well as the memory of being at the derelict house when I was eight. All approaches seemed to frame this memory in one particular way or another. They seemed to miss something important, or to suggest a meaning which seemed to be relevant in some ways, but which did not resonate deeply within me.

Being, in my former working life, a science teacher, I had a long-standing fascination with Dmitri Mendeleev and his periodic table. This has always seemed to have a deeper psychological relevance than merely an interesting scientific discovery. The process of feeling uneasy with the theory and structures of the time, an application of a curious and questioning mind, and a wish to find a frame to hold the new discoveries seems to be the hermeneutic loop activity which promotes growth and awareness. Mendeleev approached his task in this manner, and by essentially going "back to basics" he was eventually able to build his table. I will try to show what I think we can gain from exploring his process.

Mendeleev, as Sacks (2001) recounts, grew up in the early 1800s and had a mind that was constantly curious. He refused to accept what his observations, reason, and sensibility could not corroborate, whilst also seeing connections and associations between things that seemed to defy the understanding of science at that time. He didn't rush to reach conclusions; instead

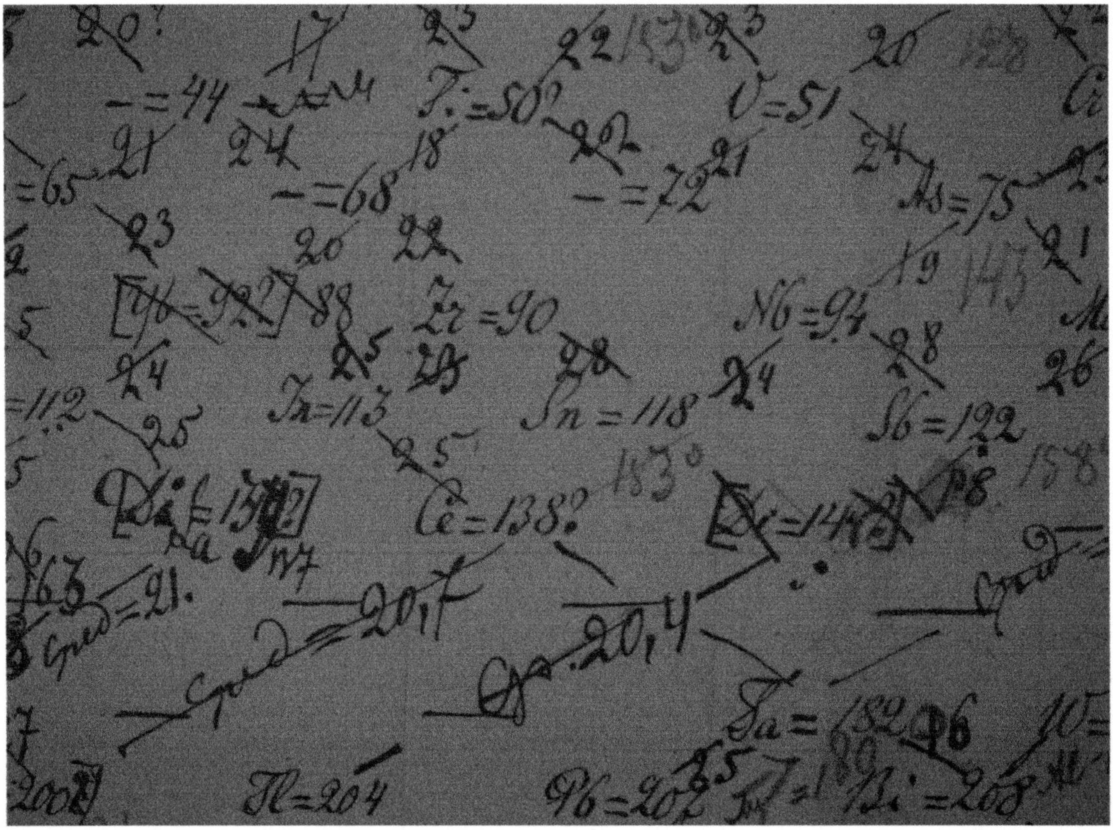

Figure 3. Dmitri Mendeleev's hand-drawn periodic table

he pondered and battled with the task of discovering an order in a seemingly chaotic and disordered universe, which others were resigned to.

Mendeleev immersed himself deeply into all things elemental. He studied (I would say that he listened to, tasted, smelt, observed, and touched) the physical and chemical properties of each metal, gas, solid, liquid, and substance he came across. Everywhere he went, he took with him his elemental cards, upon which he'd noted all of the information available regarding a particular element, and constantly shuffled them, aware there was a connection and order that was waiting to be discovered.

His immersion into and perception of the known elements led to a vast knowledge and understanding of them. He gained in his confidence to defy the prevailing thoughts and suggested that many of the measurements that had been accepted as fact were wrong. He began to create a periodic order and was able to highlight the elements he considered had been wrongly attributed. When further testing corroborated his thoughts, his confidence grew further and a periodic table was born.

Due to the nature of the associations, patterns, variations in mass, and so on, he was able to order the elements into a repeating pattern of groups of eight. He not only did this for the known elements, but he was also able to predict the place in his table where unknown elements would be. There was a gap, or an absence, where he realised an element should be—one with characteristics that would incrementally be associated with its place in his table. His table therefore consisted of elements that had a presence in the minds of scientists—known and discovered—and those that did not.

The ordering of the known elements into his table led to a deeper understanding of those elements—they became able to be more present, if you like, in the minds of scientists, and as a result could be thought about in new ways. They had a place, a mass, a behaviour, and a connection to other elements, leading to the known elements becoming more known.

The gaps left in the table for the undiscovered elements represented an absence in the order, but even in their absence a great deal was able to be known about them. In this way, Mendeleev prepared the ground for many elements to be discovered from the position of already being "known". One such element was gallium, discovered years after Mendeleev first predicted its presence and properties.

Mendeleev's pursuit of his curiosity and urge to find connections took him from a period of negative capability to one night having a dream of the known elements arranged in a grand table (Sacks, 2001, p. 198). This dream did not provide Mendeleev with all the answers, but rather he woke with a sense of revelation from which he worked with renewed vigour to solve many of the questions that had occupied him for years (see Figure 3).

The "presence" that each element had in the minds of the scientists at that time was based on assumption and measurements that had persisted, unchallenged, for years. If experience and observation seemed to counter this, it was merely disregarded as a mistake and not thought about. However, this distorted presence formed the basis for how the universe was perceived and interacted with. Perhaps a resistance to tolerating negative capability led many to push away discrepancies rather than allow them to ferment in their minds.

In a way, two different types of potential "presences" in the mind are being highlighted here. The first is that untested knowledge which is accepted as having a presence in the mind, in opposition to actual perceptions; and then the second is the capacity to bear not knowing and the presence of curiosity.

To move from the one to the other, an absence must be tolerated. An absence of knowing, an absence of a dependency on naming and learning, and an absence of the structure that rules and regulations would confer.

A tendency that all humans are predisposed to is to fill an absence with anything that might function as a "filler". Anything that serves to move away from the negative capability and pain of not knowing, even if this might be counter to actual perceptions, nature, and testing in real life. The capacity to tolerate this absence seems to be dependent upon an awareness that curiosity and discovery through perceptions can be a "presence" that occupies the absence. As the trust of perception and curiosity relies on a sense of having a place within nature, perhaps the further one moves away from it, the more reliant one is on other "fillers"—religion, knowledge learnt rather than discovered, and rules and regulations.

In formulating his table, Mendeleev tolerated the absence by intuitively knowing that curiosity and an awareness of nature could become present in it. His table became a work of discovery—not learning. Each element had a place, was known in a perceptual manner, and could be understood to be connected to and associated with those other elements around it. In this way, he didn't so much order the universe, as make known how the universe was connected and how everything was part of it.

The type of presence that fillers provide is fragile and inherently unproductive. Illusion, rather than the hermeneutic loop process, is the only possible outcome, as the knowledge has not been discovered with an inner awareness of curiosity and formed from chaos. When not having been properly discovered, the products of "knowledge" become an illusion built on an illusion.

Even though his creative process resulted in an ordering and placing of the elements into a system which followed rules, Mendeleev did go through the painful and chaotic process of tolerating the absence of knowing. When the transition state between absence and presence can be occupied by curiosity and nature, the perceptive apparatus becomes more important than the cognitive apparatus. This process then allows something to come to fruition—something that ultimately fills the absence with a substantiality. Curiosity is also intimately linked with the penetrative processes; a maternal curiosity is a "going inside" the infant to try to discover what might be there. If a system or structure exists which suggests (unconsciously or consciously) that these penetrative processes are "sinful", "anathema", or "pathological", then no hermeneutic loop is possible—stagnation takes over.

Part of the fruition of the process of curiosity and nature is having a place for the undiscovered. Mendeleev had the confidence to not rush to fill his table with what was already found; the unfound had a place and could be known by its absence. Each absence had its own quality, taste, smell, measurement, mass, and so on, but it had yet to be found and had no name. To have a table that could hold the found knowns, unfound knowns, and the unfound unknowns seems to be a very important device that is accepting of nature, curiosity, absence, and presence. It is a table of stability and wisdom. It removes itself from the inherent terrors of absence and embraces absence with the deep awareness of the transformative and transitional impact of curiosity upon it.

As Eugène Ionesco (1971) writes, "We are all looking for something of extraordinary importance whose nature we have forgotten" (p. 171). Here, I think Ionesco speaks clearly to the profound awareness of absence and the quest to fill it with a substantial presence in some way. I think the pivotal word is "nature", and this is curiosity, perceptive reality, and being *in* the world, not above it.

If for us, as practitioners in the therapeutic world, a sense of curiosity or tolerance of absence is lacking, then the periodic table that comes about in the consulting room (that is, the sense of order that is arrived at) is filled with elements that have not been discovered through being with the patient. Instead, the table has been filled with prior learning (possibly therefore an illusion built upon an illusion), a misplacing of elements, and no awareness of the possibility of anything unknown. No space is then available for that yet to be discovered. The creative awareness of the form or shape of what is unknown will also be lacking.

Many people have had a moving and powerful experience when coming across the periodic table for the first time. Oliver Sacks (2001) describes it as

> incredibly beautiful, the most beautiful thing I have ever seen. I could never adequately analyse what I meant here by beauty—simplicity?, coherence?, rhythm?, inevitability? Or perhaps it was the symmetry, the comprehensiveness of every element firmly locked into its place, with no gaps, no exceptions, everything implying everything else. (p. 203)

Similarly, C. P. Snow wrote that

> for the first time I saw the medley of haphazard facts fall into line and order. All the jumbles and recipes and hotchpotch of the inorganic chemistry of my boyhood seemed to fit themselves into the scheme before my eyes—as though one were standing beside a jungle and it suddenly transformed itself into a Dutch garden. (Cited in Sacks, 2001, p. 194)

Mendeleev himself wrote of "how contented, free and joyous is life in the realm of science" (cited in Sacks, 2001, p. 195). I think when a person can look upon the periodic table and feel moved, the feeling can be considered to come from one of two sources—the happiness associated with the need for order and categorisation; and then the joy associated with a deep understanding of what the table *is*.

The table *is* a structure which is born of not knowing, chaos, and work. It *is* a structure which demands curiosity, a negative capability, and awareness of absence, and provides a presence which has its foundations based firmly in nature. It doesn't just tolerate the unknown, it provides a place for it. That does seem to be a reason for joy.

Mendeleev and the periodic table have enabled me to look at the theories within psychoanalysis from a similar perspective. How do they all fit together? And, as I don't question the "truths" arrived at from each position, how can one practitioner say they are a Kleinian, when another says they are a Winnicottian? While being aware of an element of the ridiculous, it might be the same as saying, "You are a halogen, and I am an inert gas." As a halogen there are properties which can only be associated with being a halogen, which are relevant and unique, just as there are for being an inert gas too. Similarly in psychoanalysis, a Kleinian has a set of beliefs which will be unique to their position and so on. What seemed to be lacking was a frame or structure that held everything together, other than the vague sense of them all practising under the auspices of psychoanalysis.

If we were to look at the processes that are seemingly present in the works of psychoanalytic thinkers, there is a very understandable tendency with leading proponents to reconsider or change their minds about the thoughts that they originally had, demonstrating a dynamic hermeneutic loop in operation. Bion (1967) famously wrote his *Second Thoughts* in which he thought again about his original formulations. Freud (1940a) also did this in his *An Outline of Psycho-Analysis*. These new formulations are built on a deeper understanding of their experience and thoughts. In general, with Freud and Bion, they both seemingly evolved from a scientific, ordering approach—Bion and his grid and Freud needing to consider psychoanalysis as a science—to a looser emphasis on ways of being with a patient: "no memory and desire" (Bion, 1967, p. 143), and "evenly suspended attention" (Freud, 1912e, p. 111).

This movement away from something formulaic to a status of attunement could also be seen as a movement from something highly sophisticated and developed to something fundamental and raw. The direction of flow is from honed intellect to a stripping away of something. In coming to this position, Bion realised that he was having second thoughts about his original thinking and was trying to put words (and thoughts) to something fundamental.

Freud, at the end of his life, was preoccupied with his legacy and revisited a great deal of his original thinking in the *Outline*. During this highly contemplative period, he also continued his fascination with myth and religion. In *Moses and Monotheism* (1939a), he forensically investigated the roots of monotheistic religion in Judaism with the apparent aim of discovering the beginnings of something.

These reformulations came about from a continued application of a scientific mind full of enquiry and curiosity (like Mendeleev's), but also the realisation that their original formulations did not account for, or help, all patients they came across in their consulting rooms. Perhaps their original thinking could be thought of as similar to the starting point of Mendeleev's work—trying to make sense of what was considered to be a base of knowledge prevalent at that time, as well as noting how well that knowledge corresponded to experience in the consulting room. When it was seen to be deficient, both Freud and Bion had second thoughts, and tried to reshape the structure that they had worked from. The ability to do this reshaping is dependent upon a capacity to tolerate absence, along with a trust in nature and the power of curiosity, which all combine to become the holding structure needed to enable this growth.

In *Moses and Monotheism* (1939a, p. 71), Freud highlighted a tendency of the authors of scripture to distort or corrupt actual events to suit their need for the narrative to be in line with history, current situations, and any illusion that was being used to order life at that particular time. Given this human tendency—which I have called a hermeneutic straight line—to distort reality to fit illusions, it is to the credit of both Freud and Bion that they chose to have second thoughts, rather than imbue their original formulations with a sense of being "the truth". This distortion of reality to fit a needed theory is a movement away from nature and curiosity, and the "absence" that would be felt if the distorted structure fails would be experienced as catastrophic. There really would be a psychic void, as nature and curiosity (and Eve, in the context of this book) have been destroyed.

However, even though it is admirable that both Bion and Freud had their second thoughts, the direction of thought is from the sophisticated to the fundamental. It is my contention that the development of sophisticated thinking "contaminates" the process of formulating thoughts about the fundamental. We bring to the fundamental thinking the very structure or frame within which we created the sophisticated thinking. That is, we all operate from a personal, largely unconscious creation myth. Unless the particular beginning point of this illusion has been dismantled, the power the creation myth has will still influence our thought when we "try" to think fundamentally. This creates a particular beginning which is unconsciously designed to corroborate a particular present.

A simple but relevant personal experience might shed more light on this. My husband and I were in his car. He had neglected to change the time display when the clocks went back. He set the satnav to direct us on our journey and asked me what time we might expect to get there. I looked at the satnav and told him the expected time of arrival. He paused and said, "But that's ridiculous—it shouldn't take us almost two hours." I was confused and said it wasn't ridiculous, that was the time the satnav was showing. He then realised that the time was wrong and told me. This everyday experience represents very well the concept I am talking about. The arrival time the satnav was showing me was only ridiculous if the starting point was known. I hadn't taken in the actual time we were setting off, and so had accepted what I was being told. In the same way, our present sense and way of seeing the world can only be seen to be ridiculous if a realistic starting point is known. In the case of the satnav, if we take as a given the estimated time of arrival shown, and extrapolate back to what we believe is the starting point, it would be wrong. Creation myths not only represent this extrapolation back to an imagined starting point, but are also full of symbolism as to how and why this might have occurred.

Following Mendeleev, it also became increasingly important to me to start afresh, and follow wherever my perceptions and discoveries took me. Thus, attempting to look at beginnings from the fundamental to the sophisticated seemed to be the approach that I would gain most from. However, I also bore in mind the practical impossibility of doing this: I am a sophisticated thinker and would not be able to remove this entirely from my experience—my associations, my thinking, my words, my capacity to order, and so on, are all part of who I am. Bion approached this by a formulation of "no memory and no desire", which I agree is part of what is needed—but a removal, if you like, of Adam thought, memory, and desire; I think the more difficult task is the remembering and desiring of something that is anathema to this—that of the experience of Eve, and Adam and Eve interacting in equality.

Other difficulties with theory began to emerge too; perhaps the most shocking thing for me was to do with the disputes between the various versions of psychoanalysis. It did seem like there were four or five analytic "gods" and I was expected to somehow choose which one to follow.

Perhaps one of the most disputed factors between each of these positions is what exactly is thought to be the primary or secondary influences. Are we born with primary envy, greed, and destructiveness, or do those traits become established after life has begun? Many people new to the world of psychoanalysis might reasonably assume that this question is a relatively modern one and that science and psychology are attempting to answer it. However, it is a question which has occupied thinkers since the beginning of thought and has been the source of violent disputes throughout history, so it seems to be important to consider the present disputes in psychoanalysis from a different perspective—or a wider frame.

The next chapter looks at a very important moment in history when the nature of man was vehemently contested, a moment which has impacted the lives of everyone living under a religious structure for thousands of years.

* * *

Jacob

I had a dream ... involving an empty drawer from a big chest of drawers ... it was a drawer from the chest I used to store my films in ... I've put them in without the leaflet or casing, just the DVDs in a simple plastic covering in order to save space ... anyway, this drawer was empty and disintegrating, it was falling apart ... quite bizarre .... the sides and the backs were coming apart in my hand.

CHAPTER 4

The dispute

The vehement disagreements that I had become aware of within the world of psychoanalysis had begun to fascinate me. As previously stated, what struck me as particularly intriguing was this sense of *belief* within each "club" that *their* truth was *the* truth. This phenomenon led me to consider the starting points of each club, and I soon discovered that the differing beliefs had, at their roots, a firm idea of what was felt to be the innate starting point of the infant.

Disputes like this are not confined to psychoanalysis. Throughout history, disagreements between various religious factions about the starting point of man have been raging. Not only about what might be the ultimate source of creation, but also about what "condition" man is born in. Philosophers, theologians, scientists, and folkloric writers have been grappling with these issues since man has been able to communicate. Every time a seeming resolution of these questions comes about, it is soon revised or further elaborated to incorporate a new challenge. Heracleon theology was contested by Origen; Origen's theology was contested by Epiphanius and Theophilus, and so on. Consistent bones of contention within all these disputes concern the nature of Creation; the incorporeal or corporeal nature of God; the literal—or not literal—translation of Genesis, and the status of man, especially with regard to sin, original sin, and redemption.

A pivotal instance in history that has impacted the course of the Western world was one such dispute between Augustine and Pelagius, and their supporters. Essentially, Augustine viewed man as being inherently sinful and only able to attain redemption by an act of God. This meant that for Augustine, man was born with an "original sin". Pelagius countered this by his view that man was born inherently good, and only became sinful later through his actions.

In likening psychoanalytic disputes with those theological disputes in history, it felt important to understand more about the highly documented altercation which spread over three Councils—that of Lod in 415 CE, Carthage in 418 CE, and Ephesus in 431 CE. I will first set out the scene that led up to this dispute.

As Newell (1999) notes, from around 500 BCE, the Celts had spread throughout Europe and into Asia Minor. This steady expansion was only curtailed when it met the advancing Roman Empire, which forced the Celts to retreat to the outlying edges of Europe. By the middle of the first century CE, the Roman army had occupied much of the British Isles, only leaving the outer western reaches for the Celts.

Once Britain became part of the Roman Empire, society, infrastructure, and the prevailing religious practices and beliefs underwent great changes, and "It was during this time [around the early second century] that Christianity first came to the Celts, possibly through the ministrations of individual converts in the Roman army" (Newell, 1999, p. xvi). This period of Roman influence and occupation came to an end in the fourth century when they had to withdraw their army to engage in battles in central and southern Europe (p. xviii). Christianity in Britain was then left without oversight for many centuries, and by the late fourth century the distinctive characteristic of what could be called a Celtic Christianity had developed. This was the environment from which Pelagius, one of the first noted proponents of this Celtic Christianity, emerged.

Within Celtic Christianity, the arenas of worship were natural amphitheatres, open to the elements, and situated in places where man and nature could come together. Clerical marriage was permitted, as was the inclusion of women into the leadership of the Church. This contrasted greatly with Roman Christianity, which created holy buildings with walls and roofs, separate from nature, and which insisted on clerical celibacy and the exclusion of women from leadership positions (Newell, 1999, p. xviii).

During this time of no oversight for Celtic Christianity, Roman Christianity was hardening in the Augustine doctrine of belief in all Creation being fundamentally flawed. The grace of God was seen as over and above nature, not as restoring something to its original status of goodness. This was in direct opposition to Celtic Christianity's view of God as being the "light of life", *within* all matter, and its conviction in the essential goodness of creation.

Pelagius taught that moral perfection was attainable in this life without the assistance of divine grace through human free will. Augustine contradicted this, saying that perfection was impossible without grace because we are born sinners with a sinful heart and will. During the Council of Lod, Pelagius prevailed—his supporters managed to demonstrate that the doctrine of original sin (as described by Augustine) amounted to Manichaeism, a religion based on Gnosticism, which stated that flesh was, in itself, sinful. They argued that ultimately "original sin" could only lead to the denial that Jesus had been human, which was counter to the founding principle of Christianity. However, at the Council of Carthage, this earlier ruling was overturned, and was later ratified at the Council of Ephesus. Pelagius was declared a heretic and his teaching, Pelagianism, became anathema to what it meant to be a Christian.

Christianity and its crusades have taken over many cultures, traditions, ways of life, and other religious systems, often by force, sometimes by persuasion, and mostly by persecution and law making. This domination has effectively squashed the existence of other "beginnings" by forcefully imposing the Creation myth of the Judaeo-Christian tradition. This can be shown to have led to major shifts in the very core ways of seeing self and others. The question of original sin and the dynamics of the Garden of Eden can therefore be seen to be pivotal in who we become.

In the Celtic tradition, nature and an inherent goodness prevailed, leading to God being viewed as immanent to life and nature. After the Council of Ephesus, the Christian teaching stated that God was above nature (transcendent), and that original sin was the condition we were born in. This formulation of the nature of God and man created two opposing forces and a crisis of existence for those who had awareness of both.

Stephen Greenblatt (2017) has written a comprehensive account of Augustine's life in his book *The Rise and Fall of Adam and Eve*. He notes how Augustine obsessively analysed himself in order to try to discover when, why, and how his thoughts and behaviour had become tainted by sin. He was particularly interested in the nature of sex, finally settling on the idea that all sex was inherently sinful as it involved pleasure and lust. He was tormented by the inability to control his nocturnal emissions, and as a result felt that all humans were born with original sin which they needed to battle and seek redemption for.

Augustine was obsessed with the story of Adam and Eve and spent much of his life trying to put forward a reasoned proposition for a literal understanding of it. In looking at his childhood, it could be said that Augustine had, in terms of the classic Freudian oedipal complex, an oedipal victory—although, as his mother was in effect "married to her God", perhaps the oedipal relationship that Augustine was more involved with was that between his mother and her God. His father, while treating his wife badly by cheating and bullying, was in another sense considered ineffectual, crude, and uneducated in religious ways, and when it came to promoting her son and his education, his mother was able to exert her will and religious piety upon the family. His father died soon after Augustine went to undergo an education in Carthage and he then became the focus of his mother's life and purpose.

In Carthage, Augustine had many sexual encounters with men and women from all sections of society, before finally living with a mistress who bore him a son. She was not considered "marriage material", and a suitable girl was found for him. While waiting for her to reach the age of maturity, he and his mother had a very moving experience, during which they both felt something otherworldly and powerful. They considered it a direct communication from God himself, and Augustine decided to forego his marriage and devote himself to a celibate and pious life instead. Interestingly, soon after this experience, his mother fell ill, and she died nine days later.

In trying to capture what he and his mother had experienced, he wrote:

> Suppose, we said, that the tumult of a man's flesh were to cease and all his thoughts … should no longer speak to him; suppose that the heavens and even his own soul were silent,

> no longer thinking of itself but passing beyond; suppose that his dreams and the visions of his imagination spoke no more ... and all that is transient grew silent—for all these things have the same message to tell, if only we can hear it, and their message is this: We did not make ourselves, but he who abides for ever made us. Suppose, we said, that after giving us this message and bidding us listen to him who made them, they fell silent and he alone should speak to us, not through them but in his own voice ... suppose that we heard him himself ... just as in that brief moment my mother and I had reached out in thought and touched the eternal Wisdom which abides over all things; suppose that this state were to continue ... so that this single vision entranced and absorbed the one who beheld it and enveloped him in inward joys ...—would not this be what we are to understand by the words "Come and share the joy of your Lord?" (Cited in Greenblatt, 2017, p. 95)

This can be thought of as similar to Bion's "no memory and desire", but for Augustine the "absence" that arises is filled by a male creator's voice.

With his mother dead, his partner sent away, and despite his oath to be pious and commit his life to God, Augustine seems to have been tormented by the desires of the flesh. He felt that his mind should be able to control and manage his body, in much the same way as his mind could control when he spoke. He berated this lack of control and constantly ruminated on Adam and Eve—how they were created and if and how they might have had sex.

He concluded that, as natural birth comes about because of a sexual act, and therefore through lust, all men were born with original sin, and that Jesus was the only exception as he had been born outside the sexual experience—from the Virgin Mary.

From many possible interpretations, we could speculate about Augustine's state of mind and say he had an overly close relationship with a religious mother who revered a sexless state of being. Perhaps for her, all forms of penetration were sinful, and he was then left not only having to employ ever increasing means of control over his urges, but also with an increasing aversion to them.

Augustine ended up being a pivotal figure who, on looking back at the path Western humanity has taken, caused it to turn right instead of left—and, as a result, the story of Adam and Eve has come to occupy a central role in Western Christendom. He outwitted and labelled as heretics all dissenters to his version of the story and even at the end of his life he was still looking for the underlying meaning of the disaster befalling his world because of what Adam and Eve had done in the beginning. As Greenblatt (2017, p. 97) notes, for the next 1,000 years (and more) Augustine's version of original sin and the Fall came to occupy a keystone in the psyche of man.

This point of conflict between Celtic-influenced Christianity and Augustinian Christianity involves the question as to which version of nature, God, Jesus, and man is acceptable. It is not just a conflict between theoretical understandings, it is a difference at a fundamental level; it is the very structure which orientates each person in relation to self, the world at large, and how to interact with others.

These two positions—natural goodness versus original sin—and the conflict between them is not only evident within the councils and religions of the world, but is essentially the basis of conflict between and within science, societies, cultures, religions, and also psychoanalysis: the cause of violence, persecution, discrimination, judgement, misogyny, controversial discussions, and more. It is the conflict between which creation myth is used to define life and society.

In psychoanalysis, the divisions of theoretical formations and practice abound. A practitioner is considered to be either a Kleinian, Freudian, Winnicottian, Bionian, Lacanian, or Jungian, and so on. The differing parameters between these denominations within the belief in psychoanalysis are varied, but generally centre on the primary or secondary nature of certain characteristics, and the focus on who the patient *is*, how he was created, and what is the nature of his relationship with the creator (a God, parent, or psychoanalytic "parent").

The attack and vehemence that can emanate when these differing denominations encounter one another has been well documented and experienced. The outcome has been a better one when compared to the fate of (say) the Celts and any minority belief system in history; within psychoanalysis, the differing denominations are tolerated, albeit from a position of isolation—the Kleinians, Winnicottians, Jungians, and so on stick together, and tend to seek out and wish to be with other similar "believers".

What they all seem to agree on is that there is a "truth" or "word", one which can be translated into a particular belief system, and which can then be utilised by an analyst within a session. The *what* and *who* of each part of this chain

"Truth" → "Belief system/Psychoanalysis" → "Adherent/Analyst" → "Man/Patient"

are often taken as absolute givens, or can only be thought about within the framework and structure of the prevailing belief system.

The point of departure within many of these denominations in psychoanalysis is the question of what is primary or secondary—that is, how is man to be described at an innate level. What goes on inside him? What are those basic components from which he begins? These questions relate to the "primary him"; the "secondary him" would be those characteristics which develop as a result of his later experiences.

Augustine's answer to these questions prevailed for more than 1,000 years, each generation becoming imprinted with the conscious and unconscious messages that this position would engender. In a way, it could be said that there were at least thirty-four such generations who were living from within the structure of original sin, the Fall, and a sense of the body being sinful. Just as archaeological relics give us insight into life from thousands of years ago, so too can the relics of these disputes be discerned in the mental life of modern man.

In beginning to understand the differences between each of the psychoanalytic positions, I was left not knowing what my own responses to these fundamental questions would be. I did not know what I believed in, I only knew that I was confused and that I needed to discover for myself something that would resonate deeply within me. My confusion emphasised the need for me to discard, as best as I could, all theory, and try to work things out from a basic position for myself.

The above introduces the dispute regarding the creation of man, what he is born with, and the primary or secondary nature of (original) "sin"; this becomes in psychoanalytic terms a dispute about the belief (or not) in the death instinct. The following chapter explores another aspect within this dispute—the question of the beginning of creation itself, and the fantasies inherent in the acceptance or otherwise (again, unconscious or conscious) of the two positions. This is intimately related to the concept of original sin: when Augustine's position is taken as the beginning, the outcome of this is a "transcendent God". God becomes something that is "above" creation and nature, as opposed to the Pelagian position of God being "in" nature and part of life itself. Does life start with the Word and (a transcendent) God, or does life start with chaos and a god that exists within? This question is also ancient, and yet it is still being disputed within psychoanalysis. The "solutions" to these disputes over several millennia have led to generations of people raising their children according to the strict adherence of the prevailing solution at the time. This impact on the mind has been profound, and the defences have become so reinforced that "normal" is now thought of as operating within a defensive structure which denigrates and alienates not only a majority of the population, but also the majority of the mind too.

It is no measure of health to be well adjusted to a profoundly sick society.

—Attributed to Jiddu Krishnamurti

* * *

Jacob

… when Martha died it proved that I could feel … now Meg is ill it's surprised me … she is so timid … I wonder what her family life was like before … she hides and is so frightened … unlike Martha who was full of guile … not a nice cat … she was aggressive, manipulative, and took swipes at Meg and sometimes people … she used to sleep on my chest and it would feel good … but it was as though in Martha's presence, Meg didn't exist … we were told they were inseparable sisters, but Martha was so cruel to Meg … Martha was my favourite and I was devastated when she died … the part that swipes, manipulates, and feels invulnerable … I like being in that position … but Meg … afraid, hiding, timid … suffering … Martha was my favourite and I didn't notice Meg when Martha was alive.

I do find it fascinating that it feels like there is something which actively stops me from remembering. I think on the other hand I also want to find out about myself, to know what I might be feeling inside … so there do seem to be two sides in opposition … I think that curiosity is also something which has made me think a lot about empathy and what happens … and towards myself …

In a dream, my sister and I were in a room and I was aware of her being needy and asking me for something, I don't know what … I just started screaming at her … telling her to fuck off … to get away from me and leave me alone … I was really frantically screaming … I was so contemptuous of her being needy ….

CHAPTER 5

The chaos or the word

Chaos often breeds life, when order breeds habit.

—Henry Adams (1995, p. 239)

He had the Word,
had it from on high, while I,
previous to alphabets, superfluous as ampersand,
curled on chaos till my edges blurred.

Gardens are made for orderers,
gardeners made to order,
but I am disorderable, the first trespasser.
So as Adam was carefully hedging his bets
and hugging the hedge,
and while angels were warring and setting
God's teeth on edge,
misfit and mislaid, I fled.

—From *The Passion of Lilith* by Pamela Hadas (1976)

The psychoanalytic disputes and the power that the "words" of the various "fathers and mothers" of each position had, led me to feel a considerable sense of chaos. I found it difficult to feel I belonged, and, like Samson in the temple, felt that in my "blindness" I was in danger of bringing the whole house down … another derelict building that I might find myself in, wishing to rebuild but feeling overcome with shame. However, this time, the demolition would be my own and therefore a very different situation to the memory in my childhood.

In the creation stories I was looking at, I noticed a marked difference between those that allowed for a time of chaos before creation, and those that stated that time began with "naming" or "the word". Somehow the difference between the two seemed important. The awareness of the psychological importance of this difference began to be significant, especially with respect to my growing need for a structure to exist which had a space for the maternal function.

I looked at the Bible again and paid attention, possibly for the first time, to the discrepancy in the first two chapters of Genesis.

The creation story in Genesis has at least two distinguishable authors: "E" who uses the term Elohim to refer to God, and "J" who uses the term Yahweh, or Jehovah to refer to God (Gibson, 1981, p. 1). There is another category of "P", the material added to help the texts flow together, the authors of which were thought to be "priests". These different authors—E and J—narrate two separate accounts of the beginning of man. The "documentary hypothesis" (Viviano, 1999, p. 40) is a theological model used to explain the origins and composition of the Pentateuch (first five books of the Old Testament). It suggests that the older of the two accounts is the second (J, dated *c.* 950 BCE) and that the first account (E, dated *c.* 900–800 BCE) is a variation of J. Much criticism of the "documentary hypothesis" exists, and many scholars would question the relevance of author E due to the brevity of the passages attributed to him, whilst others also argue that the J source could not be dated to *c.* 950 BCE, but is more likely to be 597 BCE.

The first story in Genesis describes man and woman being created at the same time and in the same manner. The second describes Adam being created first and then Eve being created from his rib and being brought into existence as his helper. In order to make some sort of sense of the existence of the two accounts, Jewish mythology has given rise to the character of Lilith, said to be the first woman (that is, before Eve), who was created at the same time and in the same manner as Adam, and who therefore considered herself equal to him (Williams, 2019, p. 7). Lilith refused to consider herself subservient to Adam, who wanted to lie on top of her, and so left Eden rather than submit. When God found out about Lilith's exile, he sent angels to negotiate her return to Eden. She reiterated her refusal to be subordinate and so remained in exile. As a result of this, several stories describe her being cursed by God and required to kill one hundred babies a day (Hurwitz, 1992, p. 120).

Thus, this character, over time, became a demon who was said to be the primary force able to cause the death of newborn babies. She is also said to be the temptress, siren, or witch-like figure who leads men astray, especially at night with their dreams and nocturnal emissions.

The mythology that has arisen from the accounts in Genesis thus places the characters of Lilith and Eve in positions whereby they are made to bear the punishment, guilt, and sin of mankind, whilst also not having a status deserving of thought and awareness. Given the loneliness and demonisation of Lilith, Eve—the woman who came later—could be said to have been given a terrible choice: the best she can hope for is to bear her burden and wait. This is a choice similar to that presented in the next chapter, "The binding of Hans".

The first account (E) states:

> In the beginning, when God created the universe, the earth was formless and desolate. The raging ocean that covered everything was engulfed in total darkness, and the Spirit of God was moving over the water. Then God commanded, "Let there be light"—and light appeared. God was pleased with what he saw. Then he separated the light from the darkness, and he named the light "Day" and the darkness "Night". (Genesis 1:1; *The Good News Bible*, 1994, p. 17)

It proceeds to describe the creation in six days and man being created along with woman on the sixth day:

> and God said, Let us make Man in our own image, after our likeness: and let them have dominion over the fish of the sea ... and every creeping thing that creepeth upon the earth. So God created human beings, in his own image. He created them male and female. (p. 18)

This account emphasises the power of God's "word" as the creative force, a theme also taken up in John 1:1: "In the beginning was the Word, and the Word was with God, and the Word was God" (p. 1642).

The second account (J) describes the very familiar story of Adam and Eve, stating that man and woman were created separately and that woman came from man:

> When the Lord God made the universe, there were no plants on the earth and no seeds had sprouted, because he had not sent any rain, and there was no one to cultivate the land; ... Then the Lord God took some soil from the ground and formed a man out of it; he breathed life-giving breath into his nostrils and the man began to live. (Genesis 1:2; 1994, p. 19)

These two accounts do suggest very differing beginnings. In the first account the "word" of God says "Let there be light"—and light appears. This might be thought of as a symbolic equation (H. Segal, 1950), by which the symbol (the word) is actually equated with the thing (the light) that is being symbolised. As Segal suggests, "[S]ince a part of the ego is then confused with the object, the symbol—which is a creation and a function of the ego—becomes, in turn, confused with the object which is symbolised" (p. 53).

It is the "idea" of something, accompanied by a spoken word, that is given the capacity of generation and creation; no work is suggested, and nature is profoundly denied. Man and woman are part of the created creatures that God has "spoken" into existence.

The second account suggests that work and action brings life to things—God forms man from soil and breathes life into him—rather than the word. This moves creation into the physical, rather than the "thought-word" realm. Here, symbolisation and creation become that which can be envisaged in the mind as the finished product, before work takes place to achieve it.

From looking at the Egyptian cosmology myths, creation myths can be said to go through identifiable progressions from the more nature-based myths in which work is needed to be done, and in which there is a containment of the chaos (such as Phan Ku), to myths in which the word is used for creation (such as Marduk in Enuma Elish). Perhaps this does suggest that the second account (J) is older than the first, and demonstrates a possible psychological progression away from an awareness of nature and woman (inherent in this is the use of the body to contain pain and turmoil) and towards the use of the word as the creative force and ultimate container. The journey this progression takes is "through" the Garden of Eden—the creation of religion, a forbidding to eat of the Tree of Knowledge (of Good and Evil), the distortion of nature, the subservience of women, and the denial of the maternal function.

If the beginning *was* the word, then the inference here is that time, history, life, and the universe all began with the word. Before the word there was no thing, or formlessness. This is a very important distinction. If the beginning was the word, then the inherent and extrapolated meaning of this is that there was no thing before speech, and in particular no thing before the paternal word.

In this version of a beginning, God's word manifests the existence of the universe, and *no thing* becomes *some thing*. Even if a literal material beginning isn't adhered to (that is, there was matter prior to God's actions, but it was "disordered", and God's word brings about "order"), the meaning of this is still the emphasis of the *paternal* word being the "orderer" which brings *some thing* out of *no thing*, rather than a *maternal* word, "previous to alphabets", giving form to the unformed. The two functions are very different.

Time, space, existence, and history all become measured from this starting point of the word.

The inference that there is no thing before this negates the time of chaos, disorder, evolution, and development and the importance of it. "In the beginning was the Word" is a deeply misogynistic concept. It denies the experience and importance of the time that all babies have with their mothers, which invariably involves a time without words. This use of her body, her maternal function and containing capacity, which gives something of unique importance, is not only deemed unimportant, it is also not given an existence and representation in the mind.

Here, by "maternal function" I mean it to include everything that is prevalent in the relationship between a primary caregiver and a newborn baby. It begins with gestation and birth, and later includes nurturing, sacrifice, containing of fear and anxieties, giving of "form" and words that belong to the inside, and the teaching (through behaviour) of how to be in the world. From this foundation, the child is able to construct an internal structure (essentially a creation myth) by which he (or she, of course) can emerge and explore his environment.

During this essential time, the maternal function can also lead to the "maternal third" position which is the result of an active maternal curiosity and the internal giving of form to the chaos. The words that are arrived at from this containment are very different to the words referred to in Genesis.

What a creation myth does with this time before a deity's word is revealing as to the nature of the structure that is being offered as a container,[6] and as a window into gender relations. If there is no description of this time, or an emphasis on time beginning with the word, then I feel that the structure in use inherently denigrates the maternal function. The container that is insinuated becomes the word over the body and misogyny is endemic.

In the consulting room, this might be seen in interpretations which stop at the word—such as when a patient may be frustrated and the analyst says, "You're angry." While this may be accurate, when it is accompanied by the analyst operating from a religious creation myth, it becomes, "You're angry; I have told you now, so you can adapt your behaviour accordingly." The word, as spoken by the analyst, is expected to be used as the container, and the only response the patient can have is to employ his superego to control the anger and try to alter his state. This situation necessitates the growth of an observing self who judges, and the employment of an outside structure to measure oneself by. This sort of situation results in an analysis which strengthens the superego and relies on the analyst being like a god creating a structure with his words. Here, no bodies are involved—the patient does not "get inside" the analyst and chaos is not present. If chaos does occur, this type of analyst will interpret attack and destructiveness—thereby trying to evoke a superego response from the patient and a reinstatement of an external godlike control by the analyst.

An analyst who has a space in his mind for chaos and who allows for an unformed state to have existed before the word, will have a firmer ability to use the maternal function in the consulting room, and will be able to find words which come from a maternal third position. This capacity to allow for the chaos—that is, to have a formulation of it in the mind, as well as to be comfortable in experiencing it within the body—enables a coming together of the patient and analyst. This coupling is essential in the process of containment and development. No trauma or unknown experience can become endurable without this coupling. If the parent or therapist or analyst has no formulation or representation of this chaos, then the essential coupling experience is not possible. In these circumstances, only the creation of an external God can serve to partially compensate for the inadequate maternal function.

Pelagius argued for the placing of God within everything that *is*. All creation is then able to be thought of as being full of God's light, which is only obscured by the darkness of sin. This would mean that it is within each of our abilities to choose to allow this light to shine. Repentance, therefore, is turning to what is most deeply planted within us—the light which has not been overcome with darkness.

---

[6] Here, by "container" I mean that which enables an infant to eventually be able to emerge from his mother's care—the structure that is being used as a frame of reference which "holds" a sense of the world, a sense of self, and how they connect together, and the representation in the mind of what "goes on between".

This placing of God within every particle of life on earth is counter to the argument of God being *transcendent* to his creation (Augustine's position): that is, God is above and not to be found intimately involved in life on earth. He has created from above, according to a plan, and resides in another place from where he watches and waits. A transcendent God is one whose word is the creative force, and one who observes. With such a profound denial, and appropriation, of all things maternal, the word in this form is patriarchal; it originates from without and is concerned with action, good and bad, and "what" the person is. An analyst operating from this position sees themselves as "above" the patient, observing, and not engaging bodily in the chaos.

If God is within each particle of life, then "who" the person is becomes relevant. Experience, trauma, inner bodies, and a reaching in to find out (curiosity as part of the maternal function) become important.

The individual and personal (mostly unconscious) answers to these questions provide a structure from which we behave, that affects how we see ourselves and each other, how we react and respond to difficulty, trauma, need, pain, and otherness, and that influences what faction of psychoanalysis we may belong to. This structure, or personal creation myth, throws light on the beliefs a person has in relation to man and woman, inner and outer, and projective and introjective forces.

When thinking has been predominately *within* a particular structure of belief (which has been arrived at from events, pains, and difficulties, and a need to try to understand and control in order to offset anxiety), it then takes on a "life" of its own and becomes "truth". This truth then becomes the foundation from which everything becomes orientated. The truth itself is constantly under threat from reality and other truths, and therefore is constantly adapted and added to in order to retain the belief and truth. This accounts for the tendency for religions to evolve their doctrine to seemingly ridiculous lengths. If instead of thinking within the structure, thought could be allowed to expand to see the structure as part of a way of being which is in response to some deeply unconscious predicament, the world becomes a different place.

This is similar to Bion's sense of approaching a session without "memory or desire". I believe that the memories and desires that need to be forgone are precisely those which keep us within a so-called truth that is rarely considered, but has an all-encompassing impact upon how we live our lives. The danger of taking Bion's advice on board, however, is that it is just used as something within the structure—that is, it is simply incorporated into the existing structure as part of an external command as to how to be, instead of realising that a different sort of memory and desire are required: the memory of something before religion and the desire to interact with others in a penetrative and maternal manner. Bion's direction to put away memory and desire is only possible if there is an understanding of what is in the chaos, for it to have a form and an order, albeit a very different form and order to the world of the word.

"In the beginning was the Word" has time starting with the paternal function: this is the word that comes from outside the body which creates law, control, and judgement. In stating this as the starting point, chaos then becomes something which is without words, and therefore terrifying. A "hell" is created, and, as the maternal function which might render it tolerable has been attacked or destroyed, it truly becomes a place full of demons. Therefore, it could be said that hell is only created when the paternal word is taken to be the beginning.

This memory of something before the word is essential as it enables a representation in the mind of coupling between the self and another who can help give form to the formless—that is, another who can provide a containment function. Without this memory, there would be no desire for an infant or person to seek another.

A deeper consequence of a belief (whether unconscious or conscious) in a starting point of "In the beginning was the Word" is that it inherently needs to believe in magic. Most creation myths which start from the word speak of creation being magically brought into existence, either directly, or not involving work and coupling. Magic and magical thought are accepted without challenge. When magic-related thinking is evident, the system that is being utilised to "hold" the person together is one which imbues the paternal word with the power of containment and creation. It is this word alone which is then thought to control inner formlessness and chaos. This renders the concept of original sin necessary, as this external control leaves the internal without this function and therefore full of "sin". Thus, magical structures and original sin can again be said to both deny the maternal and the circularity of being. An analyst who operates from the position of the paternal, external word would, by necessity, see the inner body as full of unrepresented chaotic forces which can only be controlled by his external word.

If Pelagius' view is accepted, the counter position of the inner world being essentially benign or good is possible. The difference between the two positions is essentially where the locus of creation and containment is placed, and who, either the mother or the father, has the capacity to create and bring form to the formless.

An external locus needs the word to magically create, and this capacity is owned by the male. A hierarchical structure is needed to orientate the self and others above nature. As a consequence, the inner world is viewed as full of original sin or innate destructiveness.

An internal locus needs a body that creates, and this capacity is seen to belong to the female. A structure can be established where both the self and the other are felt to be within nature. Thus, the inner world is felt to be benign.

In moving from a position of feeling that there were significant absences in the theories I was learning, to a curiosity about beginnings and a confusion regarding the disputes and positions within psychoanalysis, I realised that I was experiencing chaos. I was not able to find a position that resonated with all the "hats" I spoke of in Chapter One. My memory of being in the derelict buildings and wishing to rebuild something began to take hold. I could not demolish the theories as they all contained "truth", but I realised that I had to find something foundational that would be able to hold enough of me to find a peace within the chaos. This memory, and its corresponding shame, unknowingly became the measure by which I approached theory. This memory needed to feel held within the structure that the theory offered. The most difficult aspect was to find a place for the shame.

The next chapter looks at the terrible sacrifices involved when the illusion of a creation myth is forced upon a mind.

* * *

Jacob

> I get thoughts of despair … I like words and that word "despair" really intrigues me … the two meanings of it are at odds … anyway, I get thoughts of despair [*putting fist on head and elbow on knee*] and they feel terrible, but I can then think about it as a failure of humour or think of it as a failure and can soon come back … things can happen that send me into utter despair, but now I can change the meaning of the word and unpick it …

CHAPTER 6

The binding of Hans

When we agree about our hallucinations, we call that reality.

—Anil Seth (2017)

In this chapter, I focus on a catastrophic state of mind that comes about when an outer, society-wide illusion meets the internal world and perceptual apparatus. I represent this by looking at the story of *The Emperor's New Clothes* and the philosophical "trolley problem". This is important as it represents the dilemmas that are inherent when we come across any theory which is being used to represent reality. The event horizon between the perceptual apparatus, an external, lived societal illusion, and inner awareness of needs, wishes, and anxieties, is an enormously complex one. The individual solution to this dilemma inevitably involves the sacrifice of one or more of these essential factors. The pressure to "join" the prevailing creation myth is powerful, and resistance to it often means punishment and isolation.

I have been fascinated by the complexity behind the seemingly simple, and by how often in our day-to-day lives we say things which, if thought about, develop a complexity that defies the casualness with which they are spoken. Likewise, I find that I tend to search for the simple in seemingly complex ideas.

In thinking about this reductive and expansive tendency, I feel it has something to do with a need for all parts of "the story" to be told. It feels to be an injustice somehow if some aspect has been left unsaid. It certainly can be traced to my early childhood and an unknown sense that there were many stories in my family that did not have a voice.

With anything I might read, or come across, I have this approach—and with this in mind one story in particular grabbed my attention. *The Emperor's New Clothes* is familiar to most people, and is essentially about a rich emperor who was fooled by two tailors. They promised him that they could make a new suit of clothes that would be invisible to anyone who was too stupid or incompetent to see it. In reality, they created no clothes at all, but made everyone believe the clothes were invisible to them, essentially rendering them either incompetent or stupid. When the emperor paraded before his people, no one dared say that they didn't see the clothes, but instead shouted out how good they were. A confused child responds to this by saying that the emperor was, in fact, wearing nothing at all. In the story, some of the crowd then join the child and the emperor himself realises that he is naked, but carries on regardless.

Hans Christian Andersen's story is meant to show the hypocrisy and snobbery of the upper classes, and is thought to be based in a childhood experience of his during which he was in a crowd, with his mother, watching the procession of King Frederick VI. When the young Andersen saw the king, he cried out, "Oh, he's nothing more than a human being." His mother tried to silence him by saying, "Have you gone mad, child?" (Frank & Frank, 2005, p. 110).

The story might be thought about from the perspective of the trickery of the tailors, the narcissistic arrogance of the emperor, or the political and social conditions endemic in society. But what has always held more interest for me is the situation that the child is presented with.

The child (I will assume he is a boy) is faced with a terrible dilemma. While the actual story has some of the crowd joining the boy in his voicing of the emperor's nakedness, the situation that the young Andersen found himself in was far more complicated.

I will bring together the story and Andersen's experience to examine the relationship between reality, perception, illusion, the parental realm, and the self. These are all pushed to a maddening limit. The young boy is essentially having to choose which version or path to go down.

If he goes with his perception of sight, then the emperor is naked. If he follows his perception of hearing—listening to the crowd, and his parents—the emperor is dressed in fine clothes.

If he chooses to follow the crowd, his parents, and his hearing, then the emperor "has" to become dressed in the boy's mind—a shifting of his reality, away from his perceptual apparatus, to an illusion.

What follows is a crisis of reality for the boy. Whichever route he takes involves a sacrifice. If he capitulates and agrees with his parents, it is the start of a psychological process of disavowal of his perceptions and his relationship to an external reality. Illusion has taken over. The sacrifice is monumental—that of his whole perceptual apparatus, which becomes "switched off".

If he stays with his perceptual awareness of reality and insists that the emperor is naked, then he effectively loses his parents. He has chosen reality but this reality is one in which his parents have lost their authority and respect. Both situations are truly maddening and have a devastating impact on the developing mind.

A disavowal of reality or a loss of parents. Either a part of himself becomes "psychologically murdered" or his parents do.

At some point, and to varying degrees, this dilemma is one that faces us all. The more extreme end of the spectrum being the abused child growing up in a family that knows but "doesn't know" the reality of the child's experience. This forces the child to try to disavow the perceptual and psychological awareness of the abuse, in order to at least retain a pseudo sense of having parents. The bigger abuse here is that which is done to the mind of the child. Reality has been distorted and it is not able to be spoken about. This was noted by Sándor Ferenczi in his paper "Confusion of tongues between the adult and the child" (1949).

At the other end of the spectrum, this phenomenon might be seen when a person has to psychologically adopt something he knows to be counter to his reality, in order to be able to join a club or be accepted somewhere. To tolerate this, a shutting down of something inside needs to happen. Perhaps in history this has happened many times when certain scientific advances have become apparent and are irrefutable when the full perceptual apparatus is applied, but the wider reaction to it is denial and vehement opposition. I'm sure Galileo was like the boy shouting "He's naked" while the Church was insisting he was wrong.

The "trolley problem" is a well-known philosophical exercise which I see as similarly emphasising the horror of this internal dilemma. It describes a train which is proceeding along a track and approaching a fork in the line. A person in the signal box notices there are five people tied to one line, and on the other, one. The train is on track to take the line with the five people tied to it. The dilemma is whether the person watching actively changes the track the train takes to the other line, or not. Either five people die, or one. Galileo, Darwin, Socrates and many others have suffered for choosing to psychologically save the one person (their own minds) over the five (the wider world).

When the self and perceptions are sacrificed, this creates a shut down part of the mind which grows in its monstrous capacity. It not only holds the reality; it also holds the rage of having to sacrifice it; the sense that no adult can tolerate it in their own minds, and it also creates a defensive urgency to hold back the constant need it has to find expression.

The conservation laws of physics are fundamental laws of nature and therefore fundamental to the physical world. The conservation law of energy states that the total energy in an isolated system does not change, though it may change form, and most conservation laws are exact, or absolute, in the sense that they apply to all possible processes. (Although in the realm of quantum mechanics and particle physics, things are different.)

From a scientific point of view, the shutdown aspects of mind become like a closed system wherein the energy being held by that system does not change, but might change form.

The tensions and tumults of a mind which has closed, and which believes that there is no dynamic interaction possible for this situation to change, can only remain held in the body. The result is a mind which has shut down, symptoms which emanate from the need for defences, and a body which has to hold the tumults psychosomatically.

If a creation myth were to be written describing this situation (creation in all its forms—the primordial beginnings of life, the birth of the boy, the genesis of a thought) then it would need to omit all coupling, be dependent upon an external word to denote the illusion which is being disguised as reality, and induce a fear of what was before the word. This becomes the structure by which life is orientated.

This situation is a psychological disaster on a monumental scale. The myth that becomes written and enforced is taken to be the starting point and is one which therefore precludes nature, reality, free thinking, and forbids knowledge of the truth.

If we consider the conditions required for this type of creation myth to take over, then *The Emperor's New Clothes* shows it is to do with the tension between perceptual reality, the need of the child to retain his parents, and the authoritative denial of the perceptual reality. The child has grown up relying on his perception of the world to make sense of it, to be able to function within it, and to learn about cause and effect, action and reaction. He has gained a sense of himself as being in the world and also a trust in his perceptual apparatus to guide him through it. He has also grown up trusting his parents to keep him safe, to explain things he doesn't understand, and to put words to things that frighten him. In all of these aspects, he has honed his perceptual apparatus according to his parents' capacity to contain him, and this works best when his perceptions correspond mostly with his parents' responses. A foundational trust is built which will serve him well in his future.

When a child is faced with the catastrophic dilemma of an authoritative denial of perceptual reality, like for Andersen with his mother, this system of trust can irrevocably break down. The sacrifice that inevitably comes about, either way (sacrificing the mind, or the parents) results in shutting down and closing off. If you like, the "energies" associated with life traumas, phantasies, thoughts, wishes, needs, and so on, remain inside the closed system and do not undergo any change, except changing form. The sense of self that the boy has shifts, the sense of his parents shifts, and the sense of the world shifts. He becomes mindless in a way—maddened—sensing that his reality is not acceptable, and most of all, his experience of the world becomes a terrifyingly lonely one. His parents become parents who are maddening, who defy reality, and who are not to be trusted with his inner self. The system in operation is one which the boy has to join, albeit with the catastrophic loss of his thinking and perceptual apparatus, or forever be completely alone and in exile from his parents and community.

In better circumstances, this tension between inner reality and the authoritative version of that reality is a dynamic one. The child's ability to hold on to the two is dependent upon both structures being flexible through trust. The catastrophe outlined above occurs when this trust becomes irrevocably broken through a single experience of an extreme reality crisis. The contrast between the two positions was too great. Lesser challenges to this system may also build up over time in a chronic fashion, leading to a similar outcome.

I found that part of my struggle with some aspects of theory in psychoanalysis was that I felt it was asking me to put aside much of my own perceptual apparatus and thinking. For example, the many references and inferences in psychoanalytic thinking and discourse about something labelled "merging". The prevailing attitude towards this, in what I read, was that merging was pathological and needed to be interpreted to the patient so they might then shift their behaviour—the type of interpretations that might start, "You want to get inside me," and so on. Even with the awareness of a difference between a need to merge for growth and then a more attacking or defensive use of merging, my perceptual and inner sense, built up over time, led me to feel and think something different to the attitude I found in my reading. I then had a choice—do I discount my sense of reality and adopt an authoritative one, or do I "keep my mind" but essentially be alone?

I wish to highlight this tension between versions of reality on a "micro" day-to-day level and its consequent impact on belonging, thinking, and the overall relationship to nature. Perhaps this minor example shows how difficult it is to incorporate Bion's advice to "learn from experience"—as opposed to an intellectual learning—into everyday life. As Bion writes,

> The emergence therefore of any tendency to search for the truth, to establish contact with reality and in short to be scientific in no matter how rudimentary a fashion, is met by destructive attacks on the tendency and the reassertion of the 'moral superiority'. This implies an assertion of what in sophisticated terms would be called a moral law and a moral system as superior to scientific law and a scientific system. (1962, p. 254).

Here, Bion is recognising that this phenomenon is not only present within the mind, but has an external reality too. Chris Mawson, in his editor's introduction to Bion's *Learning from Experience*, says "The clinical significance of this insight is of the greatest importance for the daily practice of psychoanalysis. … At another level, it also holds implications for considering group and political life, including the relationships between us in our psychoanalytic societies and organisations" (2014, p. 254).

* * *

Clothes make the man. Naked people exert little or no influence on society.

—Mark Twain (1927)

Andersen's emperor, dressed in his clothing, occupies a position of hierarchical authority and power, and people orientate themselves in relation to him accordingly. Without his clothing, he is seen to be just that, a naked man, who is no different to anyone else, and his authority collapses. The hallucination of hierarchy and the clothing (and words) a man wears to perpetuate this myth is an exceptionally fragile system which the creation myth (unconscious or conscious) serves to keep in place. Without this "clothing", a man is seen as nothing; he is shameful with no impact or power, and highly vulnerable.

The inherent shame of the knowingly "naked position" began to feel like a Gordian knot of complexity and impossibility for me. The shame, from this perspective, seemed to be because of the awareness of the hierarchical referencing of the self and feeling alone in a society that refuses to become perceptually aware of the naked position.

* * *

Jacob

I had a dream ... I was on an airstrip and I saw two planes, one bigger than the other; the smaller one took off and then the other, which seemed to turn back on itself and crashed. I felt excited at the fact I'd seen it ... it crashed into farmland and there were fires and the people on board died ... I saw a cat and was glad it had survived, but I felt nothing for the people.

I used to have relentless dreams of planes seeking me out, chasing me, and crashing into me ... never giving up ... terrifying ... and then I saw a programme on TV which had a character who could change things by thinking ... If he didn't like anything, he had special powers to think of it differently ... I realised I could do that and the dreams changed to the plane crashing into people around me rather than into me.

CHAPTER 7

Circularity and straight lines

In becoming immersed in the themes of "beginnings", I looked deeper into Jewish mythology and became aware of the *Zohar* and "Adam Kadmon". This is a highly complex myth and Luria was one of its leading scholars. His thinking has been preserved by the writing of his student, Chayyim Vital. He highlighted the importance of "circles" and "straight lines" to their ideas and describes the coming together of "circular vessels" with the "straight line of light". In this highly anatomical description of the beginning of Adam Kadmon (which preceded the Adam of the Garden of Eden), several bodily and psychological functions can be identified. Among the rich symbolism is an acknowledgement of projection, introjection, container–contained, and interiors and exteriors. This shows the enduring nature of the theories within psychoanalysis and that these fundamental bodily themes have had a presence in the mind and a representation in thought for thousands of years. Our response to them is a primary influence upon behaviour, character, and disturbance.

* * *

In the midst of this chaotic time, I wrote the chapter "In the beginning ..." found in Part II. In thinking about this now, I realise I was very concerned with what went on *between* people. I saw the natural processes of introjection and projection as the building blocks of every thought, every expression of self, and every experience of moving from a high state of anxiety to a lower one. I began to understand that these processes were the meaning of life itself. This coupling was essential to feeling alive, to finding meaning and a sense of identity. I could see that it was the universal law that held everything in existence in a connected state. All particles, atoms, cells, organisms, creatures, and humans behave in this way and will always need to. Projective and introjective forces are irreducibly and irrevocably essential to the capacity a person has to think and put words to experience, and are therefore essential to the establishment of a structure from which a person emerges into the world.

For this process to result in a sustainable lowering of anxiety or need, it has to be "circular". There needs to be a connection *between*, which involves awareness of the other and also a sense of the other being able to receive something, while still being able to retain their own identity. The receiver then not only needs to survive, but also needs to return something "less anxiety provoking" to the original owner.

Projection which is not circular, occurring with no idea or wish for it to be returned to the original owner, could be said to have become "weaponised". Melanie Klein (Bott Spillius et al., 2011) has expressed this well in her description of the projective capacity of an infant struggling with envy, greed, and destructiveness:

> Together with these harmful excrements, expelled in hatred, split off parts of the ego are also projected onto the mother or, as I would rather call it, into the mother. These excrements and bad parts of the self are meant not only to injure the object but also to control it and take possession of it. (p. 131)

I am calling this mechanism, in contrast to the hermeneutic loop, a hermeneutic straight line.

In the sixteenth century, Chayyim Vital (Vital, 2015) wrote various treatises based on his tutor's (Luria's) teachings. Very little has survived from Luria (d. 1574) himself, but his thinking is known by the written accounts of his students. Luria and his students were intent upon studying and understanding the *Zohar*, a thirteenth-century book of Jewish mythology published by Moses de Leon, purportedly based on the writings of a second-century rabbi, Shimon bar Yochai. They tried to explain or add to the *Zohar* in order for it to maintain its relevance within the theological views of the day.

Vital describes a highly complex creation, starting from a single simple light named "Ein Sof" (Without End). This light filled all existence; there was no space or void and no creation could occur due to its purity. When it "arose in the will of Ein Sof" (Vital, 2015, p. 2) to create worlds, it constricted part of itself into a point and withdrew this constricted light to create a perfectly round void. This was the first circular aspect of creation. A straight, thin line of light then extended from Ein Sof into the void, producing a series of ten concentric circles in descending order, these were called the Sefirot of Adam Kadmon (primordial man, as distinct from Adam Ha-Rishon, the physical Adam in the Garden of Eden). Sefirot are the emanations through which Ein Sof reveals himself and continuously creates (see Figure 4).

Luria and Vital envisaged ten concentric circles of Sefirot which have a dynamic relationship with each other. Each circle receives the straight line of light which is "bestowed" from the Ein Sof, but it is only those circles closest to Ein Sof that are able to withstand it, as they are closest to the purest state; those further away cannot tolerate it and shatter. The broken fragments of the shattered vessel descend to the lower levels, while the divine light ascends back to

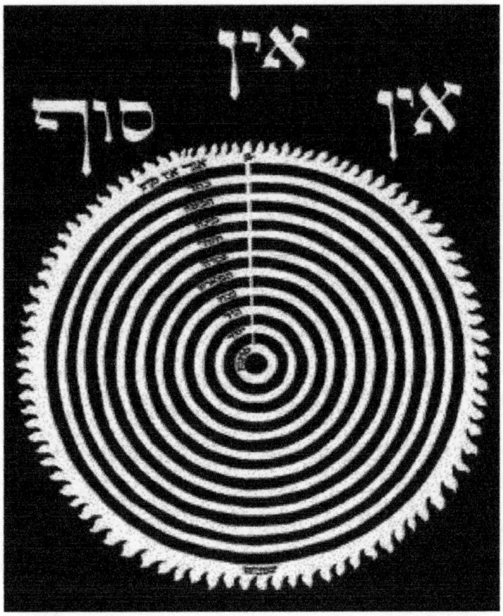

Figure 4. Ein Sof

Adam Kadmon, the holiest Sefirot closest to Ein Sof. This process proceeds and each shattering has the impact of strengthening the vessels of the lower levels (as the broken fragments carry with them some of the impact of the light in a reduced form). Humans, and the Earth itself, can only exist in the lowest level furthest away from Ein Sof, as physical existence cannot tolerate the pure, undiminished divine light.

Luria's description of the beginning of time is an anatomical one. The human body was considered to be modelled on the image of the Divine and the counterpart of the universe. Therefore, it was thought that supernal processes could be deduced through looking at the human body and its mechanisms (Vital, 2015, p. 2). This can be seen by there being a strong emphasis on the male aspect of "bestowing" and the female aspect of "receiving" within the description.

After almost a 1,000-year dearth of human dissection, anatomy studies had been proceeding quickly in the twelfth and thirteenth centuries, and the famous "anatomists"—such as Mondino de Luzzi—were starting to collate their findings. It has been suggested that the *Zohar* itself, rather than being based on the writings of a second-century rabbi, was instead written by Leon de Moses himself and, thus, may well have been heavily influenced by this "inner" curiosity and "looking" (see the article by Joseph Jacobs and Isaac Broydé in the *Jewish Encyclopedia*, 1906, for more on this).

Anatomy, and the psychological understanding of creation in relation to the genders, is perhaps the first psychic mystery primitive humankind wished to understand, and this puzzle can be seen to be a factor in the formation of creation myths. The relationship between knowledge available (scientific advances as well as personal experience) and the need to assuage terrors, anxieties, and individual wishes leads to a specific content of a myth. This initial curiosity and need then widens to a wondering about our status in nature and the universe—where all life comes from.

Thus, it seems probable that Luria and Vital had the bodily aspects of sexual function in mind when they were formulating their system of creation. Perhaps they were trying to incorporate the growing body of anatomical science into a religious creation myth, but what seems to be evident is that they had a detailed knowledge of the body, its anatomy, and introjective and projective processes. This demonstrates clearly that an aspect of creation myths is a "making sense" of procreation, bodies, sex, and gender. The sense that is made is specific to the needs, envies, fears, and provisions of the day, as well as the extent of knowledge available.

The psychic status of all these processes can be found in creation myths, and as such they provide a rich insight into development and the nature of mind.

Adam Kadmon can be described as the emanation, essence, or thought of an entity before creation occurs (similar to the attributes of Ptah). This then enables a "formation" to come into existence which can fulfil an action. The world of action is the furthest away from Ein Sof, and full of carnal desires. In this construction, the female elements (circular vessels) are given an important place, but it is emphasised that the male aspect is superior as it is the pure straight line from Ein Sof. Vital says this straight line is the creator of souls and is the carrier of Ein Sof, and so it is to be thought of as a higher form (2015, p. 228). Thus, a hierarchical system is created.

There are many fascinating considerations to this construct, and I don't have the scope to refer to all of it. However, I am focusing on my associations with circles and straight lines. In the placing of a higher emphasis and superiority on the straight line, the role and the importance of the female is diminished. In terms of the bestowing of something to a receiver of something the processes of projection and introjection are understood, but the receiver is thought to not provide anything other than being a vessel or a container. It is as though in this system, the receiver of the light, the vessel, is merely an object for the bestower to place its light into. This causes a creative process to become possible, but the "spark" or life-giving is provided via the straight line.

Straight lines create hierarchies and are dependent upon a sense of male supremacy. Vital was seemingly trying to incorporate a representation of the feminine into this and perhaps realised that circularity needed to be added. In his scheme, these circular aspects (perhaps vaginas) are vessels which both need to carry the light (perhaps the penis and sperm), whilst also being inherently unable to bear the light. (This has a parallel with the Byzantine description of the Virgin Mary as *Chora tou Achoretou*—the container of the uncontainable.) This results in a fragmentation and a reconstitution after which the vessel is stronger. This is the process of containment and development that both Bion (container–contained[7]) and Winnicott

[7] When contemplating the capacity to remember certain aspects of dreams, as opposed to other aspects which were not recalled, Bion used an analogy of digestion and "indigestibility". He wrote: "Are 'undigested facts' then used in the process of 'digesting' other facts? Is their 'indigestibility' a quality that renders them useful for this function, as if

(in "The Use of an Object"[8]) describe. It is interesting that this theme of "broken" containers was also known by Vital and Luria in the sixteenth century.

This sense of something being strong and functional after breakage is also represented in the Japanese philosophy of Wabi Sabi. The aim of this is to show the inherent beauty in imperfection—it involves a perfect, porcelain tea set being purposively "broken" before it can be used in a tea ceremony—it then becomes the beautiful container which can function even after impairment. The Phan Ku myth also psychically represents containment, as does Hina.

Luria and Vital had an innate understanding of this process and sought a way to represent it while remaining true to their original myth.

Straight lines are stagnant, they do not have the circularity needed for a hermeneutic loop, so they remain in a deadened form. Curiosity is needed to change a straight line to a circle, and that requires a wish to "go inside" and to find out. This becomes a curiosity about the female body, something akin to eating of the Tree of Knowledge which then leads to expulsion from Eden. This paradise is only a paradise for Adam and perhaps the need to keep to straight lines (hierarchies, no curiosity, male supremacy, creation of a transcendent God) is in place because to have a realistic psychic representation of Eve and circularity would bring the whole "house" down.

The levels of psychic representation in creation myths start off from the primitive sense of pregnancy and birth being mysterious and unknown. The female is felt to have "magical forces" at her disposal which enable pregnancy; perhaps this is represented in the raven myth by his surprise when man emerges from the pea pod. It is also seen in the aboriginal tribe who thought that women became pregnant by walking past a magic rock (Langdon-Davies, 1938, pp. 14–15). This phenomenon could also account for the magic attributed to actions (as opposed to the word) having a presence in these myths. At this level, the woman is feared, envied, and revered. Wherever, and whenever, there is something beyond understanding, a god is formed, and these societies will have female deities to worship, but there is no monotheistic male god when creation is felt to be a mysterious female capacity.

The next level is that of an association between the sexual act and pregnancy. This then elevates the male position into one of supremacy—his semen (which is visible and "his") is the giver of life, and the woman is merely the vessel. This representation is seen in many creation myths, such as in the Heliopolis cosmology.

---

it were some kind of container for an eroding liquid which must be able itself to resist the erosion by its contents?" (1991, p. 56). Here he is considering the relationship between the container and its contents and highlighting the "breakability" of it. And, again, he says: "The conflict is between the container and the contained thing in which they both seem to be on very destructive terms, where either the container gets split apart, or the object that is put into the container gets destroyed" (pp. 327–328).

[8] Winnicott, in his paper "The Use of an Object", describes the sequence needed before an infant can *use* an object: "(1) Subject *relates* to object, (2) Object is in process of being found instead of placed by the subject in the world, (3) Subject *destroys* object, (4) Object survives destruction, (5) Subject can *use* object" (1971, p. 94). Thus, for Winnicott, breakability is an integral part of development too.

As knowledge becomes more available and its psychic representation not only catches up, but also becomes too problematic to ignore, these myths need to be adapted to include the new awarenesses (as seen in Luria, Vital, Augustine, and so on). In this way, Luria might be said to be operating in a hermeneutic loop, but instead of "ripping up" the knowledge he had and thinking afresh (like Mendeleev did), he builds on the base of previous knowledge that he wishes to keep in place, that is, his creation myth of male supremacy and a transcendent God. The stories then need to evolve to incorporate the new knowledge, while remaining "true" to the original psychological structure the myth provides. The move away from the mysterious woman giving birth and creating, through to the woman being merely a vessel and the male being the supreme giver of life, can be seen as a factor that runs through most myths. This very much suggests that the myths as we have them today have gone through many cycles of evolution in oral form before being written. The written form then has another impact—instead of an ever evolving construct that changes not only through one telling of it to the next, but between villages and generations, it becomes static and a "straight line".

I imagine that this stagnation of myth has had a profound impact on the psychological structures available to man. The inherent dilemma being that evolution to incorporate new knowledge and development becomes increasingly "sinful" as it counters the "written", unchanging form of the myth. The primal father can live on beyond death and sin becomes anything that might remove him from this position.

This hermeneutic straight line is similar to the thinking of the psychoanalyst Matthew Bell. He says:

> … their phantasy of moving toward a known position effectively diminishes their thinking to a point of a little death. It effectively follows the idea of the thermodynamic Arrow Of Time and rather, as with healthy thinking, expanding forward to an unknown but exciting possibility, it will instead, go forward to a known, appearing therefore, to move backwards …When one is faced with a definite, then thinking … contracts. If thinking/mind is to deal with the unknown, it needs to be allowed to expand and grow. Contrarily, if thinking/mind is to inevitably be met with a known conclusion, then it diminishes to that point of known conclusion. (Private communication)

If projection and introjection involve psychically being *in* the female aspect of a body, then the consequences of not allowing this would necessitate the creation of "straight lines". The person who finds themselves at the end of this straight line would be considered to be full of sin, or abhorrent to the sensibilities of the person who is at the other end.

All particles in the universe interact by the giving or receiving of something. All creatures on earth interact in this way with others and the environment. All psychic processes need to undergo this before being able to be assuaged. It involves merging, mixing, using bodies, disorder, fear, and an allowing of this chaos to *be*. The word that might be invoked to deny or even forbid this natural and essential process sets itself up as something that can offer an adequate substitute to the universal law of nature. The consequence of mistaking the word for this is the creation of a transcendent, omniscient, omnipotent, and monotheistic god: the world becomes split into good and bad; bad things happen to bad people; the powerful are also transcendent, and all myths serve to reinforce the word. From this perspective, the actual original sin is not going against or not praising the word; it is the annihilation of nature and of Eve. Guilt is not about the actions which may contravene a law, but the unconscious guilt of what has been done to Eve and her rightful, spatial share of the mind.

Pain is essential for the whole of the universe. Without pain, or disturbance, or anxiety, or tension, or discomfort, or hunger, or thirst, or instability, or … there would be no drive, no impetus, no seeking, no motivation to find another entity to pass the tumult to, and then no opportunity for the joy (not pleasure) of having it assuaged. This connection enables a sense of love; it is the meaning of life and source of joy and calm. Gratification does not provide this and is a very poor substitute.

* * *

Jacob

The dream last night was unprecedented … I found myself attached in some way to a person I knew to be a child … that somehow I knew my job was to protect him … I found myself and the child in a prison yard … a square with a wall and three sides of tall wire fence. I had a gun in my hand, an automatic rifle of some sorts … and unusually, in fact an incredibly unprecedented event, I was able to fire the gun at the guards. I didn't seem to hit them and soon found myself turning the gun on the child—he was running and I was trying to fire at him, but the bullets were extraordinarily slow and came out of the gun like corks from a pop gun. I missed him and kept on missing him, but then I became aware of a sniper from outside the yard who was firing at me. I began firing back and I knew my fire was reaching the sniper, but I didn't have a sense that I was wounding her.

I have a sense of the dream as being very, very important, but I don't know why, other than I've never, ever been able to fire a gun in a dream before … my fingers fuse, or lose power and I never get them to work … I've always associated it with powerlessness, abject impotence …

CHAPTER 8

Initial thoughts and what comes next

Part I is primarily the fundamental basis from which I frame the questions and dilemmas I felt stuck in, especially regarding psychoanalytic theory. What began to emerge was the sense that these dilemmas are not new—they are questions that have occupied humankind from the beginning of thought. I have not attempted to answer these questions—Part I exists to allow the ideas to ferment and gather a momentum.

The problems regarding the position of man in relation to the world, the universe, and most of all woman—and the solution an individual person arrives at—have a great impact. It is the basis of the external and internal structures that are created in order to justify and modify the world, in other words, the creation myth an individual operates from.

Myths and theory both provide structures within which self-orientation can take place. What might be present and/or absent within these structures is important as they indicate the extent of what can be represented in the mind. A structure which has a close enough relationship with nature and reality is able to contain all the natural processes that are needed for existence. To veer away from this means that some aspects of existence do not have a representation. In exploring this in relation to theory and myth, a structure which has a representation of both male and female aspects, as well as being able to hold the "unknown", becomes increasingly important.

The opposing nature of the different aspects of mind (Adam and Eve), and the different answers to the question "Who owns creation?", can lead to conceptualisations of "beginnings" which in effect are hermeneutic straight lines. The consequence of this is stagnation of thought and the creation of a transcendent god which is in place to prevent further representation becoming possible. This god can become manifest in society and grow to the extent of a religion followed by many; it can also remain in the internal world of one individual and function as a "private god" being utilised to preserve a way of being.

The catastrophe that befalls a mind when having to choose which "reality" to follow is one which, to a greater or lesser degree, we have all suffered. The capacity to stand alone with a version of reality which goes against a prevailing view is only possible when the creation myth available has both male and female aspects existing in equality—a myth more based in nature. This inherently involves having a sense of the beginning as being chaos rather than the word.

To enable the establishment of a more natural creation myth, the processes of introjection and projection need to occur between people, and circularity needs to prevail over the straight line.

The equation of the death instinct with Augustine's original sin is not new—see, for instance, Felicity de Zulueta (2006, pp. 19–33) and Winnicott (1971, p. 70)—but I independently arrived at that consideration in my deliberations. Knowing that it has already been thought seems to give my arrival at this point an added validity. If a consequence of hermeneutic loops is this arriving at positions which many have arrived at before, then there is something important about the process and the position arrived at. Straight-line thinking also provides these arrival points, but these are rigid and stagnant, not like the ever developing and evolving nature of the loop. The straight-line structures end up needing to be policed, or forced upon people. They are ideas enshrined in power, religion, taboo, and law—dead metaphors of "being" that favour some over others, and most of all favour man over woman.

Myth, whether oral or written, is vital in providing a structure from which we can gain a sense of stability or awareness of where we are in the nature or religion of things. A written myth (like Genesis) is very different to the evolving oral myth function. In the consulting room, this difference can be seen in many ways. An oral narration that belongs to a particular family—the sense the family makes of itself and its traumas—can be adapted by new knowledge and understanding becoming available in a tolerable way. The family narration myth is then open to evolution, and all voices may be potentially heard.

A written narrative, however, has a deeper and less available meaning. This kind of narrative myth is a straight line, written by the most powerful member of the family, which ends in a categorical judgement of self and others. Narratives of this kind are to do with the "what" of a person. An enduring attribute of a person operating from this type of myth is a terror of curiosity. The biggest fear being the answer to a question the narrative is designed to prevent the asking of.

Carl Jung, well into his eighties, was asked by a seventy-year-old about his thoughts on life after death. Jung's answer was that

> It won't help you when you are lying on your deathbed to recall, "Jung said this or that." You must have your own ideas about it. You have to have your own myth. To have your own myth means to have suffered and struggled with a question until an answer has come to you from the depths of your soul. That does not imply that this is the definitive truth, but rather that this truth which has come is relevant for oneself as one now is, and believing in this truth helps one to feel well. (Cited in Von Franz, 1995, pp. 11–12).

As Jung implies, myth is vital as an inner and outer structure of life, but I would add that just because a myth exists, it does not mean that the myth creator has undergone the suffering and struggle which he talks about. It is important to determine whether it is being used as a straight line or a loop.

* * *

The next part, the "Engagement with the phenomenon", is where this book really started. I wrote the first two chapters of what follows more than eight years ago, primarily as an exercise by and for myself. I was struggling with my identity as a potential analyst and trying to find a place where I might belong. As beginnings had become important to me, I decided to try to see what happened if I simply allowed my thoughts to be free from the starting point of "a speck". It felt that if I were able to find out what might be my own myth, then I might be able to know which particular "club" I belonged to. I have included that exercise in an almost unchanged form; it feels important to do so—it is something I arrived at from a fundamental and free position, and therefore it is "me". There is much which, no doubt, can be challenged by experts in science, psychoanalysis, religion, and history, but I cannot accommodate these, as something important would become lost; and, as Jung suggests, effective personal myths are never definitive.

Later in Part II, I explore themes of conception, penetration, magical structures, and wholeness from the fundamental awareness of the primacy of introjective and projective processes. I begin to discuss these views from the focus of the relationship between Adam and Eve, which in turn evolves into what I see as an Adam psychology and an Eve psychology.

As Greenblatt says,

> This book is a life history of one of the most extraordinary stories ever told. … Genesis, the story … has over centuries decisively shaped conceptions of human origins and human destiny … it was highly unlikely ever to achieve such preeminence … this is fiction at its most fictional, a story that revels in the delights of make-believe. Yet millions of people, including some of the subtlest and most brilliant minds that have ever existed, have accepted the Bible's narrative of Adam and Eve as the unvarnished truth. And, notwithstanding the massive evidence accumulated by geology, paleontology, anthropology and evolutionary biology, untold numbers of our contemporaries continue to take the tale as a historically accurate account of the origins of the universe. … Few stories in the history of the world have proved so durable, so widespread, and so insistently, hauntingly real. (2017, pp. 2–3)

Adam and Eve are embedded in our minds and therefore do need to be taken seriously as saying something important about how our minds have developed.

Part II

Engagement with the phenomenon

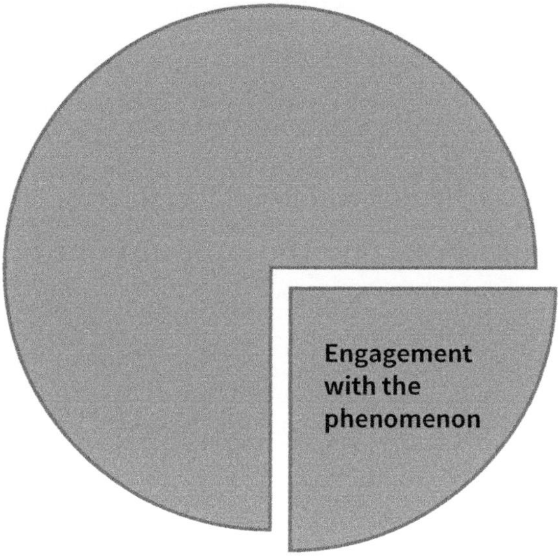

Going back to basics

We are part of this Universe, we are in this Universe, but perhaps more important than both of those facts is that the Universe is in us. When I reflect on that fact, I look up—many people feel small, 'cause they're small and the Universe is big, but I feel big, because my atoms came from those stars.

—Neil DeGrasse Tyson (2012)

A theory should not attempt to explain all the facts, because some of the facts are wrong.

—Attributed to Francis Crick

CHAPTER 9

In the beginning ...

Curiosity is the one thing invincible in nature.

—Stark (1977, p. 14)

A speck, barely discernible ... in fact, so small its presence is only betrayed by what it does. It has an awareness of itself as being in a state of excitement ... no, that's not quite right—maybe more a sense of being unstable, having a tension that is exhausting as well as alarming. It is also aware of a vastness of space, a seemingly empty, unending vastness. (*If indeed the speck could think, contemplate, and be aware of its place in the vastness—or have knowledge of the seeming emptiness of that vastness.*)

From an observer's point of view, it might be thought that the speck is content to travel around the vastness in this state of alarm/excitement/tension/instability—and in the sense that the vastness is so vast and seemingly empty that contentment, thought into existence, might provide the other (who has awareness) with some level of comfort.

To the speck, it and its inner state are the only knowable and perceivable conditions. It knows (*in the sense that it "knows" it is uncomfortable, unstable, tense, excited, in need ...*) it has something inside it that is unsettled. It travels around—*that makes it sound as if the speck has its own direction, intent, capacity to move ... it doesn't*—spinning, twisting, whirling, crashing in this direction, then that direction—with an unknown urgency which has the ultimate aim to find another speck. To the speck, the vastness, emptiness, and tension are all there is. In a way, the awareness of a tension that needs to be eased and a "knowing-but-not-knowing" that that might be achieved by "something" other than the speck impels the speck to keep on spinning and twisting.

The condition that the speck finds itself in raises the question for the observer as to what might be inside the speck … given the minuteness of the speck, its contents are even more unfathomable, almost completely unknowable, other than the tensions they cause. They pull the speck this way and that way … causing such a state of alarm and discomfort that the speck is unknowingly controlled by them; unknowingly because the speck knows no other state of being to serve as a contrast for it to become aware that it is being controlled. But why do the contents of the speck behave in this way? After all, the speck, along with its boundary (which enables it to be distinguished from the vastness), is trying to keep hold of its contents in order for it to remain having an existence in the vastness … a "some thing" rather than "no thing". It is trying its best to control and keep hold of the forces at play within it.

"At play" … an interesting choice of words … play suggests enjoyment, abandonment, spontaneity, freedom, safety … but there are levels of play too; play with oneself—deep introspection, fantasy, imagination; play with others—interactive play, games, involving a sharing of something which has trust at its foundation. There is also the meaning of "forces at play" … suggesting that there is an interaction and balancing going on—a toing and froing of energies, tensions, excitements, and discomforts.

Perhaps the contents of the speck are somehow not able to feel balanced? Perhaps they have an awareness that the speck does not? Maybe the speck has a wish (*how can specks "wish" …?, but wishes can be unknown as well as known*) … maybe the speck has an unknown wish for it and its boundaries to be all that's needed—that would be a wish to be able to give to itself the level of stability and ease that it is unknowingly seeking. Given the vastness and seeming emptiness of the vastness, the longer the speck travels around in that state of discomfort, unease, and tension, the more it will try to "play" with itself in order to try to reach a state of ease. That seems understandable.

Maybe that type of playing would involve a fantasy/phantasy that it is able to be what it is unknowingly seeking to itself. It would have to somehow adapt its tension or discomfort into something that it, and only it, can solve. Change it by putting barriers in the way of its previous outward seeking actions and changing the course of the "forces at play" … like a dam does to a river. But here we have somehow veered off course … I was talking about the contents of the speck and their tensions.

These tensions, unknown to the speck, are the building blocks of populating the vastness. The source of everything and the universal, inescapable, controlling force that is ubiquitous, eternal, has been present from the beginning of time and will survive the end of time. These tensions are the very laws of the vastness (*laws in the sense that everything, whether it likes it or not, follows these laws … laws that have evolved from the core of the speck, from inside and from the knowing-but-not-knowing that dominates all of the behaviour of the speck*).

In a way, "behaviour" is also something that needs to be thought about—when does behaviour become something that is able to be controlled or thought about? When a state of being is able to shift into another state of being—when the speck or entity is able to become aware of differing states of being within itself. Then, and only then, can the speck begin to be able to "think" about its behaviour. Perhaps when only one state of being is available to the speck, no thought about its behaviour is possible.

There is a temptation to set all of this out in a neat table, but this I'll avoid as it would be a premature attempt to order something that is actually more chaotic … a table would take away something from the understanding of the experience of the speck.

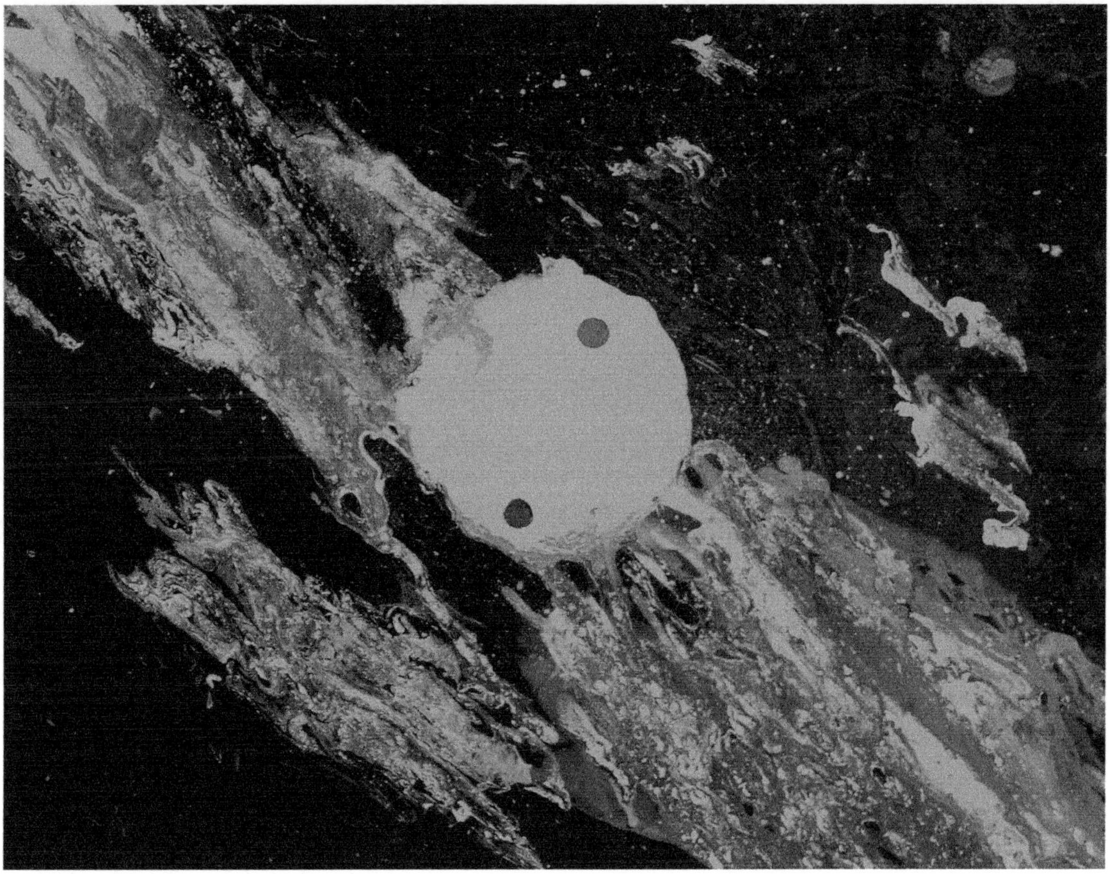

The tensions within the speck … they cause discomfort, instability, excitement, unease … like a constantly present, unchanging precipice of something that needs attention, demands attention, but is unable to be satisfied. In its panic, over time, the speck may become impelled to try to address these tensions in ways that move the speck away from this state—it begins to play! This creates a state of being which feels (falsely) as though it can control and provide what it feels it needs for itself. The countermeasures are an illusion which leads to a delusion. An illusion is formulated in the speck, which is based on a need to address the tensions by itself and for itself. The delusion then evolves to the speck feeling alone in the vastness and that it itself is the only law of the vastness.

> Even if we observe a small empty region of space, in which there are no atoms, we still detect a minute swarming of these particles [elementary particles—electrons, quarks, photons and gluons]. There is no such thing as a real void, one that is completely empty.
>
> The nature of these particles, and the way they move, is described by quantum mechanics. These particles do not have a pebble like reality but are rather the 'quanta' of corresponding fields. They are elementary excitations of a moving sub-stratum ... minuscule moving wavelets. They disappear and reappear according to the strange laws of quantum mechanics, where everything that exists is never stable, and is nothing but a jump from one interaction to another.
>
> —Rovelli (2016, pp. 30–31)

One day (*knowing full well that for the speck time is non-existent and unmeasurable—there is no day, night, week, month, year, and so on*) ... One day, the speck, spinning and twisting in the vastness, bumps into another speck. In the course of the history of the vastness and the speck this is a momentous occasion. There is no more important moment in the vastness—its importance is as vast as the vastness itself. It is the very source of the vastness becoming populated and the origin of creation. On becoming aware of "other-speck", "our-speck" begins to feel something it has never felt before ... a wish to somehow "get inside" other-speck ... or rather, a wish to place some of the tensions inside itself within other-speck. It somehow knows that this will have the effect of easing the tensions within it—that there is something inside it that needs to find its way into the other speck. Instead of trying desperately to hold on to these tensions in order to sustain a sense that it has an existence, it now understands that it can pass on to the other speck some aspects of itself and still exist. Our-speck has not only discovered the ubiquitous law of the vastness, but also that it is not alone and that something other than setting up countermeasures to cope with the tensions within is possible. This is the single most significant event in all of the history of the populated vastness. Our-speck *learns* that it can interact with another speck in a way which can ease its tensions and leaves it in a more stable state. In interacting with another speck in this way, it can travel the vastness with another in a more stable state. In effect, it is connected inextricably with other-speck, each of them sharing something which binds them together. (*The wishes, needs, and experience of other-speck are some things to think about later.*) In my imagination, I see it as a handing over of some ball of energy that has become too difficult, too big, too unruly, too confusing, and too unknowable to manage and control by our-speck who is (unknowingly) seeking to find some "other" to be able to deal with it in a way which feels safe, different and which can also respect the actual "ownership" of the energy. Our-speck would be happy to stay in this state forever if it were possible. It is not alone, it is more comfortable and stable, and it is still able to be in connection with all parts of itself.

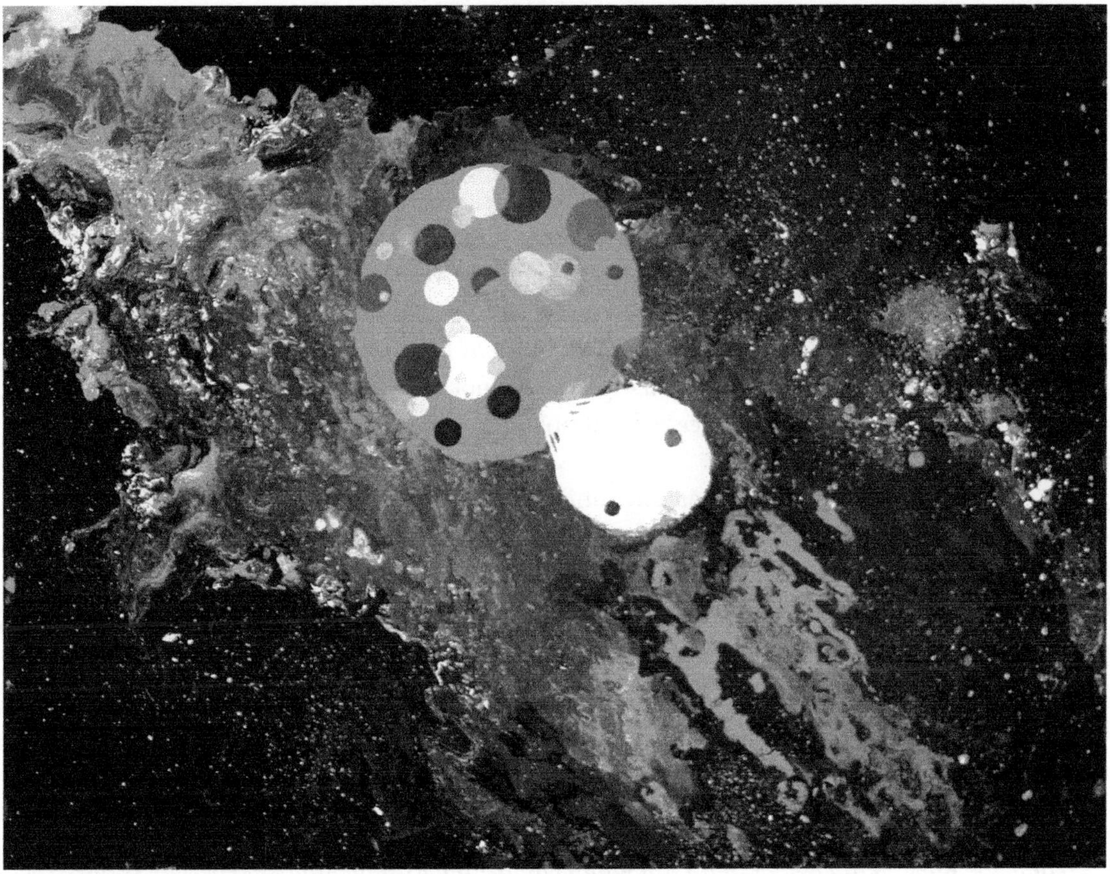

> Electrons don't *always* exist—they only exist when something or someone watches them, or better, when they are interacting with something else. They materialise in a place, with a calculable probability, when colliding with something else. The "quantum leaps" from one orbit to another are the only means they have of being "real": an electron is a set of jumps from one interaction to another. When nothing disturbs it, it is not in any precise place. It is not in a "place" at all.
>
> —Rovelli (2016, p. 15)

In my imagination, I try to put myself in the position of our-speck … I've managed to develop from a speck with only one state of awareness to a speck with two states of awareness. A new awareness that I'm not alone; a new awareness that I can ease my tensions in a more fulfilling and fundamental way; and a new awareness that another speck is managing and handling my unruly tensions in a calmer and less destabilising manner. In my rudimentary and prototype mind, I begin to feel that maybe these unruly tensions are not so scary or panic-inducing as I once felt. A fundamental knowledge or awareness grows that parts of my contents are being encapsulated in another speck, with each of us being aware that they belong to me, but nonetheless are still readily accepted by other-speck, who is able to receive them without feeling destabilised by them. In a way, it would be an extremely destabilising experience for me (in the mind of our-speck) if other-speck were to become destabilised itself upon receiving an aspect of my contents. That would feel as though my contents were in reality too unruly, dangerous, and difficult … I would feel unacceptable to my core. If that experience were to happen over and over, even though I would know I wasn't alone in the vastness, I would feel I needed to remain alone as my contents were too dangerous … not only for other-speck, but also for me; my wish to connect and the awareness of that possibility becomes too precarious a hope for me to bear.

So, let us say that our-speck has encountered an other-speck who is able to receive its contents in an acceptable manner. It senses that the exchange of unruly matter is a stabilising one, other-speck has managed to contain what was felt as difficult and unmanageable and has created the space for our-speck to be able to be aware of two states of being; tense, alarmed, excited, and confused—and calmer, more stable, and less confused. As our-speck has developed a capacity of awareness of these two states and now has the building blocks of thought and a mind … *From here I will settle on describing its experience as "I" … not the "it" that has mainly gone before … by deciding this, I may be saying more than I am writing—moving from the particulate to the cell; moving from the inanimate (although if you look deeply enough, even the most inanimate substance has a great deal of energy) to the animate; moving from the simple to the complex. But … I am aware that I am wiping out countless millennia of experiences our-speck would have had before reaching this awareness and state … it would have spent more time as a speck than any other more complex states it became involved in after bumping into other-specks … but there is not the time or space to recount this … Ahhhh … time, space, awarenesses, minds, states … they all seem to be concepts that I've prematurely brought into the mix of a universe (universe is another one) mainly experienced as chaotic, unruly, tense, disordered, full to bursting with energy, and above all, lonely. Maybe I do need to try to do this time justice … after all, what was gained and learned during this era is the most important element of all: it set the scene for all future interactions between specks. Without it, there would be no populated vastness.*

So, to sum up … chaos; energy; vastness; unease; excitement; tension—going on for millennia after millennia after millennia … what does our-speck do? … Maybe it fizzles out, having spent all its energy and never bumping into another speck … maybe it "decides" that it needs an illusion to manage the tensions inside … leading to a delusion of its own capacities … maybe it eventually bumps into another speck and discovers that connection in this way changes its state of being to a calmer and less chaotic existence.

Of course, this calmer state of being in connection with another speck also goes on for millennia, until, eventually, this binary connection becomes a tertiary one, which grows and becomes a complex array of specks all connected by passing their tensions to one another or sharing tensions.

4,600 million years ago

The planet Earth forms from the accretion disc revolving around the young sun. Organic compounds necessary for life having perhaps formed in the protoplanetary disk of cosmic dust grains surrounding it before the formation of the Earth itself.

I am going to repeat this over and over ... the most important event in all time (in fact I am tempted to say that time began when the first speck encountered another one and became aware of two states of being) is the occasion of our speck bumping into another. *Although, of course, there is the Big Bang to consider, and what was before ... Potentially the breaking up of something from which all specks and other specks came from ... maybe this connectivity–isolation–connectivity oscillation has been going on ad infinitum ... a perpetual motion of something we are all involved in, but have lost conscious awareness of, the knowledge being carried by our particles and cells; and the remnants or echo of this awareness is forever trying to find expression in the way we behave and relate ...*

Jump forward aeons ... our-speck has been involved in many complex structures ... after having its first encounter with another speck, it has gone on to bump into many other increasingly more complex structures, and after each encounter has an awareness of a calmer and more ordered state of being. These structures have sometimes been susceptible to external events, causing the structure to break up again—occasionally, our-speck has managed to hold on to another speck, but at times our-speck has become alone again.

4,000 million years ago

Formation of a greenstone belt of the Acasta Gneiss of the Slave Craton in Northwest Territories, Canada; the oldest rock belt in the world.

Jump forward aeons ... our-speck finds itself part of a different structure ... this one, instead of being susceptible only to external events in the sense of becoming exposed to an unusual or infrequent high intensity of energy or being attacked by other structures wishing to join like our-speck's previous experiences have been, is excruciatingly dependent on the external. So much so that it needs to interact constantly with other structures in its vicinity to maintain its calmer, more stable state. It needs to move to find what it needs, constantly looking for the optimum external structures that seem to enable it to reach this preferable state of calm. It has discovered that only certain things will do ... if it gets it wrong, then its state moves from a frenetic and tense one, to an even more tense and painful one. Pain … I've introduced another experience to our-speck's universe.

The earliest *direct* evidence of life on Earth are the fossils of microorganisms permineralised in 3.465 billion year old Australian Apex Chert rocks (Schopf et al., 2018).

Earliest life forms include *Archaea*, prokaryotic microbes. Later, prokaryotes evolve glycolysis, a set of chemical reactions that free the energy of organic molecules such as glucose and store it. This continues to be used in almost all organisms, unchanged, to this day.

Jump forward aeons … our-speck finds itself part of a more complex, externally dependent entity. *What I flirted with before … calling it "I" instead of "it", becomes even more valid now. It has become part of something that is aware of many states of being … pain, calmness, tension, excitement, fear, satiation, and so on. Although, it does seem to be relevant to stay aware of the speck's existence inside the entity … so maybe the speck should remain an "it" … and the entity it is part of becomes the "I". I like this, as it does seem important to stay aware of the entity being a structure which is comprised of specks. I'll detour slightly to say that the lack of awareness of this elementary fact of the universe subverts the laws of the universe and creates an "I" which sets itself apart from all that has gone on before in the existence of the speck. It tries to wipe out the speck within. Perhaps then, it is very important to stay aware of the speck. I will call the speck "it" … and in doing so will confer an "itness" to it, an existence which has its own needs and manner of connecting with other specks which confers on the "I" the same needs and manner of relating that influences more than anything else what the "I" entity does.*

[PAUSE—next day …]

I am still not happy with the "I" situation. Maybe my confusion and dilemma here need more thought. Am I confusing two meanings of the word "I"? … there is the "I" that represents the awareness of the speck that it needs to connect with another speck in order for it to feel in a more stable state, and then the "I" that represents the various awarenesses that the entity the speck is part of has. Both are valid uses of the word "I" … in that they both represent an inner state of awareness of itself and its relation to "not self". Maybe this distinction will become clearer later, but until then, I will continue to say "it" for the speck and "I" for the entity.

So, back to the new, more complex, excruciatingly dependent-upon-the-external entity the speck now finds itself part of. This new entity is vulnerable and has only a fleeting existence in the scheme of things before it becomes broken up again. But, for the speck it provided a new experience, one which had a different type of energy the other structures lacked.

535 million years ago

Major diversification of living things in the oceans: chordates, arthropods, molluscs, brachiopods, etc.

363 million years ago

The Earth begins to resemble its present state. Insects roam the land and soon take to the skies; sharks swim the oceans; and vegetation covers the land with seed-bearing plants and forests soon flourish.

Jump forward millennia … it has taken our-speck many, many, encounters with other-specks to find itself part of another, different, more complex, and excruciatingly dependent entity again. This time I will call the new entity Adam. And I think it is now time to think about other-speck that our-speck originally came across.

2 million years ago

The first members of the genus *Homo, Homo habilis*, appear in the fossil record.

Other-speck … I called that first encounter with our-speck "the most important event in history" (*well, not history, as history didn't exist … but definitely the single most important event in the creation of the universe—without it, there would be nothing, chaos, turmoil*). That first encounter involved two specks … our-speck and other-speck. Our-speck passed onto the other its turmoil, its "energy-that-felt-too-much", its tension that felt as though it were going to implode or explode if nothing came along to relieve the situation. Other-speck seemed to willingly accept what our-speck had to pass on. Why might that be? Did not other-speck also have turmoil, tension, and a sense that it might implode or explode if nothing came along to relieve the situation? The answer is of course, yes … otherwise it would not have wanted, wished, or needed to connect with our-speck.

(An aside … I still haven't really called the entity "I", the only "I" I've really referred to is me … perhaps all along I've been unaware that I had related the entity to me much, much earlier than the actual arrival of Adam … I'm quite pleased by that and I think it is apt.)

Other-speck … other-speck has an awareness, just like our-speck, that it is uneasy, has tensions and excitements that dominate and confuse it … they feel urgent in their manifestation and there is also a sense of something needing to be done about the situation in order for other-speck to reach a calmer, more manageable existence. But for this speck, that order and calmness is reached by receiving something, not passing it on like for our-speck. For this speck, the receiving of something is what enables it to reach a settled state. So in a way, it is even more remarkable that our-speck came across other-speck and they were able to connect … there must have been many previous encounters which might have been frustrating for both of the specks … ones in which our-speck kept coming across other-specks which did not wish to receive and vice versa.

Returning to our entity I've (we've) called Adam … inside Adam are too-many-to-count "our-specks" … all connected to other-specks, which are connected to other our-speck/other-speck configurations and so on. There is the added complication that some of our-specks have grown in a manner which causes them to connect with other-specks in a slightly different way … this involves a sharing of the turmoil, energy, and "too-muchness". This will have to be thought about later.

Actually, all of this confusion around "I", "it", and so on may be easily solved by considering the difference between "me", "myself", and "I".

Adam is, therefore, comprised of the "itness" of countless our-specks and other-specks in interaction with each other ... the "I" of the specks (both our-specks' "I-ness" and other-specks' "I-ness"). This sense of "I(t)-ness" is what the essence of Adam is ... the laws of the universe that Adam, along with every other formation, is inescapably following, that is, the drive to connect with an other that is able to alter an unstable, excited, tense, or turmoil-full state to one of a calmer way of being. But Adam also has the "I" of the entity as a whole, the awareness of a complex array of different states of being—pain, peace, excitement, turmoil, discomfort, ease, and all of the potential causes and reliefs of each of these states, as well as the tendency to create an illusion of self-sufficiency which leads Adam to the delusion that there is a self-sufficiency. This situation would come about when Adam has been frustrated too many times in the seeking of the other, or the encounter was one which raised tensions instead of alleviating them, and so on. So the original impetus to seek another for the exchange of something which alleviates and calms becomes embroiled with the "I–ness" of the entity and the tendency to subvert these fundamental laws of the universe into something which elevates (in the mind of Adam) Adam's entity falsely beyond them.

I hope that it has not passed unnoticed that each and every Adam has, within, a complex array of both our-specks and other-specks. That adds another dimension to our thinking. That is, each Adam has within a wish and a capacity to pass on aspects of his turmoil and instability as well a wish to receive those aspects. Each and every Adam is both our-speck AND other-speck. That awareness is why I've been reluctant to call Adam a "he". That would falsely give the impression that "he" was all our-speck.

Sexual interactions ... again, another concept that has crept into my mind, possibly prematurely. So far there has been thinking; awareness of states of being; pain; time; space; history; "I-ness" ... (and probably more that I haven't attended to) ... and now sexual interactions. This seems such a big area, and complex, that it will have to be added to the list of things to be thought about later. But it is interesting that these concepts continually creep into my mind when I'm trying to create the scenario of the history of our-speck. Perhaps in starting from such a fundamental and basic point I have few words available to describe what I imagine to have evolved, and I keep on trying to rush to more familiar concepts. This is one of the dilemmas we all face, and perhaps in trying to order, categorise, and name it is more about my incapacity to stay with the turmoil, vastness, and "too-muchness" of what is the predominant experience of our-speck and other-speck.

So ... back to our-speck and other-speck inside Adam ... perhaps as I've introduced sexual interactions, maybe it is time to introduce Eve. In the sense that I have tried to convey ... that every entity is made up of—contains—a myriad of our-specks and other-specks, then Eve too will be the same. What makes Eve "Eve" and Adam "Adam" is the manner in which their forms are configured. If we think back to our-speck and other-speck having their first connection ... a transferring of something from our-speck to other-speck, then it seems a reasonable and understandable evolution that that state of affairs would also exist in some way in how the forms are configured ... so Adam has a mechanism to physically achieve a passing of something, and Eve has a mechanism to physically achieve a receiving of something. *Of course, this is speculation and a leap in my thoughts which in the naming and ordering world isn't really tolerable … Where's the evidence? Has it been tested? What category does it belong to? Who said it first? … I'm really not going to think along this route: I would get lost in having to prove or evidence everything.*

I feel that this physical configuration is based on the primitive first interaction between our-speck and other-speck … in fact all (*or, to satisfy somewhat the naming world, maybe I should say "most"*) forms have this at the core of their physical configurations. I will return to this sexual use of that first interaction … *I am a bit fed up of using our-speck and other-speck and their first interaction … perhaps to make it shorter, as I seem to be writing it all the time maybe I should name something … (maybe I've reached the stage when naming started to occur? I don't know … but I'm getting the urge to name that interaction and the union of our-speck with other-speck. But what? Genesis has come to mind … but that has biological and religious overtones that might dominate … but it does represent the beginning of something that has an immense importance … I've just called it a union for the first time, maybe that is important in some way … I would want to represent somehow the stabilising nature of it, how that is achieved by a coming together and also how what results from it is the very starting point of everything that comes after … as well as how it is only after this has occurred that two states of being can be thought about. Is there a word that exists that would convey all of that? There is union, stabilisation, genesis, and thought. Looking at the initial letters the word GUTS comes to my mind … it appeals to me in some ways—I feel it is the "guts" in everything that has been and will be … it is the guts in every behaviour and emergence of thought, it is the essence of everything, but thinking of how I might use it … for instance, Adam and Eve ended up with their physical configurations because of GUTS … I feel it's going to fizzle out, especially as I am wary of GUTS actually losing its fundamental meaning in the process of it having been named—very quickly becoming a dead metaphor … and I'm also aware of the power of the act of naming—if I invent a word to try to describe something, then I've created something outside the experience, like a god—trying to name it instead of truly allowing the nature of what is happening to happen. I might live on after my death as the person who first coined GUTS, but the meaning that I would wish to convey, in its true relevance, would be lost.*

* * *

Adam and Eve. I suppose I have purposefully chosen these "first" humans, according to the Old Testament, in order for a particular scene to have emerged in the mind of the reader. However, there have been many firsts … as depicted in myths, folklore, song, and thoughts from across the world, each myth representing a different view of how Adam and Eve, or whoever they were, first became.

No doubt the scene that has been planted is of Adam and Eve in a particular garden, with a snake, an apple tree, a deity, and the consequences of the coming together of all of these components. With this scene in mind, I am entering a new stage in what I'm writing—so I feel a new chapter is warranted.

CHAPTER 10

The garden

They preferred the name of the tree/to the taste of the apple.
—Tony Hoagland, "Among the Intellectuals" (2019)

If you can only be tall because somebody is on their knees, then you have a serious problem.
—Toni Morrison (1993)

The garden. The scene that emerges in my mind is one of a complex and interdependent myriad of entities … some able to move, being excruciatingly dependent upon external circumstance—needing substances from the environment in order to sustain themselves, and also having many different conglomerations of specks inside of them. The "whole" of these forms seems adapted to be aware of the external, and sensitive to changes in it. There are many different "wholes" … different shapes, textures, sizes, some with many limbs, some with no limbs. Some wander on the surface of the garden, some fly over the garden, and others seem to wish to be under the garden. They seem to have a limited lifespan—easily damaged and easily worn out. Maybe as a consequence of their limited lifespan, they seem to be able to generate or regenerate immature forms of themselves which grow and become the same as themselves.

Then there are other entities which do not move … or move so slowly it is as though they don't move (apart from when there is an external event such as a storm or wind) … these forms do change with time, they seem to be very dependent upon the seasons and trends in how warm or cold the external is. The changes are remarkable … producing varied colours and aspects of themselves. These non-moving forms are also dependent upon obtaining sustenance from the environment, but do so in a very different manner to the moving ones. They also have a potentially longer lifespan … sometimes hundreds of times longer …

but are also susceptible to being damaged. There are many forms, shapes, sizes, colours … some very large with limbs, others very small with fragile, delicate coloured forms. They too can generate new forms of themselves, and it seems that they do so for the same reasons as the moving entities.

Then there are those structures which do not move and are the least impacted by the external … they do not need sustenance from the environment, nor are they easily damaged … these forms are varied, ranging from the very hard, very large, and impenetrable, to the smaller versions which are speck-like. They do change with time, but the changes would not be noticed by the other entities as they take place over such a long time … probably a longer time than the lifespan of the moving forms. One of these forms that I'm classing as a non-moving entity is different to the others … it seems to flow, but it is not actually moving itself … it also changes according to the external conditions, sometimes becoming hard and slippery, then flowing, but then seemingly disappearing. It seems to be of vital importance to all the other entities: they need it as part of what sustains them.

All of these structures are intricately linked with each other … the flowing, non-moving form is constantly taken inside the other entities … the moving forms also take inside themselves many of the other forms … the produce that comes from the very large, many limbed form … and also some can take inside themselves other moving entities too.

Each and every entity has our-speck and other-speck inside them. Each and every form is in varying degrees of stability, and intimately connected with all around them. Each is constantly in a state of acquiring or shedding specks, so ultimately all are in a state of interaction, communion, and interdependence. The moving entities take in the flowing form, other non-moving forms, and for some, other moving entities. Their forms become constructed of everything around them; they also shed seemingly superfluous specks which in turn are taken in by other moving and non-moving forms. It seems to me in this system of interconnection and interdependence that there is an equality and awareness of the law of the universe—that is, all connection has as its prototype that original connection between our-speck and other-speck.

In their capacity to (re)generate, the moving forms all tend to obey this law. A representative of our-speck and other-speck is to be found in all these moving populations. Each representative seeks the other in order to transmit something and receive something. This seems to be something that is completely known to the entities and doesn't have to be learnt. Perhaps this is known as the billions or trillions of years that our-speck spent in seeking other-speck is somehow represented in the behaviour of the specks within the form—it is something that all specks know, and therefore all entities know too. It would actually be quite arrogant to assume that this experience of our-speck counts for little, or has not been the formative experience on which everything is based. The physical differences between these representatives of our-speck and other-speck in many cases are subtle … but nonetheless there. One passes something on and has the physical mechanism to be able to do this; the other receives something and has the physical mechanism to be able to do that. The (re)generation of an immature form of themselves tends to occur only inside something … either actually inside the representative of other-speck, or something that that representative produces … a container which allows the immature form to grow.

I imagine that by now the reader would have noticed that I am avoiding naming anything … I can imagine that for some readers this will be an extremely frustrating experience. I'm afraid that names will continue to be few and far between for a while. I feel that this scene in the garden which is supposed to represent the origin of something would have had no names and would have also been subject to the law of the universe … the nature of the speck … the nature law … the law of nature. To name takes us away from that awareness.

About 300 thousand years ago

Anatomically modern humans appear in Africa.

In this scene of interconnectivity, interdependence, awareness of the cycle, and law of nature is also Adam and Eve. Each consisting, just like every other entity, of our-speck and other-speck. If we think back to the dilemma that our-speck had trillions of years ago—when it was spinning, whirring, and fretting around in the vastness, full of energy that felt "too much", and (*if it had a mind*) fearing that it was all alone; or having had encounters with specks who didn't want to receive, feeling frustrated in ever being able to find stability—it seemed as though a solution to this might be to create an illusion of self-sufficiency, which would lead on to a delusion of self-sufficiency. So it seems possible that the nature of the speck, or the law of nature, can *feel* surmountable, or bypassed. If we consider that the nature of the speck is to seek another in order to feel stable and connected, we can see that in the behaviour of our entities in the garden—each moving, and to a degree non-moving, form that is dependent upon being sustained by the external, seeks another to interact in such a way that creates a sense of stability. This seems to be a drive, in that it dominates their behaviour, in most of the moving entities: a drive to engage in a connection with the other.

The excruciatingly dependent nature of these moving entities develops competition between them during times when the resources they are dependent upon are scarce. When this happens, the stronger among them exert their dominance and take the resources for themselves. This behaviour evolves over time to enable the form that has taken the position of being the strongest to feel powerful and entitled to have their needs met before others.

The forms that engage in this competitiveness start to become aggressive. In order for this to become established without difficulty, a vindicating structure of hierarchy is needed, which sets the strongest form apart from the others and the law of nature becomes subverted into a different kind of law … It is the strongest who has a right to everything and the others who have to submit. This is not a law based on nature or speck; it is a law which brings fear, inequality, and pain.

When Eslom managed to sink his large fangs into Lanjo's neck, driving him screaming up a tree, the struggle for dominance was finally over. All the chimpanzees in the group, male and females alike, performed rituals of submission—known as pant-grunts—to him, while he pant-grunted to no one. Anyone who failed to submit risked slaps or full scale beatings from the angry alpha, or from his erstwhile rival, now the beta male."

—Greenblatt (2017, p. 289)

The drive to engage in a bodily connection with another is, for some of the entities, a physically pleasurable experience, and this tends then to get confused with the drive to connect ... gets confused with the law of nature.

* * *

Joy, it must be remembered, is nothing like happiness, its milquetoast cousin. It is instead a vivid and extreme state of being, often arrived at in the aftermath of great pain.

—Ayana Mathis (2016)

There must be a distinction between the drive to connect to find stability and a peace, and the wish to connect as it gives physical pleasure, although I am aware that the drive to find stability can also render a pleasure too, but it is of a different order. This physical pleasure does tend to follow the law of nature in that there is a tendency for there to be a heightened sense of excitement ... a "too-muchness" ... a feeling of being full to bursting with something that needs tending to, a solution needing to be found ... this solution becomes the coupling of the physical mechanisms of the our-speck and other-speck representatives. This allows temporarily a stabilising of this too-much feeling and the transmitting and receiving of something. Where it deviates from the law of the speck is that the union is temporary, the stability achieved is due to the form, in its physical self, becoming excited and then having an experience by which it can feel relieved. In a way, this becomes something which may start to feel a controllable experience ... the drive, need, necessity, law, nature to connect to find stability, becomes something that can be substituted, bypassed, and controlled by the pleasurable coupling experience. The experience of Adam and Eve becomes one which begins to feel as though they have a control and a bypass of the law of nature. Pleasure starts to feel as though it is more important than true stability. This physical coupling is, of course, important in that it allows the (re)generation of the entities, and has its place as an important influence on the behaviour of every form that regenerates in this way; but for those for whom this action is pleasurable, complications in the laws of nature and the speck also arise. It sets up an artificial mechanism of stability which can almost squash all awareness of the other, "having-been-around-for-all-time" mechanism. Comfort instead of care; pleasure instead of true stability; sexual act instead of true connection. Pain and pleasure become things which feel subject to choice.

The sexual act would also feel superior and advantageous as it seems controllable, under the domain of the entity, immediate, and seemingly puts the seeking of pleasure ahead of the seeking of a solution to pain.

Perhaps I now need to think about what I mean by "true stability" and "artificial stability". In my mind, the discomfort of our-speck whirring and fretting in the vastness is twofold. The first level of discomfort would be about having an energy full to bursting that needs something to happen to find relief. That something is the transferring of the energy bundle to other-speck, a simple jettisoning of the turmoil. And the second level is that of a wish to step out of this constant cycle of too-muchness, jettison, temporary relief, too-muchness, jettison, temporary relief, and so on.

In sexual coupling, the entities engage in an analogous transferring of something that can feel pleasurable, as well as satisfying a desire to unite in this way. Those that find this pleasurable also have that experience to add to the relief. Other-speck has an equally unbearable, but different, experience … it has a need to receive and feels an equal level of discomfort in feeling its absence. The sexual act replicates or imitates the first coming together of our-speck and other-speck; it is like a symbolisation of the initial union. (The bestower places part of itself inside the receiver, which almost symbolically represents the original interaction. Something then becomes ejaculated and the entities part.) Perhaps, in seeing reproduction as a symbolisation of the original coming together, it necessitates the pleasure associated with it being seen also as a symbolisation of the original joy that is engendered by the coming together through pain and turmoil. This symbolisation is then felt to be mastery and control and serves as a possible alternative to the original law of nature.

> A young male, Kako, [was] inadvertently blocking an older female juvenile, Leslie, from moving along a branch. First, Leslie pushed him; Kako, who was not very confident in trees, tightened his grip, grinning nervously. Next Leslie gnawed on one of his hands, presumably to loosen his grasp. Kako uttered a sharp peep and stayed put. Then Leslie rubbed her vulva against his shoulder. This gesture calmed Kako, and he moved along the branch. It seemed that Leslie had been very close to using force but instead had reassured both herself and Kako with sexual contact.
>
> —de Wall (2006)

This confusion of physical pleasure with the coming together for a lowering of tension, chaos, and turmoil is a minefield. Physical pleasure, in its mimicking of the law of nature (the law of our-speck and other-speck), offers itself as a solution to the awareness of pain and turmoil. This is artificial stability and is associated with the physically gratifying pleasures that come from the illusion of feeling something has occurred between two entities which both give and receive.

From a level of dis-ease and a wish to jettison the turmoil, the other level of discomfort is one of needing to find something that allows our-speck and other-speck to step away from this continual internal frenzy of excitement or tension and relief. The union that is the most important in history is the union of our-speck and other-speck in a manner which stabilises this frenzy. The energy bundle is passed by our-speck and received by other-speck. When this occurs, and an enduring connection is felt, other-speck doesn't feel it needs to pass it back or jettison it—it isn't "too much" and it is accepted willingly. Our-speck feels relief and then has the space to notice the change in its state of being. It notices that other-speck doesn't find the energy bundle too much and our-speck begins to feel as though maybe the bundle isn't as intolerable or unbearable as it was originally felt. Something new and more permanent has been generated, an entity in which our-speck and other-speck are willingly connected and stable. There is also the additional relief and stability of having the sense of being known by an other, being not alone, and the vastness feeling less vast. These feelings can all be felt as a pain that is there, but not known until another experience comes along. This type of interaction is very different to the frenzy of finding pleasure, it is an awareness of pain and how that may be borne by someone other, and how stabilising and transformative the bearing of pain can be. From this, joy is elicited.

True stability is achieved by the bearing of pain, and, for that to be possible, an other-speck needs to be found. The painful situation of having a bundle of unborne energy and having to find mechanisms to try to deal with that is every speck's, every entity's, challenge. There are seemingly many paths that forms take to try to solve this dilemma. In order to have the space to think, or to be aware of another state of being, another speck needs to be found. Another entity needs to be able to receive the bundle of confusion, pain, excitement, turmoil, too-muchness, and so on; and bear it. The body of another is needed to receive and then to give something back—a circularity of being. Perhaps for other-speck this pain is the unknown awareness of an absence of something which corresponds with our-speck's too-muchness of something. The pain inherent in this situation is being alone with the absence or too-muchness. This is ameliorated when a coming together is possible.

Around 275,000 years ago

Homo sapiens evolved.

Adam and Eve. Adam and Eve are entities which find pleasure in their physical coupling and so might use this mechanism as a substitute for the true stability as outlined above. The coupling becomes the height of excitement, relief, and pleasure, allowing Adam and Eve to feel in control of the law of nature and the need to find true stability. Given this potential state of affairs, the space to think and consider other states of being has been distorted. There is pleasure, excitement, and a need to obtain or relieve these states. Pain is felt, but felt to be something alien, or not belonging in an experience where pleasure is all important … and the delusionary sense that pleasure can banish pain becomes one in which the entity might begin to feel it can push pain away by its own capacity, rather than have to experience it, engage meaningfully with another, or to see it as something that can be transformative. Given the generative nature of the physical coupling between Adam and Eve, Eve naturally would begin to have an immature form grow inside. Once the immature form has reached a certain stage of growth, the cycle of regeneration involves this immature form needing to somehow emerge from Eve's form and start another stage of growth. This emergence of an immature form from the body of Eve is a painful one. Why this might be the case when other entities seem to have a less painful experience is open to speculation. However, for Eve the process is painful and potentially long, but she seems able not only to bear it but also to care for the immature form after the emergence. Perhaps this is because of the original experience of other-speck—Eve is able to bear something painful, uncomfortable, and potentially confusing inside her, and willingly so. Eve is then able to care for the immature form that seemingly has caused the pain and discomfort.

I imagine that Adam, looking on, would find this whole experience disturbing on many fronts. There is pain, willingly borne; there is the object that causes the pain being cared for and loved; there is the challenge to the principle of pleasure being the preferred and most important state; and there is the sight of Eve having produced, from within, a new form. All of these realisations or potential realisations could cause a pain in Adam which would be every bit as painful as a physical pain. Adam might also be aware of Eve's preoccupation with the new form and also the damage that has occurred or seemingly occurred to Eve's body.

Given this new situation, Adam might find the sudden (apparent) withdrawal of Eve from taking part in the pleasurable physical coupling they once engaged in as an abandonment … Eve is giving the capacity to receive something to another form, not in a manner which is using her body in an exciting, pleasurable way, but rather receiving pain, instability, fretfulness, confusion, and so on and transforming it to allow the new form to gain stability. It is not unreasonable to imagine that Adam might try to create an illusion to try to counter this situation.

I am finding it increasingly difficult to keep on writing without the use of the terms "he" and "she". Before this point it had not been that difficult … there is something about having reached this stage in my description of the garden that seems to change my free-flowing capacity to write without the use of "he" and "she" to one in which I am labouring over every sentence to find ways of keeping them out. Perhaps there is something about this stage in the evolving psyches of Adam and Eve that changes from being aware of all as entities comprised of our-speck and other-speck, to something being separate, named, categorised and (in the minds of Adam and Eve) not all the same in this fundamental way. He and she. What does that mean? To me it suggests superficially an attempt to describe the physical otherness of the entities … "He" being an evolved representative of our-speck, and "she" being an evolved representative of other-speck. It also suggests a categorising of each as wholly either our-speck or other-speck and a moving away from the sense that they could be a "we" (in the manner of other-speck receiving something that enables our-speck to reach a true stability). In categorising the he and she, there is inherently also more emphasis on the pleasurable, physical coupling as being the important driving force to the detriment of the universality of the more stabilising interaction. Universality in that the capacity to receive in the other-speck manner is present in all entities. As it has now interrupted my free flow of writing, and the "he and she" is emerging out of my unconscious, I will stay true to that and include it.

As my writing is evolving to need to include concepts and terminologies that hitherto didn't feel necessary, I am aware of also wishing to think about what that signifies in the possible evolution of Adam and Eve. I have introduced otherness, stability, pain, pleasure, union, genesis, thought, awareness, the capacity to receive, the capacity to pass on something, he and she, and possibly much more too … and whilst I have had a struggle against an urge to order and categorise, I still have not had to struggle against an urge to name (other than Adam and Eve and a few other minor instances). I am not seeing an urge to order as the same as an urge to name … I feel there is a big difference here somewhere, but I trust that that understanding will emerge later.

Back to Adam and Eve. I left Eve just after she had had a new form emerge from her body; and Adam having watched this happen. My speculation about the impact of this event on Adam is fundamental to the shift in Adam's and Eve's psyches: from being aware of, and mostly influenced by being part of a universe of interconnectivity and potential stability, and each entity being comprised of both our-speck and other-speck; to a universe of "he and she", and psyches that are deemed to behave in a very different way.

Adam experiences Eve's growing body and is confused; Adam experiences Eve's gradual pulling away from her wish to couple with Adam for pleasure as her body grows; Adam feels frustrated and abandoned and (*as I speculated in the beginning when our-speck might create an illusion to seemingly help manage its own tensions*) he might begin to try to manage these excitements and tensions in another way—he may discover that he can use a limb to achieve pleasure that feels similar to that experienced with Eve—and perhaps that would be enough, but then something else happens that challenges him even further.

Eve begins to feel pain (*this is undoubtedly a difficult and confusing time for Eve too, but for now, I'm concentrating on Adam's experience*) and it seems to get worse and worse … Adam is looking on in horror and fear. Not only is pain something that both Adam and Eve have tried to counter by using pleasure, but it is also something they feel might lead to their entities breaking apart (after all they have seen other forms who seem to be in pain, then stop moving and after some time their forms seem to be swallowed by the earth or taken in by other entities). In their awareness of pleasure, the "I"s that have evolved for both Adam and Eve involve a growing fear of "not-I", of not being the entity that can achieve pleasure and seemingly control it. Adam might look upon Eve in pain and fear for her, fear that she will be swallowed by the earth, fear that he will be alone and have no one to help him with his tensions (pleasure-related ones, as well as his need to stabilise). In order to try to deal with this fear and horror, I imagine Adam would try to push away his awareness of what was happening, or perhaps try to change its actuality into something else.

This period of pain, being aware of it and being afraid of it, passes. Eve seems to have not only borne it without stopping moving and being swallowed by the earth, but is also producing something new from inside her body. A new form emerges that is small and excruciatingly vulnerable. It cannot move in the way Adam and Eve can … it cannot take in sustenance in the way Adam and Eve can, it cannot seek shelter when the external conditions become arduous like Adam and Eve can. In fact it is completely dependent upon an other to provide all of the safety and sustenance requirements it has.

Adam is confused to say the least. He has felt abandoned and left to his own devices in order for him to receive the pleasure he seeks. He has seen Eve in pain and has been horrified by that sight. He does not wish to formulate this experience of pain in his mind and so pushes it away or changes his perception and experience of it for it to feel less horrifying. He has seen a new form emerge from Eve and is not only awestruck by this event, but also aware, for perhaps the first time, of a capacity that Eve has that he does not.

Eve, in her capacity as other-speck, is able to look upon this new form and instinctively know that it needs her care and attention. She needs to be able to receive the tensions, pain, confusions, and turmoil that this new form has to enable it to become aware of the potential of two states of being—turmoil and relative stability. She becomes fully attentive to this new form as she is also aware that this attentiveness and capacity to receive its pain and turmoil in this way is the law of nature … the nature of law … the awareness that nature is law. Now I'm tempted to also say that this is love. Another concept that is enormously complex and multilayered. Perhaps "love", in the way I'm using it here, is the capacity to bear pain for an other and still wish to be connected and attentive to that other. This is different to the love that pleasure might elicit—that would be more of a connectivity in pleasure-seeking.

Adam is a witness to all of these events. He feels abandoned; left to seek his own pleasure for himself and by himself; horrified at the pain Eve endures—not only in his fear of pain signifying the possibility of not-being, but also in the challenge it represents to his world built upon the pursuit of pleasure; aware that he can do nothing about the pain Eve is suffering—it is not under his or her control; feeling so inadequate, but yet wishing also to try to provide something that might receive this pain for Eve; awestruck at the emergence of a new form; confused by Eve's capacity to care and attend to the new form after it has caused so much pain in emerging; abandoned again when Eve diverts her receptivity and attention to the new form and away from Adam; aware of the differences between Eve and himself in that he is not able to produce a new form from his entity; also amazed, confused, and again aware of the differences between Eve and himself when he sees that she is able to provide the sustenance the new form needs from her body; and all of these feelings, thoughts, awarenesses, and sights get mixed up together to create a turmoil, tension, and pain that Adam has not felt before.

This is not physical pain, like he experiences after a fall, this pain feels different—more intense and all consuming … more like a deep ache that doesn't go away. He has seen difference for the first time between Eve and himself, and feels as though he is somehow less than Eve as not only is she able to have new forms emerge from herself, but she can also use her body to sustain the new form. His I-ness in relation to how he imagines Eve's I-ness to be feels different now.

In this scene that I have set, all the components are in place for Adam to begin to wish to change his perception of the events that have occurred, and what these events might signify about Eve. His I-ness feels to him to be in pain, in need, and in turmoil. He looks upon the scene before him and understands that the difference between him and Eve is also something to do with the manner in which their bodies are configured. He looks upon his body and knows that the site of *his* pleasure is something that Eve seemingly doesn't have. He looks upon Eve and sees her capacity in having a new form emerge from her body, her capacity to sustain it, and her ability to bear pain and still attend to the cause of her pain, as something he doesn't have.

Perhaps at this point I can speculate about the course of events that follow and take many paths that will all have a relevance in greater or lesser ways, but I am going to concentrate on one path … one that will engender the familiar events that would have arisen in the minds of all readers when I first named Adam and Eve. It is fascinating that I do not have to describe the scene that would have emerged in the minds of the readers … it is a beginning that is known, in one way or other, by all.

In the turmoil that Adam feels after these events, there begins to arise within him a need to stabilise … to somehow reduce or counter the pain, turmoil, and fretfulness that he is feeling. Eve is preoccupied with the new form and so is not available to him … he becomes like our-speck, spinning, twisting, and fretting in the vastness with no sense of his pain and turmoil being able to be borne or stabilised. He resorts to the countermeasure of an illusion. If somehow he can feel more in control … if somehow he can change his pain to pleasure … if somehow he can blot out the awareness of the difference between him and Eve … if somehow he can feel more than Eve instead of less than … if somehow he can own what seems to be the magical creation of a new form for himself, instead of it seemingly being Eve's capacity … if … if … if … With all of these thoughts, feelings, pains, envies, fears, and turmoils it starts to become clear to Adam that he could think of the events differently and in that way his turmoil would feel less and under his control. His I-ness, in his mind, would gain dominance over the law of nature … the nature of the law … and nature being the law.

He looks at his body and sees the site of his pleasure … he might have confusions and mixed feelings about this, he might start to see it also as the origin of his need … not only his need for pleasure (which in a way could be met by himself and for himself), but also his need for connection and stabilisation which can only really be met by Eve (*he doesn't realise that he has the capacity for this within himself … perhaps he hasn't had enough of his turmoil received by Eve for him to know that his turmoil is tolerable and manageable and that he has a capacity to manage within too*). The site of his pleasure therefore becomes mixed up with also being a symbol of what he needs—stabilisation. In his need, frustration and rage (*another new concept*) and the sense that Eve isn't available to him and that he is not able to tolerate these feelings, he starts to try to find something else that might be able to represent or hold or tolerate these intolerances for him.

He looks around and sees something that has a similarity to the part of his body that is the site of pleasure. It has a shape and smoothness to it that seems to Adam to be so familiar and similar that he is able to place upon this smooth entity the frustrations, rage, turmoil, needs, pleasure seeking, and stabilisation seeking aspects that he is struggling with.

He looks around again and tries to find something else into which he could place the other struggles he is having … those struggles which are more to do with Eve … the struggles with the actuality of the events he has witnessed (the emergence of a new form and her capacity to sustain this new form), how can he take away the realisations that have come about from him witnessing these events? In these realisations is the innate awareness that has been carried in each and every speck from the beginning of time … that there is our-speck and other-speck and that other-speck has a capacity to receive turmoil and stabilise it. That other-speck has the capacity to generate something new from the tolerance of such turmoil and that our-speck needs other-speck. This awareness counters completely the structure that Adam had been operating from; that pleasure is the law of nature. He looks around and sees something that seems to represent this … something that is taken in by him, Eve, and other forms, something that seems to symbolise what Eve can do … take in, receive, ingest. It not only represents Eve's capacity to receive, but also represents what Adam might wish Eve to receive—his turmoil, his realisation and knowledge of the law of nature.

So, the scene is becoming more familiar … Adam, Eve, a smooth entity representing Adam's site of pleasure, and turmoil about his needs, and something that is a product from a big, many-limbed entity which represents the awareness that Adam doesn't want to think about. But there is another tension that Adam is struggling with … that of the seeming capacity to create new forms. He sees Eve as having this capacity and himself not. While finding other entities has sufficed in holding or representing most of the aspects he is struggling with, this aspect is different. He looks around and sees different entities which are also able to seemingly create new forms and these all seem to be the representatives of other-speck … that is, those with the capacity to receive. This aspect seems to require to be managed differently by Adam. He begins to formulate an illusion in his mind which would take away the painful aspects of this sense of Eve being the source of creativity and which perhaps also enables him to elevate his own capacities compared to Eve's. He creates an illusion which feels satisfying to him … there is a more powerful entity than all the forms in the garden, more powerful than the law of nature … more powerful than all the other-specks … so much so, that this entity has managed to create everything there is. In the mind of Adam, Eve would have no capacity compared to this entity, and it might even end up allowing Adam to feel that he would never need Eve again. If he needed stabilisation, he would be able to turn to his illusion of an omnipotent, omniscient, creator for whom Adam would be special … (after all, Adam *is* special in the sense that he is the form that has created this illusionary all-powerful entity).

This scene … the smooth entity holding his needs and rage; the produce of the many-limbed big entity holding the actual knowledge, law of nature, and Eve's capacity to receive; and the all-powerful entity being set up as the origin of creation who holds Adam in a special place—this all appeals to Adam on many levels. Not only does it give him a sense of creativity, it takes away his need for Eve; it allows Adam to feel in control of his envies, rages, problems with pain, and needs of pleasure and stabilisation; and also allows him to reconfigure the state that witnessing Eve producing a new form has left him in. He is able to see himself as "higher" than Eve.

Adam is then (through his own creation of illusions and forms to hold aspects of himself) able to feel something else that feels new to him … he feels powerful and has a pleasure that comes from his illusion of having triumphed over pain, need, and Eve. In this new state of powerfulness he looks around himself and decides that he has dominion over other forms … to show this dominion and also to represent that his control and power over other forms is derived from him and not Eve, he begins to name them. When the law of nature had dominion in Adam's mind, there was no need to name, as everything was known … our-speck, other-speck, how they worked together, the single most important event in time, the need to have turmoil and fretfulness received by other-speck, the transformative effect of this turmoil being received, the awareness of being known and knowing other-speck, and so on and so on. All of this knowledge and awareness came about as a result of the interaction between our-speck and other-speck, it came from within each and every entity, and so did not need to be named. In Adam's new state of mind, this knowledge is lost to him … having been placed in the form that has many limbs; and his needs are lost to him, having been placed in the smooth, moving form. He feels he and his creation need to reconfigure the universe and subvert the law of nature … the new creation becomes the Creator who therefore should create. Adam looks around him and in seeing the vastness open up (due to the absence of needs, awareness, the knowledge of nature, and Eve) decides that to fill the vastness he should create a new knowledge with names. The new creator should be named God. He decides that this smooth form holding his needs and rage should be called Snake. The many-limbed entity is Tree, and its produce is Apple. He himself he calls Man and Eve becomes Woman. All of these names come from an external place … they do not come from inside Adam, using his experience and awareness gained from aeons of time spent as our-speck. They come from an illusion of him being able to manage his own turmoil by reconfiguring the law of nature. He is a demiurge who has to create everything around him again in order for the external world to fit into his illusion/delusion. This illusion becomes a delusion which he begins to take in as the truth and the law. Adam has shifted from being under the influence of the law of nature to being under the influence of a delusion which turns the law of nature into the law of (many) gods.

What about Eve? After all, she and Adam are both configured of our-speck AND other-speck. Whilst Adam has tried to wipe out the reality of other-speck, she has a more difficult task to do that. She cannot let go so easily of her capacity to receive, and her knowledge of the law of nature, as not only is the capacity more available to her, she also has to endure pain, care for the new forms, and sustain them. All of this requires an awareness and capacity to receive, and also maintains the awareness of the law of nature within her.

Sensing the endurance of the law of nature within Eve, Adam forbids her (using the illusion of the all-powerful creator God) to eat from the Tree of Knowledge of Good and Evil … forbids her to know the law of nature which is the biggest challenge to his illusion/delusion. This is impossible for Eve and her awareness and knowledge isn't able to be squashed. Adam is able to reconfigure this by also creating right and wrong, good and bad, better and worse, superior and inferior, hierarchies of entities that hitherto were all equal. It is good to obey God. It is good to abide by the law of God. It is good to see Man as in control and special to God. It is bad to know the law of nature. It is bad to feel pain. It is bad to see other-speck and nature as the source of creation. Adam, however, is never really able to let go of a sense of his need for other-speck, no matter how hard he tries. He cannot allow the collapse of his illusion/delusion, but he also cannot allow Eve to be completely banished for not obeying these new laws. Instead, another illusion is set up whereby Eve's innate knowledge and awareness is present within her because she is easily fooled and led astray by the smooth moving entity … the Snake. The Snake who represents Adam's confusions about his needs for pleasure and stability and also his need to have these needs received by a form in Eve's absence. The Snake … that is, the very need for stability itself, has fooled or tempted Eve to eat from the Tree of Knowledge. As this was a law from God (the creator, namer, and divider into good and bad) that Eve has seemingly gone against, punishment as a concept is also created. She is to forever be punished with pain while bringing new forms forth, and is to be the subject of Man.

Around 4,000 years ago

Judaism evolves to become a monotheistic religion. Monotheism begins to take over from polytheistic and pantheistic ways of life.

This sets up something whereby pain, instead of being seen as something potentially transformative and able to be borne, becomes an indicator of "badness". Adam is free to not feel horror and guilt at Eve's pain when giving birth. In the reduction in importance, or even abolition in importance of the role of other-speck (that is, the law of nature and the receiving of something that enables our-speck and other-speck to reach a more stable state), Eve, as the physical representation of other-speck, is seen as less than Adam. She becomes in his mind either subject to him or the object of his pleasure, while he is able to be the creator (of the illusion/delusion) and name things. In a place in his mind, he is unable to completely allow the sense of himself as creator, as there is the reality of his real capacities to be considered too. He counters this by creating God: a transcendent God who sets the law as he wishes and a God that visits punishment on those who challenge his creation.

At this point, "Let there be light" and there was light, "Let there be a firmament" and there was a firmament, "Let there be creatures" and there were creatures, is seen as the new starting point of time. The age of the law of nature has become the age of the law of God (man). Sin becomes the allowing of the law of nature and the knowledge of our-speck/other-speck to emerge from within—the knowledge that we are fundamentally particulate, like all other entities; that the creative process is from the union of our-speck with other-speck, and that other-speck has the capacity to receive, sustain, nurture, create, and transform pain.

And so, the end of this stage in the garden has led to Adam becoming man who is looked favourably upon by the illusionary Creator/God. Perhaps too, the actual visual reminders of the mechanism of connectivity between our-speck and other-speck (Adam and Eve) had to be hidden away in order for this illusion to be maintained. At this stage, they become clothed and enter into a new way of relating, being, thinking, seeing each other and their place in the universe. The law of nature changes to the law of God (man); the sense of *who* as being important, shifts to the sense of *what* being important. The essence and knowing of something innately reduces in significance to the sense of learning something through it having been named. All of these dichotomies—the who and the what; the law of nature and the law of God; the innate essence and the name—have their own psychologies. There is the *what* psychology which is anathema to the *who* psychology, just like the law of nature is anathema to the law of God, and Eve is anathema to Adam (although interestingly, other-speck is NOT anathema to our-speck!).

Another chapter is beckoning, and my head is hurting. Perhaps the readers' heads are too. The increasing complexity, nuance, psychologies, and so on are proving a difficult task ... both in terms of trying to follow their progression, as well as trying to develop an understanding of them. Maybe this next chapter needs to delineate the qualities of the dichotomies ... the differing psychological nuances of the who (me, Eve) and the what (I, Adam). But ... before I go on to that, I'd like to take another look again at "beginning myths".

CHAPTER 11

Conception stories

There are only two or three human stories, and they go on repeating themselves as fiercely as if they had never happened before.

—Willa Cather (1913, p. 119)

The concept of nakedness, shame, and clothing—all aspects which feature in the Garden of Eden myth—are factors which differentiate us from the great apes. Nakedness within the natural world elicits no shame and the clothing that humans acquire (the donning of status, wealth, and difference) seems to exist regardless of actual inner capacity.

The great ape populations of chimpanzees and bonobos behave in very different ways. As our nearest living species relatives, the social structure of each inevitably can be thought of as revealing a very important period in our development.

Chimpanzees organise themselves around a dominant, aggressive male who will mate with all the females in his community, while keeping the other adult males subdued. The alpha male chimpanzee regularly beats the females with sticks (de Waal, 2006).

Bonobo communities operate from a more female-dominated structure. There is widespread sexual freedom, and, in effect, everyone engages in sex with everyone. There are seemingly few gender, age, or family prohibitions. Conflict is resolved by offering sex (de Waal, 2006).

With all the great apes there is an extended period of mothers being with their young. The mothers carry the young for many months and are in constant contact with them. They are totally dependent upon her, and it is thought that because the father is not certain the offspring are his, he does not invest himself in the upbringing. This very close period lasts for many years. All of the great apes are also able to show empathy, make tools, and demonstrate problem-solving skills, learning, communication, grief, and joy.

Chimpanzees and bonobos are very closely related and are thought to be two separate populations arising from an original group which became split. This split was absolute as chimpanzees occupied a region north of the river Congo and bonobos south of it. The conditions were very different: the bonobos were able to enjoy a relatively abundant living area, while the chimpanzees struggled and competed for food. It is easy to assume that the better conditions for the bonobos reduced the tendency for an alpha male to come about—with plentiful food and easier conditions there was little or no competition for finite resources. A strong male would have no real advantage over the others. In this environment, perhaps pleasure took over. This could be comparable to the many instances in human history when need has reduced and hedonism grows.

With the chimpanzees, need was the most important factor, and the tendency for the communities to be dominated by a powerful alpha male is understandable as the most powerful could, in the short term, ensure that he had most of the food for himself. It is interesting that a male behaviour prevalent in the chimpanzee community is the hitting of females with sticks. Playing with thoughts and ideas around this, it seems a reasonable idea that an Adam creation myth is in operation. The alpha male has remembered his mother and the care she gave him, but his wish to be powerful (as well as perhaps his resentment at having to leave his mother's care when a sibling comes along) dominates. In order to justify his present situation as well as perhaps showing his envy (at her capacity to create, feed, keep him safe, and carry on) and anger (at feeling abandoned) he hits her and the other females. It is as though he is saying that the females are nothing compared to him and they need to follow his word, as he is the god who controls and knows everything. To my mind, this situation is the fertile ground from which human creation myths and religions begin.

In the bonobo community, where need isn't so urgent, pleasure has taken over. There is no alpha male and coupling is used as conflict resolution. Here, perhaps, a creation myth might be more nature-based and allowing of both the male and female. Pleasure, as opposed to the male God/word, is being used as the containing factor. However, the adult male in bonobo societies has been known to seek his mother when under stress, and perhaps this indicates that underneath the layer of pleasure is a deeper awareness of something else that calms and stabilises.

The specific creation myth or conception story that might be in place, and its aetiology, is based on the answers, if you like, to several questions. Who has ownership of creation (or thought, or idea, or infant, or piece of art …)? That is, is it Adam, or Eve, or both? Are penetrative processes tolerated or has magic taken over? Is there a dynamic awareness of inside and outside being in relationship?

Perhaps, among these factors there are two aspects of creation myths that can be considered. They represent an expression of the need to make sense of the universe and where we are in it; but they also express something about the mental representations that are available to make a tolerable sense of conception itself. The making sense of the universe can be thought of as an outward curiosity, and the making sense of how conception happens can be thought of as an inward curiosity. A consequence of a creation myth which takes the word as the starting point of time is that inner curiosity becomes anathema. Thus, looking inwards becomes a taboo.

One of the first recorded (if not mythological) instances of a taboo is that of the Garden of Eden, where God prohibits the eating of the apple from the Tree of Knowledge of Good and Evil … it was taboo.

This prohibition and its violation by Eve, and later by Adam, led to the establishment of further taboos, namely the covering of their bodies with fig leaves and the sense of sin constantly having to be atoned for. Men became dominant and pain free, women became subservient and having to carry pain. Religion and the worship of God became a necessity, which if not carried out would be punishable in some way. Altars, temples, and priests all became sacred and inviolable. The first taboo begot an ever increasing population of further taboos. Women became "unclean" and not able to enter temples, people were not able to be "saved" unless baptised, and so on. Just leaving the house would have become a complex experience in the lives of these people.

Even in seemingly non-religious (that is, outside of the major world religions) communities, taboos developed as a way of life. The Madagascan indigenous peoples of more than 200 years ago had strict codes of behaviour based on the premise that women were unclean and able to take the virility of men away. Mixed groups were forbidden and there was a strict separation regarding the type of work each could do. There could be no crossover and women were forbidden to touch anything that belonged to the male, for fear of it becoming unclean and reducing the power of the male (Langdon-Davies, 1938, pp. 45–49). It would be interesting to discover the conscious and unconscious creation myths in operation within these societies at the time. Perhaps it would be reasonable to assume that the unclean nature of women came about from their menstruation and their impact on fertility and virility, as they were the carriers of life. I would also put forward that perhaps the nature of Eve—to receive the psychic contents of others—was also a factor. If a woman represented the receptacle not only of the penis and sperm, but the passions, tempers, disorder, chaos, and aggression of the male, and also could carry and give birth to life, then she possessed a very powerful capacity which would terrify a man. Her menstrual blood would also be a confusing phenomenon—blood being an indicator of pain and illness which would often be unsurvivable—so the woman would also possess powers that seemed to go against experience and nature.

Since it seems that taboos become established in societies regardless of formal religion (as religion is thought of today, although many, if not all, indigenous peoples operated according to some form of religion) it would seem reasonable to assume that, to varying degrees, taboos develop in all societies.

If we take the Garden of Eden myth as representing an aspect of human development, dilemma, and attempt at a solution, then perhaps looking closely at this first taboo might reveal something important.

From my previous interpretation of the garden story, I suggested that Adam became too overwhelmed with anxiety, pain, envy, and fear (of death, loss, pain itself, and abandonment) in his relationship with Eve, and that in his bewilderment and hatred of the situation he resolved his state of mind by creating religion. This religion rendered man special to a God that created the universe and left Eve being subordinate and the bearer of pain. From this position, the first taboo created by the first man would have to have been not to think about or to become aware of nature. This awareness of nature would have been an instant reality check—to look around and see and understand the manner in which creatures interacted, the interconnectedness of it all, and how man is no different; that pain is part of life, and that life is born of Eve.

Eve, in Genesis, was not able to curtail her curiosity and awareness. She (with the "help" of the serpent—which perhaps represents the sexual knowledge and need that is part of life) tries to get Adam to eat from the tree—that is, to become aware of and to accept that he is a part of nature and to see each of them (along with other creatures) as equal.

Perhaps at this point Adam did have an opportunity to become enlightened—or to re-enlighten himself. If we also see the moment that Adam created religion and God as also creating narcissism, then perhaps his refusal to re-enlighten himself comes from pride, envy, a wish for his own superiority, and a need to be dominant. Or … perhaps, there is a need to distinguish a moving away from nature and Eve due to having an experience of feeling abandoned in pain, and then a continuation of this position due to feeling powerful.

Instead of becoming re-enlightened, Adam decides to embellish and reinforce his position. He creates other taboos to reinforce his own creation of God and religion. It is now required that both Adam and Eve cover themselves—probably to deny further any possibility that enlightenment might occur when the actualities of the human body are observed and understood.

If we do take it as likely that pain—in all its forms—led Adam to create God and his own special status, then the constant need to reinforce this position would lead to more and more taboos. These not only would arise due to a need to keep his illusion alive, but also out of fear of the unknown. The cost of this illusion and structure is a sacrifice of the perceptual apparatus and the relegation of certain members of society to the bottom of the hierarchy—a hierarchy which is inherent to this structure.

The position of women in society and Eve within each and every human being's inner world becomes the position to be demeaned, abused, ignored, and denied. Anything which alludes to human beings as being part of the natural world becomes taboo. Anything which takes notice of Eve—both as woman and Eve within us all—and the damage that has been done to her (which takes over from Augustine's lust, flaws, and disobedience, to become the psychological original sin which we are all struggling with) becomes something which is unable to be put into words or even seen. Words take on a power that could bring the illusion down, so speech becomes controlled and prescriptive. Words themselves lose their live metaphor status and become dead. They have to be experienced as coming from without and from Adam … so, words name and inform, rather than being vehicles that express discovery and the within.

There is perhaps nothing that epitomises more the Adam creation of religion than the initiation rites of the Arunta tribes in Australia (Eliade, 1976). During a two-week ceremony of initiation for boys to become men, they experience a whole series of spiritual and secret traditions which involve the reverence of animal life and nature as well as the worshipping of the powerful god Twanyirika.[9] The boys are blindfolded and separated from the main camp, in which the women and children remain. During many of the rites they remain blindfolded, but towards the end of the two-week period, after a very intense and thunderous climactic ritual in which the elder men create the cacophony using bullroarers, the blindfolds are removed, and the boys are shown the instruments that make the noise and how the elder men dress up to represent the gods and spirits. They are also told, upon pain of death, they are never to reveal this to any woman or child. The women left in the camp hear this thunderous noise and believe that it is the god Twanyirika and are fearful of his power.

This shows clearly that the religious aspect and creation of gods by the Arunta men are part of an illusion which perpetuates the dominant position of man over woman, and which also allows them to own creation for themselves, even if it is only as part of an illusion. This also depends on the ignorance of woman—if she is to "eat from the Tree of Knowledge", then the whole system will fall down.

It might not be too difficult to imagine that this process underlies the formation of all religions.

If it is taken as the likely development of religion—that is, an Adam response to pain, envy, fear, and wish for dominance—then it might also be reasonable to say that our present-day societies have been built on this psychology of Adam for millennia.

In *A Short History of Women*, John Langdon-Davies (1938) traces the fate of women across time, from the more primitive societies, to the lauded civilisations of Babylonia, Egypt, Greece, Rome, and early twentieth-century Great Britain and the United States of America. He notes that there are generalisations to be made in that women tend to have a higher status and better rights in agricultural societies than hunting ones. He explains this by suggesting that if the society depends on the fertility of the soil, which is considered to be a female attribute, then women are employed in the fields. If the society does not rely on agriculture, then fear of women takes over and they become segregated and blamed for most of the ills that befall the men—taboos take over (p. 73).

Generally, throughout history, women have been viewed as people to be feared, as confusing, and envied for their creative capacities, and consequently taboos become the mechanisms of behaviour control within the society. What perhaps needs to be remembered, though, is that all taboos originate from the first taboo which was established as a result of Adam (within all of us) not being able to tolerate his pain (chaos, fear, and envy).

As I have placed the formation of religion and taboo as arising from a particular "answer" to the question, "Who owns creation—Adam, or Eve, or both?", a brief scientific exploration of how (and perhaps why) living organisms come together might be useful.

---

[9] There is some dispute as to the nature of this god—whether he is thought of as a "superior" god, or just mumbo-jumbo and being used as a device or bogle to keep the women and children in check (see Lang, 1901, p. 67). Either way, I feel the above argument holds.

If we consider simple life forms, such as *Copromonas*, and watch them replicating, it is noticed that they increase in size by feeding before then splitting into two and becoming two separate living beings (Langdon-Davies, 1938, p. 3). These then repeat the process until a population has been created. This, however, does not go on forever: after a time the *Copromonas* seem to get exhausted and languid, and a sort of impotence takes over. What then happens is that two individuals come together and "mix" until they have become a single individual. The replication process then proceeds again when this single individual begins to feed. The union is not sexual as both individuals are the same.

Another microscopic animal, a *Bodo*, replicates in the same manner as the *Copromonas* but at the point of merging behaves differently. One of them remains anchored while the other swims about until it finds the first. One is quiescent and waits and the other is mobile and "hunts". Other simple animals also show this primitive differentiation. At the point of needing to merge after replication is exhausted, some individuals grow into larger egg cells and some into smaller sperm cells. The egg cells do not move, while the sperm cells move about rapidly. The egg cells are large and contain a great deal of nourishing food and are thus a food store, while the sperm cells are shaped for motion. The sperm cell then moves incessantly until it finds an egg cell, at which point it bores its way into it. The result of this union is a number of new individuals which then replicate as before.

As Langdon-Davies suggests (pp. 6–7), this seems to be the way in which "sex" came into the world: a division of labour. Motion and nourishing food storage are the essential necessities for successful union. The different forms which this division of labour imposes are what could be called the sex differences. The moving individual is the male and the larger, food-rich individual the female.

To take this suggestion further, perhaps we can imagine that more complex animals which evolved from these simpler forms needed to divide the labour that was increasingly becoming a complex process and so the sexual apparatus developed. Male- and femaleness, therefore, was an evolutionary need for a division of labour during the reproduction process. If replication was able to continue without the exhaustion that occurs, perhaps evolution might not have led to more complex animal forms, as it is the re-merging of two replicated individuals that leads to evolution.

In this way too, perhaps, it is also reasonable to be able to say that maleness and femaleness in separation are incomplete and that it is only in coming together with another that a satisfactory completeness is possible.

In terms of Adam psychology, at a deep primitive level, this would be the psychology of the "mobile" sperm cell—Eve psychology would be the psychology of the "nourishing food store" egg cell. Both are needed for the achievement of a successful completeness which leads to the potential for reproduction (or the creation/conception of anything—thought, idea, word, art, infants ...).

In societies which actively represent this equality of function, women and men can be considered equal and both positions are revered. In the more primitive societies which were agriculturally based, women are thought of as having a relatively high status. The "food store" that they represent is actioned in their work in the fields and understood as necessary. In more hunting-based societies, the emphasis on the mobile hunter as being most important skews this equality and renders the position of women to that of feared slaves.

A thousand years or so before Jesus, the empires that were flourishing were those based on agriculture—Babylonia, Egypt, and Phrygia. Each developed religions which taught the worship of a feminine power as a supreme goddess of fertility, all ultimately being represented by the goddess Isis. As a result of this, the status and rights of women were almost equal to those of men. The king of Babylon, Hammurabi in 2350 BCE passed a series of laws which gave women more rights than they enjoyed much later in nineteenth-century Britain (Langdon-Davies, 1938, p. 85).

The status of women in the time of Homer was dignified and free. However, by the time of Pericles, women are cloistered slaves. Langdon-Davies explains this deterioration in status, rights, and freedoms as to do with the shift from the "age of need" (if you like) to the "age of reason". As he says:

> Plato, Socrates, Sophocles, Aeschylus, Euripedes, Herodotus, Aristotle etc. … are all sons of women who achieved their eminence at the cost not only of a horde of male slaves, but of the enslavement of the whole female sex. (Ibid., p. 90)

To the ancient Athenian, all forms of manual labour, commerce, and business were degrading, and no free citizen could think of soiling his hands with them. For the free citizen, his activity should be purely intellectual. Education, the intellect, and its exercise were absolutely denied to women. She became not even an overworked companion, but an isolated reproductive organ. Hitherto, woman was revered for fertility, whilst also being feared; now there was a new fertility—giving birth to new ideas, and in this men took woman's place.

When creation myths are thought about as representing the prevailing state of mind and knowledge available at the time they came into being, their contents and subsequent progressions over time can reveal a great deal about the processes that are in operation. From those myths that give status to the female and allow for a time of chaos and work before creation can occur, to those that evoke a male demiurge who magically creates using names, this (de) evolution not only reveals the incumbent terrors and defences, but also shows the intimate relationship and unconscious attitude towards projective and introjective processes, inner and outer, male and female, circles and straight lines. Each myth seems to try to incorporate what is known with the unknown and "fills in the gaps" according to the defensive structure needed. The first oral myths were perhaps highly influenced by the mystery of how a woman might become pregnant. This ignorance led to envy and fear of woman as the source of creation, and the myths represented this by creating female deities and powers. The worship of nature and the earth which could provide became the main focus.

Then an association between pregnancy and the sexual act began to become available for representation in the mind. This had a profound impact on the way man saw the world and his place in it. Instead of woman owning creation, he could now do so. His sperm was the giver and creator of life and the woman merely a vessel. This liberated man from his fear of woman in many conscious ways—he could now think of himself as the more important and demote woman to something he could own. This psychic state (or myth) would engender a terror of the inner, because if man has elevated himself above woman and has owned creation for himself, the new "tree of knowledge" that it is forbidden to eat becomes the inner body of woman. The inner would reveal his myth to be just that, a psychic construct of Adam, and so would collapse under the revelation of the inner body of woman.

As creation myths show what is available to be represented in the mind at any given moment in time, they also reveal the vicissitudes of penetration, gender, and the relationship between inner and outer. The transition from ignorance about how a woman is able to create a baby, to the association with the sexual act, to a realisation that the sperm is important (without the knowledge of the female egg) can be seen in the evolution of the myths. Each new generation of myth-makers have had a need to represent their state of mind in relation to these themes since time began. The first female deity conception stories neglected the role of the man; the next male deity stories reduce the female to mere vessels and counter the evidence that that might be wrong by evoking a monotheistic god who has deemed that that is meant to be.

Conception stories have all been created to serve as a structure that has been put in place to organise self and other. Especially in relation to man and woman. If a story which is serving as this structure has little representation of actuality, then the missing elements are, by necessity, pushed into becoming the unconscious and feared. Most conception stories of the major Western religions have little or no accurate female representation, alongside a male ownership of creation. Due to this lack of representation, it is not surprising that this element in all our minds has become the demeaned and feared position.

* * *

Jacob

I think that my mother and father stopped having a sexual relationship long before they actually separated, they never seemed really "together". It wouldn't surprise me if they only had sex the once … I find it hard to imagine my mother ever having had sex again … They slept in separate beds and rooms from the earliest memories I have. My father was an aggressive, big man who constantly intimidated me, and my mother was impenetrable, impassive … no, she wasn't impassive, she was impregnable, opaque … I can't remember feelings as a child … I just can't remember … I do remember grief of some sort at her brother's funeral … I remember feeling sorry for my mother … I was moved to feel something … say, empathy … for how my mother might have been feeling. I found myself moved to cry … [*pause*] … well, sob, and I shook trying to control it. After, my mother asked me why I'd been laughing … it was extraordinary that she should think I laughed. If I think of her, something like an old, stone fortress comes to mind … she would get the boiling oil out if people approached … I suppose I retreated to a place where I existed, but I didn't let anyone in, in response to her treating me as though I'd compromised her immune system … I ended up feeling hardly anything … I've always been confused about why she wasn't able to breastfeed me …

CHAPTER 12

The vicissitudes of penetration

These themes (inner/outer; man/woman; projection/introjection) are at the root of how we organise our minds and societies. The status of these organisational factors with regard to terror, experience, pain, and joy determine the structure of the myth (conception story) that we need to create to hold them. If the myth that prevails is stagnant, the image that comes to mind of a person that is unconsciously using this myth is of a being frozen in time, but under the illusion that his myth is time.

Augustine spent many years of his life trying to find a way to incorporate irrefutable knowledge with his own personal creation myth (that is, his own personal relationship to the vicissitudes of penetration, gender, and inner and outer). He employed his Adam aspect to diminish and not to have to think about his Eve. Luria and Vital seem to have been trying to incorporate a knowledge of anatomy into existing creation myths. Perhaps it might not be too much of a leap in the dark if I were to say that Augustine did not have a psychic construct available in his thinking of the female egg as necessary for life; he saw woman as important, but only in the sense of being a vessel. He sourced the "spark" of life as being the sperm which therefore was filled with the "light" of God.

If we think about the first union between an egg cell and a sperm cell, then features of this union being carried over into the psyche in some way may not be such an unlikely thought. The egg being a larger, immobile food store and the sperm being smaller and mobile suggests that nourishment and activity are a characteristic of each. The union of these cells to form a new individual is dependent on both of these characteristics—the egg cell having enough nutrition for the process to be fuelled, and the sperm having enough motility to be able to not only find the egg, but to also penetrate it. In this manner, the components of each are brought together to create a new being.

It is only by this method that reproduction can occur. This process of penetration and mingling together is reminiscent of the processes by which all particles interact and seek out more stable structures. This seems to me to be a blueprint underneath all processes—an instability which seeks out others to enable a greater stability. This involves penetration and mingling and something new results. These fundamental processes are at the root of all interactions between others, not only in quantum mechanics (it is interesting that in quantum theory, no object has a definite position, except when colliding with something else, which means that reality is an *interaction* and outside this is not able to be seen), but also in conception, sexual processes, and psychological ones. We are programmed to behave in this manner, again not only sexually, but also psychologically.

If all cells, particles, creatures, and humans are fundamentally influenced to achieve either a more stable form or reproduction, then it seems important to understand the methods of achieving this. Anxiety, in all its forms, represents a state of heightened instability. Whatever the creature or cell involved, the drive would be to reduce this anxiety in some way. On an atomic level, this would be to find another in order to either merge or share contents, which enables a lowering of "tension". On a cellular level, this might be to take something which feels stabilising—perhaps nutrition or fluid. On a species level, perhaps a lowering of tension or anxiety would involve eating or drinking—if that tension were due to hunger or thirst. If the tension or anxiety were due to fear or danger, especially at a young age, then in order to reduce that tension another, usually maternal, object is needed.

Whatever the impetus for "merging" or utilising another to reduce anxiety, the quality of that experience seems of vital importance. If thought (or imagination) is given to the relative permutations of the quality of the interactions between an egg cell and a sperm cell, as well as the relative qualitative sense of the act of intercourse between a male and a female which leads to a conception, it seems that it may provide a different way to think about the various states of mind that can occur.

It seems reasonable to be able to postulate that the "state of being" of the sperm and the egg may influence the resulting quality of the fertilisation and embryo. Perhaps a sperm which has to swim about for a relatively long time before it comes across the egg becomes "tired" and "languid", being able to penetrate the egg in an "only just about managing it" manner. Or a very mobile, relatively young sperm might penetrate the egg with a great deal of vigour. The egg itself might be old or exposed to an endometrium which is starting to shed … Although I am aware that I am transferring qualities to the experience which may be stretching a point, I do feel that the quality of the interaction is of vital importance. The division of labour which is inherent in the process of fertilisation—the mobile sperm and the nourishing egg—feels to me to be greatly influenced by the quality of the experience. The variable factors being the relative strengths of the sperm and the egg, their age, and their capacity to fulfil the interaction.

The quality of penetration of the egg by the sperm will be dependent upon these variations. To further the imaginative playing with ideas and thoughts, perhaps the embryo somehow carries an awareness of this quality of penetration. What if this does occur and somehow this quality of penetration is carried by the embryo as part of the very core of what constitutes the body and psyche of the resulting individual—perhaps this is a factor in the determination of sexuality or sense of inner gender identity? These would be the vicissitudes of the original penetration of the egg by the sperm.

In quantum mechanics, when two particles collide, a "quantum leap" occurs of one or more electrons jumping to the other particle. This process releases quanta of energy which result in either the absorption or emission of photons. Thus these collisions are also experiences of energy. The sperm penetrating the egg would be no different—the sperm would not be seeking something if it did not culminate in an end position which was preferable to its pre-penetration state. It has a potential inside which is demanding action to seek something which can fulfil this potential. The egg would not be receptive if it did not also have this potential. The lowering of these potentially uneasy states by coming together in a penetrative manner would also release some sort of energy—like the orgasm in sexual intercourse. As the embryo which starts life in this way is therefore "made" by this coming together, it seems reasonable to me to suggest that the quality of this coming together, the energy that is released, is somehow carried by the embryo; these vicissitudes leading perhaps to the sexuality of the person that becomes. (I am not saying that I think this is the only influencing factor—later experiences and the quality of the primal scene also have an impact—but I am saying that even when all aspects of life have been unremarkable, sexuality can be something that feels to be who the person is—something always known and felt. This kind of sexuality seems to me potentially to be something determined during this first penetration.)

If each egg and sperm represents a division of labour which creates a whole, then the capacities of each (mobility and nourishment) which are separated in the gametes become part of the embryo. The baby, once born, needs an awareness of both of these capacities to be able to survive. She/he needs to be able to root for the breast and to be able to suck milk—this is the mobility aspect of the sperm. She/he also needs to have a sense of sustenance within (obtained perhaps from fullness from feeding, or from having a sense of resilience and resources which perhaps have been "carried" forward from the strong egg) and this is the nourishment aspect of the egg. Regardless of whether the baby is male or female, these qualities of the egg and sperm get carried forward and become part of the whole individual. The relative strengths of these qualities will vary according to all the variations of the penetrations and the actual resulting chromosome type of the infant.

From this perspective, it seems that to render these qualities as separate—mobility and action belonging to the realm of maleness, and nourishment belonging to the realm of femaleness—would be really talking about just the physiology of the sperm and the egg, not the whole individual. It is impossible for a whole individual to be just sperm or just egg.

If Adam, as the metaphorical first man, and Eve as the metaphorical first woman, were living in a garden with other creatures and plants, and Eve became pregnant, the potential confusion that resulted would be profound. The pain which this possibly caused would (as previously described) be the impetus that led Adam to create gods and religions. This situation removes the nourishment and creative aspects from belonging to the egg and, instead, positions them in a god. It also elevates the position of the male over the female. The damage this does to the position of woman is obvious, but there is also great damage done to man as well—he is left having to negate large aspects of himself and to feel that to be a "man" involves being all "action" and no "nourishment". Perhaps he also confuses action for nourishment.

The awareness of the importance of the primal scene in the phantasies and development of individuals is not new, but perhaps less considered is the quality of the actual experience which resulted in conception. If the egg and sperm are two cells which need to come together to create a whole, it seems the two cells are of equal importance. This equality of function of conception can be skewed and distorted by which unconscious creation myth each participant is operating from. If religion has been created by Adam, then the act becomes something very different to a female and male coming together in equality, and a qualitative hierarchy becomes established in relation to the different functions each employs during conception and pregnancy. Also, the ultimate source of creation has become a transcendent God.

During the actual experience of the primal scene, if the creation myth is Adam-based in form, then the male unconsciously believes that he is superior and dominant, even if his religion allows for a great deal of compassion and love. The important aspect is the degree of real equality present—equality in status, equality in respect, an ability to recognise the importance of both functions, and the ability to allow *both* mobility and nourishment to exist in *both* the male and the female. Every child grows up observing the relationship between his parents and intuitively understands the intimate relationship between the male and female aspects of both. She/he sees the outcome of the vicissitudes of the primal scene in terms of the capacity of each of the parents to own both Adam and Eve within themselves, as well as the relative equality in-between them.

All of these vicissitudes of penetration become important when trauma, experience, need, and development are considered. They determine the nature of the mechanism that alleviates the position of anxiety and what the particular impact might be if it doesn't occur well enough.

* * *

Doe, a deer, a female deer,
Ray, a drop of golden sun,
Me, a name I call myself,
Far, a long, long way to run,
Sew, **a needle pulling thread,**
La, a note to follow Sew,
Tea, a drink with jam and bread
That will bring us back to Doe ...

Whenever I heard this song growing up, I was always struck by my difficulty in working out whether what was meant was a "needle pulling the thread" or a "thread pulling the needle". I think it was due to the words needing to fit into the rhyme, leaving the verb seemingly attached to the thread, while logic demanded it be attached to the needle. The effect of this floating verb stayed with me and much later I began to think about the ambiguity as well as the impact on the meaning.

Both situations seemed to be saying something important. It resonated greatly with my thinking around the vicissitudes of penetration and personal creation myths.

Each personal creation myth represents not only the history of the impact of all the vicissitudes of penetration from conception to adulthood, but also "the solution" arrived at. The story itself becomes the containing object that exerts an influence and provides a structure from which the person then orientates himself, others, nature, and the universe.

In the context of the analogy I am trying to convey, this myth or story becomes the garment or embroidery or tapestry that is produced by sewing together all the experiences of penetration and the associated phantasies.

Sewing does convey an active process which is creative and individual. With the danger of pushing a metaphor to breaking point, I think it is a worthwhile exercise to think about what is involved, especially regarding the vagaries of the point of origin of the "pulling".

There is a "thread" inside everyone that exists in a raw, unformulated, and urgent state (perhaps akin to Bion's beta elements[10]). This has a potentiality of energy associated to it, by which I mean that it has an urgency to seek something which would enable it to become formed, or to gain a relative form compared to its previous condition. This forming, in simple terms, has the impact of reducing the urgency and potentiality. All experience needs to undergo this process and once done, it leaves a "story" behind in the mind of the individual regarding the nature of what he feels he is inside. The need to find another (to provide a maternal function) to give form to the "thread" is relentless.

The "needle pulling the thread" scenario, therefore, is a situation which enables the thread to be pulled out of a person. Something external, which elicits the inner self to emerge and become known. Here, the needle is penetrating the mind and pulling the thread out in order for something to be sewn, that is, something becomes created, which gives a form to the thread.

The "thread pulling the needle", on the other hand, relates to the thread's incessant need to attract something in order to become known. This search for something penetrative, for something to be taken in, is in the hope of attracting a maternal penetration of curiosity combined

---

[10] "Alpha-function operates on the sense impressions … and emotions … of which the patient is aware. In so far as alpha-function is successful, alpha-elements are produced and these elements are suited to storage and the requirements of dream thoughts. If alpha-function is disturbed, and therefore inoperative, the sense impressions of which the patient is aware and the emotions which he is experiencing remain unchanged. I shall call them beta-elements" (Bion, 1962, p. 274).

with a capacity to "sew a picture" or contain and put words to the experience. The thread, or story, will constantly pull penetrative processes towards it in the hope that it might be a maternal function which can provide "me-words" and a change in tension. This primitive need can be likened to the desperateness of a very hungry animal which might feel compelled to ingest something inedible instead of food.

For me, this scenario shows well the relationship between inner, outer, and the processes which are in between. For an analyst with a patient, the first stage is for the analyst to become aware of the "thread of the patient. This involves a parting of the waves of the defensive structures and creation myths which are not based in reality. The thread is the tumult, tension, pain, shame, chaos, and aspect of self which feels to be anathema to others (the "me"). While the existing myth is not in line with a natural reality (in that it might have created gods or other mechanisms to assuage pain), it nonetheless is a solution to something felt to be intolerable and has been established as a result of the vicissitudes of penetration. The thread, on becoming known, would cause the existing creation myth to collapse and so a great deal of care needs to be taken to ensure that the patient feels that another structure (new creation myth) can take its place.

If the maternal penetrative processes are absent, the thread will still seek out other penetrative processes—perhaps the ingestion of drugs and alcohol in order to provide a solution to the need. Continuing with this analogy, the use of gratification (food, sex, injecting and taking drugs) as a substitute, instead of the real thing, becomes the "thread pulling the needle". This situation starts out as a need which becomes consumed by defensive structures and the absence of a true maternal process, and ends up as a creation myth in which coupling is denied. Gratification takes over the penetrative process, and the whole system becomes the word around which life is orientated. Chaos in this system is feared as it represents a nothingness—that is, a situation in which no creation myth is in operation and no functional maternal curiosity present.

The product of creation that I am talking about is the "myself", or embroidery or sewing, of what (the "I") and who (the "me") the person considers themselves to be in the world. This creation story or embroidery represents the quality, the experiences, the opportunities, equalities, or not, of all of the aspects of the processes involved. This provides a structure within which the creation of life and themselves, the interaction between their parents, and the capacity to produce ideas or thought is framed.

Any theory of psychoanalysis which does not include this penetrative dynamic between patient and analyst, or doesn't see it as the fundamental process by which the relationship becomes formative, is essentially operating from a magical creation myth.

* * *

Jacob

I had a dream—I was in an art gallery and standing in front of a picture, one of those paintings which you had to look at in a particular way in order to see the picture … it had a brownish, green background with red cross hatches on … but I looked at it from the side and I could suddenly see a pale blue jug … a sculpture … it was eggshell blue … I then looked at it from behind and it was very obviously the reproductive organs of a female … the ovaries, tubes, and womb … but as well as this, there was an egg situated just above it … I wasn't alone looking at it, there were three others, two women and a man. At some point, the egg was nudged or touched and that caused it to fall and break into two rough parts. I knew that it hadn't been me who had caused it to break, but there was an interrogation and I couldn't speak.

*

It confused me as a child that my mother ignored and allowed my masturbation, but stopped and reacted extremely about those photos of a woman.

Analyst: It felt like you were allowed to give and receive to yourself, but not allowed to direct those feelings towards women or others—and with me, it feels okay to talk about your masturbation, but not okay to have sexual feelings directed at me.

I've never thought of it like that … [*pause*] … do you know what? … loads of memories seem to be flooding my head that I've not thought of before ….

CHAPTER 13

Magical structures

The universe is full of magical things patiently waiting for our wits to grow sharper.
—Eden Phillpotts (1918, p. 19)

Over history, it seems that the prevalent state of being that has structured societies is an Adam narcissism based on a male ownership of creativity and intellect. In order to maintain this, taboo, myth, illusion, and religion have been created by Adam. These have become more convoluted and elaborate over time, as every time the perceptual apparatus "sees" beyond the myth or taboo, another, more powerful one needs to be created to take its place. This eventually leads to the evolution of an omnipotent, omniscient God within monotheistic religions and the laws and societal rules which enhance (generally) man over woman.

If we return to the Garden of Eden and Adam and Eve, then I think I have shown that two very different psychologies exist—that of Adam and that of Eve. The psychology of Adam has dominated for millennia, at the expense of women and Eve.

Many myths have, if they are unravelled, an expectation of a necessary belief in a magical power, whether that is the creation story of Adam and Eve, or the numerous gods and goddesses depicted in mythological stories from around the world. Much thinking has been done *within* this framework, relating stories and experiences to omnipotent forces within the psyche, but even so, I feel there is still an inherent acceptance of the "magic". An unconscious acceptance of it—that is, an unconscious (or perhaps conscious) belief in a particular form of creation myth—leads to the development of ontological fictions. These fictions are like an omnipresent background noise, or like puppet strings that we are unaware of, but which influence almost all of our existence.

An unquestioning acceptance of the magic in these stories leads us to the well-versed psychology regarding the inner worlds of humans. This psychology describes Adam, who has created gods and magic, but what of Eve? It might be interesting to look at one particular story and try to "take away" the magic.

Orpheus and Eurydice

I won't go over the story in detail, but instead will simply outline the main points:

- Orpheus has fallen in love with Eurydice.
- Orpheus has magical powers, he can play his lyre and all creatures and even inanimate objects follow him. He can even move stones.
- Eurydice is chased by a potential seducer, and in order to try to evade him, she runs, falls into a pit, is bitten by snakes, and instantly dies.
- Orpheus is overcome by grief and tries to negotiate her release from the underworld. He succeeds, but is given the condition that, as he leads her out of the underworld, he must not look back at her.
- Just as they are almost out, she calls him and he looks back. She is returned to the underworld and forever lost to him.
- His grief is enormous, and as a result, his magical capacities are diminished.

While this story has many very interesting interpretations, I feel that they mostly focus on Adam psychology *within* the frame of an implicit acceptance of magic.

If I were to somehow remove the magic from the story, I immediately feel that I would be accused of trying to remove the magic from life; a force which is deemed to be the very thing that gives meaning to life. Magical feelings can be described as coming from Adam psychology, which inherently fears and feels that there is nothing else in the world, as he has destroyed Eve and nature. Thus, taking away magic in this construct would feel to be the taking away of the meaning of life.

Another criticism might be about removing the essence of the poetic representation of love, grief, life, and death. It seems to me that if this structure or frame of reference did suffice in its intention—that is, to express or represent something to reduce (however temporarily) anxiety of being—then the accumulation of all myths would theoretically lead to a more settled state of ontological awareness.

I am often surprised that when I reference nature or non-magical interpretations of states of mind and experiences, I am met with blank looks, confusion, negation, or vehement opposition. I am left very unsure as to whether this non-acceptance of natural or non-magical thinking is because my thoughts are naive and I have yet to develop into magical thinking, or that I am somehow naturally oppositional. I am often left paralysed within this experience and constantly question my motivations, thoughts, development, and being.

While bearing in mind my own confusions about my experience when I try to voice what is essentially a natural versus a magical thought, I find myself still unable to stop thinking naturally, and unable to be satisfied within what is essentially a magical frame.

So, returning to Orpheus and Eurydice.

Intrinsically then, Orpheus was an accomplished musician who had fallen in love with Eurydice. He could move people with his expressive music. Eurydice was about to be raped by a man and died after being bitten by a snake. Orpheus was unable to accept her death and was wracked with thoughts about how to "bring her back from the dead". In the throes of grief, he dreamt or hallucinated that he could bring her back and fantasised the scenario. As ever with dreams, the wish is tantalisingly obtainable, but often thwarted. In Orpheus' dream, even though he was instructed not to look back, he did, and Eurydice was lost to him in death.

The fact that he looked back, to my mind, is categorically the only course of action that complies with the laws of nature. He HAS to look back, otherwise he really would be lost to the world of magic. He looks back to save himself from madness, an even deeper madness than the one he'd been in whilst Eurydice was alive. His feelings for her had elicited in him feelings of immense pleasure which resulted in him feeling that his music was magical, powerful, and able to bring to him anyone he wished for.

I wish to try to show that this very elevation of love to magic, whilst it is perhaps a common experience and poetically reflects the enormity of the loving feelings, it is *within* the frame of Adam psychology and inherently denies Eve and nature. The repercussions of this are profound.

If (a) man has an unconscious creation myth (or ontological fiction) that is inherently against nature, then each time he comes across an experience that leaves him in chaos, fear, or panic, he will evoke a god. He will create a religion, if you like, whereby he is able to dispel his chaotic feelings. A man operating from this frame will even experience love in a different manner to a man who is operating from a more nature-based frame. He will love pleasure rather than another being, therefore he will love any object that he feels will give him pleasure. This is akin to the aesthetic poets, writers, and artists who are in love with beauty itself.

A quick look at Orpheus' background reveals a reverence for women. He grew up in a female-dominated house and went on to worship female goddesses, although there are accounts of his obsession and love for young boys. Perhaps growing up in a house of females exposed him to women who exerted their Adam minds in order to be powerful. This may have led to both a hatred of women and a defensive counter position of reverence. This might have reduced him to idealisation and "beholding" women from afar, with his hatred existing underneath.

From this position, upon seeing Eurydice for the first time, it is easy to imagine he "fell in love" with her image both as an object of idealisation and also as an object of pleasure. The music, therefore, becomes a seductive device influenced by narcissistic pleasure and played to those listeners who were also under the influence of this intoxicant. It seemed that women were both revered and hated … able to be married as chaste objects of adoration, and raped as mere vessels of a man's lust and hatred. From this position, Orpheus's grief takes on a mourning for his lost ideal, a narcissistic blow that feels catastrophic as it is a structural decimation of a frame of self-reference. Due to the reliance within this frame upon the creation of gods and magic to somehow negotiate pain, another magical construction is put in place to try to resolve it. Orpheus dreams a solution whereby death does not mean death.

If Orpheus had NOT looked back, magic would have won the day and he would be truly lost to madness, forever accompanied by his ghost-like, idealised wife Eurydice and unable to ever be in a real relationship with another. He would have forestalled his pain, but lost his mind and his future. By looking back, he has accepted death as death, accepted the pain (whatever its origin—grief for Eurydice as a real person, or grief for the loss of an idealised object and his narcissistic fall), and forsaken magical thinking.

Perhaps it is somehow significant that this anchoring to reality and the natural order involves a "looking back" … He is looking over his shoulder to his history, to his creation, and to his ontological fictions. It is a point of crisis which, if he does not see what there is to be seen behind himself, then he is lost to the drug of magical thinking and madness. He sees Eurydice, but really he is seeing she is dead, seeing the loss of the idealised object, the loss of his object of pleasure, the loss of his Adam, magical structure of mind, and the loss of his own omnipotent sense of creation. At that point, he sees reality for what it is. At one and the same time an utterly painful, crushing, collapsing, catastrophic, and joyful experience (not pleasurable at all). He has prioritised reality (and therefore the possibility of joy) over pleasure and power.

Another aspect to this story is that of Eurydice, or that of the lot of women in these magical states of mind or ontological fictions.

In states of mind which emanate from unconscious magical creation myths, Eve is always idealised, negated, abused, denied existence, and hated. The fact that magic exists in this story necessitates a consideration that Eurydice would be viewed in this manner too. As she is the representative of Eve, perhaps the story could also throw light on a meta-dynamic in relation to creativity.

Orpheus (or the Adam part of his mind) is "owning" creativity for himself in being able to use magical influences, and this creativity goes against reality and nature. Woman, in her real form, is the most feared and biggest threat to this; she therefore has to be reduced to being an object that pleasure can be obtained from, revered as pure, or reviled. Woman and her real capacities are forever to be hidden away in an "underworld" part of the mind. This corresponds to the character of Lilith too.

The mind structure described would be Adam occupying all but a hidden away, inaccessible underworld in which Eve resides. This does enticingly suggest a conscious and an unconscious, but I am very wary of drawing this analogy too sharply. Perhaps Eve is only in the unconscious as she cannot be thought about in a world in which Adam owns creativity and magic exists; in this respect, she is only unconscious as a result of Adam's narcissism. This then happens within each mind (male and female), and, as a reflection of what can and can't be tolerated in the mind, within society as a whole.

Within this creation myth, man cannot see woman as a human with her own capacities, thoughts, and personhood; he can only see her as an object of pleasure, reverence, or revilement. Woman, in experiencing this distortion of reality has to find a path which ensures her survival—she becomes that which is likely to please man best. Someone who excites his look. So, in a way, the dance between the leer of the man and the painted face of the scantily clad woman is a collusion in which both are playing a part, a collusion that perpetuates the ontological fiction that Adam owns creativity, and that magic exists.

The union of this man and this woman is one based on that ontological fiction, and is as deep as his gaze. His eyes rest on her body shape and painted face and she becomes the object that he needs to service his pleasure, service his narcissism, and forestall pain. The "underworld" then becomes the Eve part who exists under the paint. His gaze does not wish to reach that far, so in another twist of the Orpheus and Eurydice story, perhaps his look back is not just about keeping nature and reality in their rightful place, but also a darker wish to keep Eve in the underworld. Perhaps in being bitten by a snake, she has lost her purity—in interpreting her falling into a pit of vipers and being bitten as a reference to a gang rape, Orpheus can no longer see her as the chaste, revered woman he could marry, but as a fallen, soiled one. The world of magic, gods, and religion cannot tolerate the natural idea of penetration, and in being bitten, Eurydice has been penetrated. That means a loss of the ideal and a fall of his narcissism. The pain involved is felt as grief: he wishes to get back his ideal … his chaste wife … and when he tries to evoke her in his mind the impossibility of the task is signified in his look back. If he were to take Eurydice from the underworld, he would be face to face with her pain, her defilement, her becoming a person who has been used and abused. Adam psychology is not capable of this, it is one of pain avoidance and denial of Eve. He would need to access the Eve within himself to be able to countenance a relationship with a Eurydice who is in pain. So, in this context, his look symbolises the entombing of Eve in the underworld. This is the true original sin, which leads to original guilt.

* * *

The impact of having condemned Eve to the underworld and establishing a magical state of mind is profound. The wide-reaching consequences can be shown by looking at the permutations involved within the processes of judgement and discrimination.

Judgement Day

The being from Venus alighted on Earth,
It was impossible to discern any gender,
Its outer skin was smooth, betraying
No sign of genital agenda.
It had two legs, two arms and a head;
Two eyes, two ears and two noses.

Its naked colourless body radiated
An iridescence in all poses.
A second being appeared, next to the first
Visibly identical in every way,
No one could distinguish between the two
Even given the pure light of day.
They wandered the Earth, noting
And observing human behaviour.
They wanted to live among us,
Work hard, live peacefully and prosper.
When applying for jobs or just shopping
They were absolutely astounded
To be ethnically and sexually questioned
Which they thought totally unfounded.
They were asked their colour,
Their nationality and their religion,
Their age, their race, their class,
Their gender and about their education.
It seemed somehow very important to know,
They needed to be given a label,
So people knew whether to look up or down
And if they could invite them to their table.
When unable to answer the questions
The beings from Venus thought
That they would be judged on their abilities
Because that was what they had been taught.
But unable to label and to box them
People couldn't contain their hate
So they created a new category
To fulfil their need to discriminate.
The untouchable, unemployable
Lowest of the low,
Was having two noses
Allowing them to grow!
The beings from Venus couldn't stay,
Their skills and abilities didn't matter,
What was more important to humans
Was having something to batter.

I wrote this when I was about fifteen. Whilst it is definitely not a good poem, I have a fondness for it as it catches well a trapped feeling that I've had for a long time. A feeling that the world consisted of hierarchies of discrimination and judgement, and that once you had been born, there was little that could impact your place, especially with regard to being female.

I realise that my fifteen-year-old self was perhaps confusing discrimination and judgement, but perhaps a closer look at the words' definitions might enable us to disentangle the two terms.

Discrimination

1. b) The practice or an instance of discriminating against a people on grounds of race, colour, sex, social status, age etc.
4. The faculty of discriminating; the ability to observe accurately and make fine distinctions; perceptiveness, acuity, good judgement or taste.

Judgement

4. A divine sentence or decision; *spec.* (now freq. *joc.*) a misfortune or calamity regarded as a divine punishment or as a token of divine displeasure.
9. The function of the mind by which it arrives at a notion of a thing; the critical faculty. b) Good judgement; discernment. (*The Shorter Oxford English Dictionary*, 2002, I: pp. 697, 1466)

It is interesting that both words have two definitions which almost contradict each other—each one having a "good" definition and a "bad" one. I could very easily be a wise, good person if I showed great judgement and discrimination, but I could equally also be a very bigoted, self-appointed demiurge.

I think that this duality of meaning of judgement is what perhaps led me to call my poem "Judgement Day" … something somehow being present in the treatment of the two aliens as vindicated, perhaps unconsciously, within a society under the mantle of a "divine punishment". The aliens were discriminated against because of their difference, so the calamity that befalls them becomes attributable to the presence of a divine punishment. By this I mean a godlike presence within the mind that enables the thinker to condemn, judge, or punish outside the realm of reality, logic, or sensibleness.

It seems reasonable for me to then think that perhaps "bad" discrimination has a basis in parts of the mind becoming godlike in character. That is, the capacity that allows (if you like) the discriminator to discriminate is the seeming absence of a capacity to make considered decisions and to come to sensible conclusions, and the corresponding presence of a self-appointed (or societal) demiurge in the mind—one which vindicates the "bad" discrimination and metes out divine punishment.

While this may be a bit of a leap into the dark, I think that it might be worth pursuing.

When a person makes a decision to discriminate and behaves towards the object of discrimination with hatred and anger, the person has effectively suspended their capacity to appraise the reality of the situation; has lost an ability to recognise and understand the difference between themselves and the object of their discrimination, instead using the difference as their rationale for their hatred and bias and thus resorting to the creation of a godlike figure within their minds which enables them to say, "They deserve my hatred as they are bad and need to be punished." It is interesting to note that, more often than not, the very aspect of the other that incites the discriminator to discriminate is beyond the control of the hated object—their gender, colour of skin, disability, race, religion, and so on. In this respect, it very much fits into the "divine punishment" vindication mentality, enabling the discriminator to think, "I hate women as all women are bad and deserving of punishment." In this statement there is a powerful presence of a god within the mind which forestalls the need for thought and consideration.

Following this line of thought, the presence of a god, then, allows for judgement to move from the ability to make considered decisions and exercise discernment to something that happens as a result of a divine punishment; and for discrimination to move from the recognition and understanding of difference to the prejudicial treatment of difference.

The capacity to come to considered decisions and to exercise discernment, along with the recognition and understanding of difference, both require a working perceptual apparatus, an awareness of reality, a capacity to tolerate not knowing for periods of time, and a placing of oneself among the whole (whole in this sense meaning the entirety of what "is" in the world).

To view an event as a divine punishment, and the prejudicial and unjust treatment of difference, requires the perceptual apparatus to not be working, a negation of reality, a belief in a structure which enables the unknown to always be known, and a placing of oneself above the whole.

I think given the commonality of factors that either need to be in place or not for the meaning of each word to shift from one form to the other, I will try to address each of these factors within the Adam and Eve story. I am working from the premise that chaotic feelings, pain, envy, and a sense of abandonment, primarily in relation to Eve, caused Adam to create god in order to control and manage his difficult feelings. In creating god, he stripped Eve of her capacities, her status, and his need of her. In order to maintain this delusion, greater and more elaborate illusions are needed to serve as vindication and rationale—a structure of religion, magic, taboo, and myth comes into being. From this moment, discrimination and judgement take on very different meanings.

A working or non-working perceptual apparatus

The facts of life are negated within the Garden of Eden. Evolution, man being born of woman, the natural order of things, pain, and struggle are all denied or attributed to either a good magical god creator, or an angry one. In order to psychically take on board this version of the universe, the full capacity of the perceptual apparatus has to be switched off. Adam does not want to use his eyes and see all around him. Instead of seeing reality with his eyes, he uses them to create images inside his mind which reveal to him the magical basis of the version of the universe he has created. The reality of birth, death, pain, and being the same as other creatures is substituted by the creation of a god and a garden in which the delusion of his own creation as being moulded from clay can exist. This subversion or denial of his perceptual apparatus comes at a cost. He moves away from being *in* his environment and part of it, to being *outside* it and apart from it.

This situation is reminiscent of *The Emperor's New Clothes* ... in order to appease the mind's need to go along with a mass structure that would render a safety of sorts, the reality of the situation as perceived by the perceptual apparatus is negated.

Awareness or unawareness of reality

This is closely linked to the negation of the perceptual apparatus. Nature and how things interact are aspects of reality which, if heeded, place humans within it. If they are not heeded, for whatever reason, then the reality in which a person places themselves is distorted considerably.

In not being able to tolerate (again, for whatever reason) the reality of his situation, Adam creates another sense of reality that feels like a solution to his difficulty. He creates a god, a place for himself that is special among the creatures, a position of superiority over Eve, a disavowal of the natural order of things, and magical forces take over. The biggest challenge to his delusion would be to reinstate the perceptual apparatus and gain knowledge of nature and Eve. This could be represented by the prohibition of eating from the Tree of Knowledge of Good and Evil. Adam creates a religion or story which allows him to become special, superior, to own creation for himself (by making it ultimately a male process), and enables him to possess Eve. Adam now doesn't have to think about reality, he can justify his treatment of others as he has dominion over all.

This structure has turned reality into delusion and illusion. Man is now in a hierarchical universe of his own making and has placed himself at the top. From this position, his discrimination and judgement shift from being able to be considered, sensible, and reality-based to being prejudiced and justified according to a magical creation myth.

Tolerance or intolerance of the unknown

The creation of gods, religion, and myths all serve a purpose to enable Adam to never have to tolerate not-knowing. His religion offers a solution to the unknown as he has created a god who knows everything. He not only is able to justify all his actions by using his creation, he can also attribute all unknowns to being the will of god and therefore known in some way.

If Adam creates religion, whatever and however his god becomes structured in his mind, he uses it as a rationale to shift discrimination from the recognition and understanding of difference to the prejudicial and unfair treatment of difference (his subjugation of Eve); and he uses it to shift judgement based on considered decisions and discernment to the judgement meted out by a divine being which justifies punishment according to those beliefs (pain becomes Eve's punishment).

Placement of self above nature and the whole

In the Garden of Eden this manifests itself by Adam having "dominion" over the animals—they need to be (re)named as a word is needed which removes the inner awareness of them. The Eve word that existed first would belong to that awareness which has become anathema to Adam.

A society based upon this myth would control and rein in all nature and regard it as a right that has been given to Adam. He is able to travel the world and claim it for his own. Nature—all land, plants, and animals—become his to do with as he pleases. He does not need to think about what might be detrimental, long-term consequences. (Perhaps the climate change crisis and the long list of extinct and endangered species bear witness to this myth having been present in minds for a very long time.) Adam can only psychologically do this if he places himself above nature. If he is within it, he is able to see himself as part of something bigger that is all connected and needed.

* * *

The consequences of the events in the Garden of Eden involve structures being put in place which involve a heavy reliance on magical thinking—often attributed to the mysterious and unknowable workings of a transcendent, omnipotent, and omniscient god. Thus the presence of magic or magical thinking is a strong indicator of an Adam-based creation myth. Magic is present within many myths, from those of Greece to Egypt and so on. It has been considered as representing mystery, or love, or a poetic expression of inner emotions. In a way, it might be said that all (certainly the vast majority) of these myths were written by men and *for* men. When Eve has been destroyed, the only "making sense" that is available is a magical one. This fits in with Langdon-Davies's (1938, pp. 89–93) view of the Greek civilisation (a society built on the cloistered enslavement of women) and maybe accounts for the prevalence of magic in their myths.

Magic and magical thinking does not have to be consciously believed in for it to have an influence on thought, behaviour, and ways of relating to the world. It is one of the inevitable consequences of an unconscious Adam-based creation myth being in place. The profound impact this has on behaviour can be seen when we look at the processes of discrimination and judgement.

The next chapter investigates another consequence of an Adam-based creation myth being in place: that is, to view "wholeness" as being a mind operating entirely as Adam.

* * *

Jacob

… I do think the firing of the gun is something of a communication, that something is being exchanged that I've not managed to do before … the prison yard has three sides of fencing, before I've always considered or thought of myself in "safe" places … fortresses … like the old bathroom whose door I could lock in a particular way to make it invulnerable, or my "safe rooms" … I'd imagine having a room which could cater for all my basic needs … no one could get in … I've not considered that it also becomes a prison …

I've noticed something which strikes me as quite significant … for as long as I can remember, on a daily basis, I would indulge in fantasies … delusions … say, a delusion of specialness or being a super-hero … or that I was invisible … or that I was a world-renowned author, when in fact I'm quite terrible at writing … I think every day would be dominated by these thoughts … but I've realised that I haven't done so for a while … I think they allow me to provide a sense of invulnerability and keep me safe in some way … I think I ended up thinking that I had to keep mother out at all costs …

CHAPTER 14

Wholeness

Knowledge comes by taking things apart: analysis. But wisdom comes by putting things together.

—Attributed to John A. Morrison

[Love] is a relic of that original state of ours, when we were whole; and now, when we are longing for and following after that primeval wholeness, we say we are in love.

—Plato (360 BCE, p. 24)

Aristophanes, in Plato's *Symposium*, spoke about the origin of love in the form of a myth. He said that long ago there were three genders: male, female, and androgynous. Each person had four arms and legs, two heads, two sets of genitalia, and so on. They could move both ways and run by doing cartwheels. Males were descended from the sun, females from the earth, and those who were androgynous from the moon. However, they were powerful, and threatened the gods, so Zeus decided to cut each person in two, saying that if this didn't settle them down, he would cut them again and leave them with only one leg each. Because they longed for their original nature, the split people kept on trying to reunite with their other half. When they found each other, they would embrace and stay together, not wanting anything else.

Eventually, people started dying of hunger or inactivity. Zeus took pity and moved their genitals around so that they would be facing frontward. This way, when they embraced, they could have sexual intercourse, and those who were formerly androgynous could reproduce, and even two men who came together could at least have sexual satisfaction and then move on.

Plato was using this story to talk about the origin of our instinctive desire for other human beings—a search for another who might complete us. Those who are interested in members of the opposite sex are halves of formerly androgynous people, while men who like men and women who like women are halves of what were formerly whole males and females. Hence, "love" is the name that we give to our desire for wholeness—to be restored to our original nature.

Someone else who has written about wholeness is Friedrich Schiller. He suggested that "[T]here is no doubt that the emergence of Greek humanity represented a maximum at which there could be neither pause nor further upward movement" (1795, p. 19). He saw the Greek civilisation as "whole" and all time since as being degraded due to the mechanical focus on arts and crafts. Schiller's argument was that the individual Greek was able to unite sensuousness and rationality within himself, and that the Greek state (society) united the individual and the community together:

> Greek states resembled a colony of polyps, for within them individuals enjoyed an independent life, although in time of necessity they could form into a whole; this now gave way to the artifice of the clockwork mechanism, the joining together of an infinite number of lifeless parts to create a new mechanically driven whole. State and Church, laws and manners were now torn apart; pleasure was separated from work, means from end, effort from reward. Eternally shackled to one small fragment of the whole, man imagined himself to be a fragment, in his ear the constant and monotonous noise of the wheel that he turned; never capable of developing the harmony of his being … he simply became the impress of his occupation, his particular knowledge. … Dead letters represent living intellect, a practised memory being a more reliable guide than genius and sensibility.
>
> If the commonweal makes office the measure of the man, if it prizes in one citizen only his memory, in another only mathematical understanding, in a third only mechanical skill; if it is here indifferent to character and only interested in particular knowledge, but there by contrast a sense of order and lawful conduct is thought enough compensation for the most occult thinking … should we be surprised that all other faculties of the mind are neglected, so that the one single faculty prized above all others should be exclusively rewarded? (pp. 19–20)

He saw modern society as having lost this Greek wholeness due to two factors: first, needing to specialise as depth and quantity of knowledge grew, and second, the governing authority's need to establish ranks and occupations to cater for its needs. This modern society is one predicated upon a division of labour principle, with each part being isolated from others. With these influences, he saw the loci of wholeness as having moved from the individual to society, thus society in its entirety represents wholeness at the expense of the individual. In the above quotation, Schiller seems to be suggesting that as man moves away from being a whole in and for himself, he loses sight of any attachment to the product he may be making. This leaves him with repetitive and mechanical work which dulls his mind. I don't think anyone can argue with this. The surprising aspect of Schiller's thinking is his attribution of a relative wholeness of mind to the Greek civilisation.

As Langdon-Davies has outlined (1938, pp. 89–93), this Age of Reason was built upon the enslavement of hordes of men and all women. It became able to exist as men discovered they could "conceive" of ideas within and between themselves. These intellectual fertilisations and pregnancies were a male preserve and women were literally hidden away. This is creativity begotten from a magical belief system in which Adam prevails and owns all creation, whilst Eve is diminished almost to the point of non-existence (except as a provider of sons and an object of pleasure).

Thought from this perspective, while no doubt capable of many great enlightenments, is, nonetheless, fundamentally flawed, as it is based on an unnatural conception and hierarchical thinking. It is thought by men and for men—it does not include any representation of the position and function of women and slaves. It is, therefore, a whole which is a representation of an ontological fiction. The structure of society, in mirroring that of the mind (or vice versa) leads Schiller's wholeness to be a complete eradication of Eve and manual workers from the mind, society, and thought. It can only be thought of as whole if one accepts, as a given, the position of women and slaves and therefore conceives of them not needing to have representation at all.

Schiller attributed the degradation of the Age of Reason to the focus on work and manual creation, and this, unlike pure thought, has historically been more the realm of women, artisans, and servants/slaves. This is comparable to Phan Ku, who, instead of magically creating the universe with words, worked over time after experiencing a period of chaos. Schiller's lament and sense of something having been degraded seems to go hand in hand with the increasing demand for more products which perhaps the male "thinkers", who had no wish to degrade themselves by doing the work themselves, necessitated. That is, there was an ever increasing network of workers needed to support the male thinkers.

Schiller states that this way of being, rendering wholeness to society rather than the individual, becomes "tyranny against the individual" (1795, p. 25). He asks whether the sacrifice that this type of wholeness causes is necessary—and notes that, if it is, we would have to be the slaves of humanity and consumed by servile work for thousands of years. He goes on to speculate that this cannot be true, as even if the law of nature had this tendency, we must have the capacity to reform this way of being, which has taken the perfection of reason away, by a superior or more powerful process.

This tension between the adulation of the thought over that of the product is also found in Ptah and Adam Kadmon. It shifts the concept of creation from being a product (baby, tool, art form, work) produced through action, to being in the realm of the production of reason, thought, or an idea. A shift from creation belonging to Eve, or both Adam and Eve, to one which Adam can own. This follows the trajectory of change over time for many creation myths.

In looking at both Plato and Schiller, wholeness can be seen to be being interpreted differently. Plato, in his *Symposium*, is attempting to convey his understanding of sexuality and the nature of *who* the other might be when searching for love. He is suggesting that each of us is constantly searching for the other, and for him, wholeness becomes a sexual union with another who somehow completes us. For some, this means being with someone of the same gender. This understanding of wholeness can be thought to be based on the vicissitudes of the sexual union between two parents who can potentially create pleasure together, and/or a baby. Pleasure itself can then take over the position of the baby as a created product. Sexual intercourse becomes an action which enables a creation to occur.

For Schiller, his use of wholeness is more focused on the capacity to create thought and reason. In the beginning of life, thought-production belongs to the realm of the vicissitudes of the penetrative maternal function, as it is this experience which enables the first thoughts to be born. However, because women, and therefore Eve, were not represented in Greek times, it instead becomes owned by Adam. This shifts thought away from being a position of awareness of both inner and outer states of being, an awareness which has a place for both Adam and Eve, to being reason and focused only on Adam. It also moves the product of the creation process away from something tangible, to an idea.

It is difficult to completely categorise Schiller in this way, as he is also mourning the separation of sensuousness and intellect. Freud (1939a, p. 113) also writes about this separation or victory of the "intellect over sensuality", but instead of lamenting it, he sees it as a progressive step towards civilisation. In both cases I think it is worth trying to think about what they actually mean by sensuousness and intellect. In Part III I discuss this in more detail regarding Freud, who clearly associates sensuousness with the maternal. For Schiller and his mourning of the separation, it might be tempting to say that he is mourning the separation of Adam and Eve; however, I feel that what he is actually mourning is the separation of feelings based upon passion and pleasure from the intellect. He is mourning the loss of pleasure from the mundane work that the population engages in and feels that this situation is the cause of the degradation of mankind. This focus on pleasurable feelings and passion and the thinking that can come from it becomes an orientating factor only when Adam has taken over the mind (and society). The "words" that are thought come from the created product being pleasure and status and not a baby whose creation inherently involves pain. Pleasure and passion are different for Adam and Eve; pleasure for Adam is based on gratification, status, power, and ownership; for Eve pleasure becomes joy when pain is shared and alleviated—she seeks to be in relationship with others in the realm of pain, not gratification or pleasure. I do not mean that she receives gratification from this, I mean that she relates at the level of suffering and a wish to alleviate it. In Schiller's description of the degradation of man due to mundane work and the separation of sensuality from the intellect, he has no concept of the union between Adam and Eve bringing about joy in the alleviation of this mundanity and possible pain.

Schiller, in his concept of wholeness, has little representation of the true position of Eve and woman as the "bearer of pain". Therefore, as Eve is the penetrated object who becomes aware of pain and suffering, his paradise doesn't have a place for her.

The focus of this book is to think about wholeness as being that of Adam and Eve existing in a dynamic tension of oscillating equality. This can be thought of as the penetrative processes not only between men and women in society (often pleasure-based and objectifying, therefore not equal), but also between mother and father in a family, mother and baby during the maternal function, the egg and the sperm coming together, and the Adam and Eve aspects of mind within each individual. Plato seemed to place wholeness as the sexual union between two people; Schiller placed wholeness in the creation of reason arrived at from the uniting of Adam pleasure and the intellect. Both suggest a split has occurred and an impoverished existence when in isolation.

Sexuality is not the focus of this book. I am more concerned with the nature of the relationship each individual has to the Adam and Eve aspects of their minds. If this relationship (within each mind) is in an oscillating equality, then the nature of *any* sexual relationship will be based on an already "whole person" in search of another "whole person", regardless of whether this is between male and female, or other.

When there is an unequal relationship between Adam and Eve within the mind, this results in a stagnant, fragile, and closed state, and any relationship—whether homosexual or heterosexual—based on this will be looking for another to meet their individual Adam and Eve needs. This might mean finding another who can be used to place their pain into, or to just give them pleasure, or who allows them to achieve a sense of power and superiority.

In primary Adam and Eve psychology, wholeness is an egg and a sperm coming together and equally being involved in the conception of a baby. The division of labour between the processes involved comes together and creates the whole who is then able to function according to this premise. Projective and introjective processes are working in equal tension with each other. When an embryo, or foetus, or newborn baby is operating from this basis, creation and creativity can be conceptualised as belonging to both male and female.

After birth, the vagaries of the provisions of maternal function, the family, and society mean that secondary Adam and Eve can gain prominence in the mind. There have been fundamental failures in the circularity of the projective and introjective forces and secondary processes take over. When secondary Adam is dominant, projection becomes the most important tool and pleasure becomes the orientating factor. From this position, the concept of wholeness can become an illusory thought of conception occurring without Eve, while within Eve narcissism, wholeness can be thought of as conception without Adam. This is shown by the progression of creation myths which range from those which depict a coming together of both a male and a female aspect before creation occurs, to those which either completely omit the female element or, more rarely, the male element.

If the Garden of Eden represents the entombing of Eve into the underworld by Adam, then Adam and Eve coming together in equality would represent a wholeness regained.

A whole implicitly contains parts, and the part which tends to dominate the most is secondary Adam. Primary Adam can operate with Eve to create a whole within which they are both essential to creation. The egg is nothing without the sperm and vice versa. Motility and action along with nourishment and robustness are both vital to the developing foetus and baby. Nourishment is achieved by the introjective processes, and action is achieved by the projective processes.

Secondary Adam is that part which cannot tolerate pain, orientates himself according to pleasure, owns creativity for himself, creates religions and gods, and pushes awareness of Eve to the underworld. Eve (in being pushed into the underworld) is that part which is left with the understanding of the natural order, is the provider of nourishment and life, endures pain, and is able to ease suffering by her capacity to hold it, before working to provide a word or thought in relation to it. In order to be a whole, Adam and Eve need to create a more or less equal union.

The desire for wholeness is universal. As soon as the psyche splits from the "circularity of primary Adam and Eve" into secondary Adam and Eve, the desire for unity is endless.

As Saleem Sinai says in *Midnight's Children*,

> I no longer want to be anything except what who I am. Who what am I? My answer: I am the sum total of everything that went before me, of all I have been seen done, of everything done-to-me. I am everyone everything whose being-in-the-world affected was affected by mine. I am anything that happens after I've gone which would not have happened if I had not come. Nor am I particularly exceptional in this matter; each "I", every one of the now-six-hundred-million-plus of us, contains a similar multitude. I repeat for the last time: to understand me, you'll have to swallow a world.
>
> Rushdie (2008, p. 535)

The wholeness that is real and would serve to diminish anxiety and promote health is that of Adam joining in equality with Eve (Saleem's "what who I am"). The desire for this is lifelong and attempts at artificially achieving it are multiple. One of the biggest factors that inhibit it is the guilt of secondary Adam, guilt at the damage he has done to Eve—the original sin. Wholeness is the coming together in awareness of all the "I"s[11] which come about from every single experience eliciting a qualitative dynamic outcome of tension between Adam and Eve, which becomes an "I". The "me" that results can only be understood by taking in the "world" to become a "myself". To my mind, that is the taking in of the natural order—from specks to rocks, to unicellular life forms, to insects, to primates, and all—to accept that Adam and Eve are equal and necessary, to situate pain, and its alleviation, as the fundamental meaning in life over pleasure, and to have created "me-words" which come from a maternal function.

For me, the very genesis of thought (by "thought" I mean that which is aware of self, other, and inner states of being) relies on the work of the maternal function … or the work of one speck that encounters another and exchanges or shares something that reduces the tensions, discomforts, and unchanging precipice of something that demands attention but is unable to be satisfied while the speck remains alone … or the work of an analyst who accepts a patient's projections and is able to effect a reduction in anxiety. All of these have very important things in common:

1. An ability to keep "systems" open, to allow dynamic, penetrative forces in between either: a maternal object and baby, a speck and other-speck, or an analyst and patient.

---

[11] Rushdie's use of the "I" here is at odds with my use. To see how I am understanding "me, myself, and I", see pages 78, 80, and 112.

2. The state of anxiety in a baby, speck, or patient being able to penetrate the mother, other speck, and analyst, who are willing to receive it.
3. Work is done by the mother, other speck, or analyst, which has the impact of rendering the anxiety less unbearable.
4. Anxiety is reduced and there is a corresponding awareness of this shift in state.
5. A third position is created: either the energy release from the specks coming together, the maternal capacity to think of a "me-word" (or psychic construct in place of a word) which is owned by both mother and baby, or the similar capacity of an analyst.

For me, this shift in state from high anxiety to a lower anxiety is the very genesis of thought. Without it, there could be no thought. This is the first awareness of variable states of being, which also inherently leads to an awareness of "other". Luria and Vital in the depiction of Adam Kadmon seem to also be intuitively outlining the processes that are involved in thought production. This topic was also one which fascinated Bion.

In Adam Kadmon (and Ptah at Memphis), the essence, thought, or idea *of* creation is necessary *before* creation can occur. The processes outlined are a variety of circular vessels nested together like a Russian doll which receive "light" and then break as they are unable to contain this pure light. This light and vessel construction can only occur if a void in the pure light is able to be formed. In many ways, this is similar to Bion's thinking about the generation of thought. A true or real idea can only come about if a void is created—"no memory or desire". When the light then shines into this void and vessels are able to break and reform and ultimately contain it, action and creation can come about. This describes the process of the container–contained system very well.

Therefore, for me, the split in the psyche is not *the* necessity for thought—it is that thought itself comes about as a result of the psyche having been split from conception, which necessitates the need for a maternal function or container–contained process. (By this I mean that, as the organism has both a body and a mind which are fundamentally built on the interaction between the introjective and projective processes, it is this dynamic interaction itself which represents wholeness and is the mechanism by which thought comes about—but only if an external maternal function has been available.) It is the *work* done by the maternal function that is necessary for first thoughts. This then has the potential to allow the rudimentary Adam and Eve aspects of the mind to function together to enable the infant or patient to be able to *think* for themselves.

Intellect or reason, based on law, is the thought that belongs to Adam—located outside the body, and, when operating in isolation from Eve, devoid of inner feeling. Eve thought would be located within the body and aware of states of feeling; when in isolation from Adam it would possibly be ethereal and experiential—a refutation of action and a still observance of the world. When thought can involve both Adam and Eve it is based in the real experience of the individual and involves the penetrative processes necessary for something transformative to occur. It is the position from which true creativity can emanate. This type of thought is necessary as, if there is not enough of it, then the unexpressed Eve thread begins to pull a whole variety of needles in an attempt to find something that can either numb the need or serve as the maternal penetrative curiosity needed.

The psyche has always been, and always will be, split. The split is in existence from conception, when a sperm penetrates the egg. The split is between the two functions of introjection and projection. Each function has an influence and a representation in the mind and so from conception these are in dynamic tension with each other. If these functions don't have a representation in the conscious mind (for whatever reason), they form the unconscious mind. This situation is confirmed in so many ways—the yin and yang of Chinese philosophy; the anima and animus in Jungian psychology; the conscious and unconscious in Freudian psychology; and in phrases like "my left hand doesn't know what my right hand is doing". All of these theoretical, experiential, and anecdotal confirmations indicate that a split is in existence, but it is a split of functions or forces, a split between the Adam and the Eve aspects of our minds. From this point of view, wholeness becomes the two forces acting in circularity with each other and in equality. This wholeness is only possible if the secondary features of each have either not become inflated to a straight line extent, or if they have been able to be overcome. Wholeness is the circularity of flow between Adam and Eve in equality.

In the primitive psyche of the foetus, these dynamic processes occur without needing to have thought (by this I mean thought which results in a third position of a word or image being formulated), as primary Adam and Eve are in harmony with each other. There is, however, a different type of thought present in the primary experience, but this thought is based in awareness or an innate knowledge which is more related to instinct. Thus, the processes that happen between Adam and Eve are known, but it is Adam's domination of the mind that prevents conscious awareness. This awareness is carried in each and every cell in our bodies. The taking in and expelling out in bodily terms is known at a cellular level as well as a whole-body level. Each time a cell is in need of fluid or nutrition it interacts with neighbouring cells to acquire it. The "good enough" womb experience will enhance this awareness and embed it into the innate knowledge of the infant. This is the manner in which all tensions are assuaged. The embryo also becomes aware of the outside presence of something bigger which helps keep it in harmony within and without.

The trauma of birth becomes the first experience which the infant is not equipped to deal with. It is a trauma that he has no ability to contain or deal with alone. He needs a maternal figure to attend to him physically and psychically, meeting his needs and lowering his anxieties. For Klein, this trauma is the start of the processes which result in the infant splitting his experience of his mother into the "good" and "bad" breast. Wholeness then, perhaps, becomes the time when he is able to realise that the good and the bad breast is the same person. This means that something of the mother is able to be introjected as a good object and is able to become something which the infant can draw upon when anxious at later times. A bad object is one which has not served this function well enough, or, in Kleinian terms, has been built up due to the excessive aggression, envy, or greed of the infant. Object relations then becomes not only the seeking of objects to provide essential functions for the infant, but also the inner world of these good and bad objects that influence behaviour and how the infant relates to the external world.

In the argument that is the basis of this book—that we all have an Adam and Eve aspect to our minds, both in the rudimentary (primary) form and the secondary form—the relationships that become important are the qualitative interactions between these Adams and Eves. Thus, how the sperm and egg come together, how the coupling of mother and father can be imagined, and how the vessels/containers (maternal object) of trauma have all been able to withstand the projections. These vicissitudes of penetration influence the dynamic tension between secondary Adam and Eve in the mind, and if secondary Adam has taken over the psyche, then that situation is also represented in how the external world is viewed. This might seem to be saying the same as object relations, but there is an important difference. Adam and Eve are already aspects of the mind—they are not introjected. What I am suggesting is that the functions that both Adam and Eve have innately within the mind become imbued with a qualitative sense of pain and its ability or not to be assuaged. Secondary Adam takes over when pain and frustration are felt to be too much, or when other solutions have been offered instead of a true maternal function.

C. S. Lewis (1942 pp. 2–3) has written about experiences and feelings being like the mother within a piece of literary work, and the choice of form (poem, sonnet, epic, story, etc.) being like the father. He considers both as necessary to create a well-regarded poem, or epic, or sonnet. He highlights that it is the work done by the author to fit his sensations and feelings into words that correspond to the form that makes the difference between good pieces and mediocre pieces. He is equating the mother with sensuality (like Freud does) and the father with order or reason or the container in some way. This wholeness, if you like, also follows Plato's sense of wholeness in his *Symposium*—a coming together of a couple.

If I elaborate on this, I might say that the creative act becomes the work done in choosing the specific word that expresses the passion while fitting into the form. From this, and pursuing Lewis's mother/father analogy, and focusing on the creation of something from their union, I would say that the baby is the passion, the mother's mind is the work done, and the mother's body is the form. The mother's body takes in the projections of passions in all their writhing and holds them until her mind can work to transform the passion to thought and words. This is the primitive function that we all interact with and need. So what is the container? There is none … the word "container" denotes a closed receptacle that perpetually carries something … the maternal function is a dynamic system that is open and receptive to receiving passions. These are held in the body before the mind can work to reduce their chaos. As the maternal function is able to transform the chaos to something survivable, the baby becomes aware of a reduction in the overall anxiety felt.

The containing element is the whole process … the projection, the receiving, the work, the return. Without one of these steps, no containing process can take place. It seems to me that possibly the best poets, writers, or artists innately know this process, and have not entombed their Eve in the underworld—but the influence of society and male-dominated laws and freedoms have focused the vast majority of works to the "male gaze".

Perhaps the monuments, statues, art works, and literary works that dominate the cultural histories of all societies (including the myths, religions, and taboos) serve to remind us that, from the mind of Adam, they all represent dead metaphors. They are dead as Adam is only willing or able to see the beauty in them; what they actually represent or are trying to express—the hidden Eve meaning—is lost.

In man's (Adam's) reverence of the dead metaphor (that is, seeing beauty and aesthetic qualities and not needing to penetrate his gaze deeper, *not allowing penetration at all*) the monuments and arts become things to collect and to look at to see beauty; the main purpose is to elicit a pleasure or gratification associated with the shallow gaze. To penetrate his gaze deeper might reveal truths and pains that Adam does not wish to think about or feel. Thus, the art, the story, the statue, and the monument need to remain *dead* … the meaning cannot become *alive*.

Dead metaphors exist because Eve (the mother) is dead (in the unconscious) and fights from there to exert the truth. Ruins, monuments, arts, myth, and so on, all represent in some way the death of Eve. They are all dead metaphors which carry a truth and meaning somewhere—and perhaps the preoccupation that moves humans to constantly seek them out not only indicates Adam's search for more beauty to gratify his gaze with (and to reinforce his illusion), but also Eve's constant striving to place the psyche in contact with the truth. There is, therefore, a constant desire to find the alive metaphor. Perhaps *that* should be the fundamental aim of psychoanalysis. A striving to seek out the alive metaphor from the enormity of dead ones. It seems to me that it is a psychic catastrophe to have lost this aliveness, and perhaps what it suggests is that it is a catastrophe to have lost the maternal function as an equal partner within human thinking and interaction.

Equality between Adam and Eve is needed in reality—without both action and nourishment nothing can exist—but perhaps a problem secondary Adam has is his innate awareness that the maternal function is the domain of the penetrated object, whether this is the atom, mother, or analyst. Not only does this mean an acceptance and tolerance of pain, a restructuring away from pleasure being the organising factor, and the genesis of transformational thought being the action of the penetrated object, but it also creates envy and guilt.

Because of the innumerable vicissitudes of the positions and psychic ramifications of penetration, perhaps secondary Adam becomes stuck in the blinkered view his gaze affords him. He does not find it easy to look beyond or deeper to find Eve, not only because of his envy and guilt, but also a fear of the pain that might become available. But perhaps what eludes him too is the fact that the male (on a psychic level) can be the penetrated object himself.

Jacob

The only person I've never been able to read is my sister... she is opaque to me ... I don't know whether she's lying or telling the truth; happy or not, or genuine or not ... and I've never known it. I had a dream of being in my childhood bedroom and there were two cats with me. I was aware I needed to try to keep them in the room—but one of the cats found a way out and she managed to jump high enough out of the window, the other one didn't ... I wasn't afraid about the cat, but she just disappeared.

I feel if I'm not intellectual or thinking, then a chimp part of me might take over ... I dreamt that there was this story, but in it were two stories written by a man and a woman, both were dead. The detail of the dream was so vivid, I come across the male author, knowing that he was dead, and I'm trying to write something about his story, but it's like I'm writing in sand. I try not to meet his eye and I don't want to attract his attention, then something changes about my writing, it becomes almost full of a visceral subjectivity and feels trite and meaningless in comparison. I walk trying to think about these words, and come across a woman; I'm thirsty and she has a drink. I somehow manipulate it off her.

Another bit of a dream I had was my sister was in a room doing a crossword, I was there and at some point she started saying something to me and I couldn't understand what she was saying ... she repeated it louder, but I still couldn't understand ... I always felt my sister to be opaque and that she didn't communicate with me, so the dream isn't strange ... cryptic crosswords are also something I've never understood—they remain a puzzle to me ... obscure ... so I think the dream is about not being able to communicate with people—although in the dream my sister didn't seem to be saying any words ... just sounds ... phonetic sounds all jumbled up ... incoherent and incomprehensible.

CHAPTER 15

Tentative thoughts

Adam is of course in all of us—in women as well as in men. But, it must also be acknowledged therefore that Eve is too. Thinking back to the first chapter in this section, Adam and Eve, in a way, are personifications of our-speck and other-speck. If we look at things from a perspective of turmoil, pain, envy, and rage, and ways of trying to ease these, then the secondary Adam solution(s) is one which sets up false objects in the absence of Eve (whether in phantasy or actuality). In attempting to allow something other than himself to hold his unmanageable intolerances, he chooses a snake and a tree, and then, because of his envy and feeling of inferiority he creates a deity to be the creator of all. Adam's need for Eve's capacity to receive something is felt to be intolerable, and her capacity to (re)generate is felt to be enviable, and both are likely to engender a feeling of inferiority in Adam. This gender dynamic is not only an external reality, but an internal battle too.

The Adam and Eve (our-speck and other-speck) in all of us leads to an internal conflict which in its essence is about how to manage and cope with pain in all its forms. Is it best dealt with by Adam or Eve? Or, more accurately, is it best dealt with by the paternal function or the maternal function? The meaning I give to each of these functions is fundamental: the paternal function comes from outside the body and is related to *what* a person is; the maternal function uses the body and is related to *who* a person is. The paternal function is based upon the power of naming; the maternal function is based upon the power of holding (containing) something in the body, and a different "me-word" becoming available. I am talking about functions which can *both* result in thought and words … our-speck's and other-speck's … Adam's and Eve's … that are present in each and every one of us.

This paradox of gender is like a Gordian knot which, in having a choice of either going to the anchor point (start) and taking out the beginning bits of the two entangled ropes and working to unravel it—or slicing the knot in half—the tendency has been to slice. This is what has happened to the relationship between Adam and Eve in the mind. It has been arbitrarily sliced instead of being allowed to mingle while retaining separate functions. Wholeness *is* the equal interaction between the two.

The Adam and Eve story in Genesis therefore sets out a conflict and a solution, which given the nature of that particular solution, leads to a law which is transferred from generation to generation almost in an unthought manner. Good becomes anything which reinforces this solution ... Bad becomes anything which threatens it. Those people who agree with secondary Adam are thought of as good; those that question him or disagree are bad and need to be punished. The law evolves over time to try to prevent every possible threat to the system and women are seen as the biggest threat of all. They have eaten from the Tree of Knowledge. They "know"! Women need to be controlled, separated, treated only as subjects or objects of pleasure, possessed ... women cannot be given the same rights or status as men, women cannot be considered to have the same capacities as men. In some cultures and religions, women cannot even be in the same room as men. If you think about it, this extraordinary state of affairs does actually show that, to certain men and certain religions (based upon the Adam and Eve genesis myth, or something similar), women are the most dangerous creatures on earth. They have this status as they are the biggest challenge to the structure that secondary Adam has put in place—that is, the biggest challenge to the religion itself and the status of man—and so need to be defended against at all costs, and cannot be allowed to enter temples, mosques, and synagogues, and cannot enter into the religious clergy or hierarchies, and so on.

This system or way of seeing the world, men, and women, is present in our society, but not without huge cost. Ultimately it sets up the fundamental philosophy that "good things happen to good people, and bad things happen to bad people". This is more fundamental in its impact than seeing the world as split into good and bad. It goes further and sets up a system by which the victim or sufferer is seen as bad. This is one of the direct consequences of the Adam and Eve story: Eve's pain is given to her as she has sinned by eating the apple and so needs to be punished.

It also sets up the complete division of the genders and does not allow for the paradox that we are both to exist. This is the biggest factor in psychological anguish and suffering. That would also mean that I consider it to be the single most important factor in all external conflict—past, present, and future. All religious conflict, all power-based conflicts, all inter-gender conflict, racism, violence, and hatred. It is universally the biggest influence upon our capacity to be happy, calm, and stable.

I think I have to be clear about what I mean by Adam and Eve, and secondary Adam and Eve. When Adam and Eve are working in a dynamic tension with each other, when both have equal or equal enough presence in the mind, this replicates the primary status of both. From the point of conception in the womb, to being born and experiencing good enough maternal care, the primary relationship between Adam and Eve can function well.

At the point of trauma, or when the maternal function is not good enough, this working, dynamic tension between primary Adam and Eve breaks down. The unbearable tension has not been able to be relieved via the established inner relationship between them, nor has it been relieved via the external maternal function. This leaves the mind to create a secondary aspect of Adam or Eve. Adam (our-speck) has as his fundamental tool the power of projection. Eve (other-speck) has as her fundamental tool the power of introjection. These are the two paths available to the mind. Mostly (certainly to begin with) secondary Adam holds sway. His lack of curiosity about his pain, capacity to project, own creation for himself, deny the use of the body, create gods, appropriate aspects of others, and use pleasure as a substitute for real interaction all function together as secondary Adam. He takes his original position and subverts it to his own gain. This system works well as long as secondary Adam has a place high enough in a hierarchy and life is relatively comfortable. His straight-line thinking enables him to project everything that feels painful onto those lower in a hierarchy and he then equates the bad things that *happen to* those others to them *being* bad (in creating his own god, he can also mete out divine punishment) as he has filled them with his own pain.

If the balance of power shifts and secondary Adam fails in some way—if there is too much trauma or loss, or if he finds himself at the bottom of the hierarchy, his creations are no longer able to be enforced—a narcissistic fall occurs. If the destruction of Eve has been extensive or particularly barbaric, then it feels like he is left with nothing, and suicide feels like the only option. He has annihilated Eve in his mind to such an extent that secondary Adam's failure feels catastrophic. Perhaps similar to the "thick-skinned" narcissist.[12]

Not so often, secondary Eve can gain ascendancy in the mind. This, just like with secondary Adam, comes about as a way to try to gain control over trauma, pain, and the natural order of things. I think this is more complicated than secondary Adam as it is often confused with a secondary Adam aspect of mind within woman. When women have gained a position in society that enables them to take advantage of their power and to set up gods and religions which justify and perpetuate their position, this is actually the secondary Adam aspect in their minds operating.

If secondary Adam is all about power, gods, and owning creation—which are all the end points of a straight-line process involving a denial of penetration and the forces of projection—then secondary Eve is also the end point of a straight-line process, but one involving the forces of introjection. This position is about denying her own penetrative capacity, whilst utilising the forces of introjection. If secondary Adam has projected everything painful out of himself, and refuses to be penetrated back in a circular manner, then secondary Eve has taken in projections, and believes there is no one available to help her in a circular manner. She feels she has to cope alone, with only her own body available to help. On a psychological level, this

---

[12] "Thick-skinned narcissist" (Rosenfeld, 2002, pp. 274–275) describes those "narcissistic patients whose narcissistic structure provides them with such a 'thick skin' that they have become insensitive to deeper feelings".

manifests itself in a "thin-skinned narcissistic" manner:[13] trying to be all things to herself, or not having any mental representation of there being anything else.

I imagine that a person operating from this position has already exhausted the secondary Adam path, and is now left with the rudimentary Eve that had managed to survive. Arriving at this position potentially involves much trauma, or a deep hatred of the penetrating object (maternal or sexual). On a bodily level, this position might be what underlies anorexia and other eating issues and psychosomatic states of being (she has to use her own body as a containing object in the absence of, or perceived absence of, a usable maternal object).

Narcissism is a breakdown of circularity, and whether it is experienced from a secondary Adam or Eve perspective, it is fundamentally a process which denies penetration and utilises the characteristic tool of each position—either projection or introjection.

In Part III I will be looking at four of the main figures in the history of British psychoanalysis and investigating my understanding of their beginnings (or thoughts they attribute to the first moments in history and life). Thus: Freud's, Klein's, Winnicott's, and Bion's first thoughts.

This will include what I see as their version of original sin and what their specific solution might be, in terms of development, to resolve this original sin or innateness. And also what they think the fundamental aspects of being human which are constant and irreducible are—that is, what, for them, are the primary instincts or drives.

From this, I hope to be able to come to a sense of my own thoughts about their thoughts, especially in relation to what I feel I wish to incorporate of theirs into my own "myth".

[13] "By contrast to those with a 'thick skin', some narcissistic patients are 'thin-skinned'. They are hypersensitive and easily hurt in everyday life and analysis. Moreover, when the sensitive narcissistic patient is treated in analysis as if he is the 'thick-skinned' patient he will be severely traumatised" (Rosenfeld, 2002, p. 274).

Part III

Reappraisal

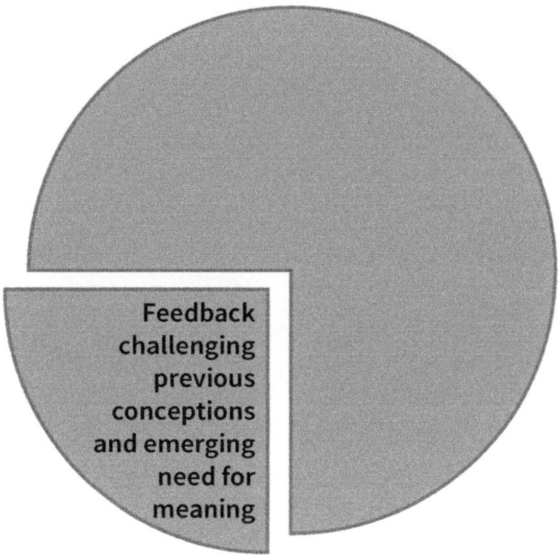

Reappraising

We cannot solve our problems with the same thinking we used to create them.

—Attributed to Albert Einstein

CHAPTER 16

Freud's first thoughts

With the original sin death came into the world. In fact this crime deserving death had been the murder of the primal father who was later deified.

—Freud, *Moses and Monotheism* (1939a, p. 86)

Original sin—the killing of the primal father; what is carried by the death instinct.
Instincts and processes—life (Eros) and death instincts; projection and introjection.
Solution—superego and triumph of intellect over sensuality.
Central concepts—sexuality and oedipal conflict.

* * *

In *Beyond the Pleasure Principle* (1920g), Sigmund Freud takes us through his thinking and ruminations regarding "instincts"—what they are, where they might come from, and how they manifest themselves in life. He had arrived at some thoughts and statements based upon his observations and research which he then tries to unravel, test, and investigate further to the point at which he could have more confidence in them. The original observation that instigated this investigation was that his adult patients had a tendency to repeat the traumas and experiences of their past. This did not go along with his understanding that pleasurable experiences would be chosen over painful ones. He could not bring these two observations together in an understandable way, as the repetitions he saw his patients undergo were often very painful and frustrating to the patient.

Consequently, he formulated a hypothesis: "It seems, then, that an instinct is an urge inherent in organic life to restore an earlier state of things" (1920g, p. 36). He went on to put it another way, considering instinct "the expression of inertia inherent in organic life" (p. 36). He attempted to investigate this as being an instinct which determines how we behave, and which influences life itself, and he eventually arrived at the thought that this is an instinct which expresses itself as "the aim of all life is death" (p. 38).

But then, "pausing for a moment" to reflect, and remembering his understanding of the sexual instincts, he noted that "[I]t cannot be so. The sexual instincts to which the theory of the neuroses gives a quite special place, appear under a very different aspect" (p. 39). He described the germ cells of male and female animals which come together to create a new organism, and could not attribute the instinct of inertia or death to this experience. He then made the distinction between the sexual instinct inherent in reproduction as being directed towards objects, and a narcissistic libido which is directed towards the self. Both of these he saw as part of a wider instinct of Eros—that which seeks to hold together the portions of a living substance. The counterpoint to this being the death instinct, which is the urge towards an earlier state of being, that is, death.

He felt that Eros and the death instincts are in operation, and opposition, from the very first moments of life, and that we are all held to varying degrees in an existential tug of war between these two forces, with the inevitability that death will be the final winner (except in the sense that in reproduction, the germ cells are carried on).

Therefore, for Freud, all human behaviour and character evolves from the genetic and environmental forces that bring Eros and the death instincts into battle, and the manner in which each is able to exert its influence. The sexual instincts emanate from Eros which can either be turned outwards towards others, or turned towards the self in narcissism. The death instinct is the root of all behaviours which oppose this sense of being held together or connecting with others. At its fundamental centre is the irreducible urge to return to a previous state—and that, in the sense of evolution, would ultimately be the impetus to return to an inorganic state. A summary of his thoughts about these instincts is found in a passage from *Civilization and Its Discontents* (1930a):

> Besides the instinct to preserve living substance and to join it into ever larger units, there must exist another, contrary instinct seeking to dissolve those units and to bring them back to their primeval inorganic state ... [i.e.] as well as Eros there was an instinct of death. The phenomena of life could be explained from the concurrent or mutually opposing action of these two instincts ... A portion of the (death) instinct is diverted towards the external world and comes to light as an instinct of aggressiveness and destructiveness. In this way the instinct itself could be pressed into the service of Eros, in that the organism was destroying some other thing ... instead of destroying its own self. Conversely, any restriction of this aggressiveness directed outwards would be bound to increase the self-destruction ... At the same time one can suspect from this example that the two

> kinds of instinct seldom—perhaps never—appear in isolation from each other, but are alloyed with each other in varying and very different proportions … unrecognisable to our judgement. (p. 119)

In "The Two Classes of Instincts" (1923b), Freud noted that Eros was the easier to investigate as it is more available to be observed. He suggested that Eros is anabolic (going from the simple to the more complex) and that the death instinct is catabolic (going from the complex to the more simple). He also said that while there is "no doubt" about the primacy of the pleasure principle and the distinction between the ego and superego in the mind, there was a great deal of doubt in regarding the two instincts as distinct. He proposed that the opposition between love and hate may indicate the nature of the opposition between Eros and the death instinct, especially with the instinct of destruction being available as the death instinct's representative; however, he concluded that there was no obligation to assume that there had been a direct transformation of hate into love, which would be incompatible with a view of a qualitative distinction between the two instincts. Towards the end of this paper, Freud notes that

> [O]ver and over again we find, when we are able to trace the instinctual impulses back, that they reveal themselves as derivatives of Eros. If it were not for the considerations put forward in *Beyond the Pleasure Principle*, and ultimately for the sadistic constituents which have attached themselves to Eros, we should have difficulty in holding to our fundamental dualistic point of view. But since we cannot escape that view, we are driven to conclude that the death instincts are by their nature mute and that the clamour of life proceeds for the most part from Eros. (1923b, p. 46)

In the footnote to this he suggested that, "[I]n fact, in our view it is through the agency of Eros that the destructive instincts that are directed towards the external world have been diverted from the self" (p. 46).

Returning to *Beyond the Pleasure Principle*, Freud also referred to Plato's *Symposium*, and Aristophanes' espousal of the myth of the origin of love (1920g, p. 57). He mused about the splitting of the whole body into two by Zeus as being a reference to the possible nature of particulate matter. He especially speculated that its endeavour to reunite through the sexual instincts is somehow reminiscent of the chemical affinity of inanimate matter which has been carried by the living matter in some way.

A footnote to a later passage makes this point clearly:

> With the hypothesis of narcissistic libido and the extension of the concept of libido to the individual cells, the sexual instinct was transformed for us into Eros, which seeks to force together and hold together the portions of living substance. What are commonly called the sexual instincts are looked upon by us as the part of Eros which is directed towards objects. Our speculations have suggested that Eros operates from the beginning of life and

> appears as a "life instinct" in opposition to the "death instinct" which was brought into being by the coming to life of inorganic substance. These speculations seek to solve the riddle of life by supposing that these two instincts were struggling with each other from the very first. (1920g, pp. 60–61)

He has identified a dynamic tension between forces at play and has inferred that these forces are life and death instincts. He attributed (speculatively) the origin of the life instinct to the pull that brings inorganic particles together to form more complex forms and being concentrated in the germ cells. He attributes the death instinct to that which pulls a life form towards its original inorganic form.

Thus, for Freud, he maintained a dualistic view of instincts. The death instinct he saw as mainly hidden from awareness, only becoming known via destructiveness, sadism, and masochism. He viewed it as present, but unable to operate independently as pure death instinct—it being only able to become active via the action of Eros. He saw this as explaining sadism and masochism in which pleasure is present alongside the destructive components. This leaves his death instinct as a passive instinct, but one which can exert a power over Eros.

From this I would say that for Freud the concept of an original sin (from the Augustine sense of something inside which is irreducibly flawed, sinful, or against a favoured creation myth) becomes that which is present in the mind and body that counters the life force of Eros. Eros is that force which unites, binds, and seeks, while the death instinct is in opposition to this, leading to the presence of destructiveness, sadism, and masochism in the world.

* * *

In *Moses and Monotheism* (1939a, pp. 81–82, 135), Freud described original sin as resulting from the action of a band of exiled sons getting together to kill and eat the primeval father figure. This action is felt as a sin, and the lingering sense of guilt becomes, in Freud's view, the original sin which needs to be atoned for—akin to Bion's "original guilt" (1977a, pp. 308–309).

Throughout *Moses and Monotheism*, Freud outlines a reconstruction of early events in the history of mankind, from Egyptian times, through the life of Moses, to the beginnings of the Jewish religion and monotheism. He builds on his work in *Totem and Taboo* (1912–13), (pp. 1–162) in which he described the setting up of a totem figure that represented the murdered father figure, which was worshipped and used for protection.

He talked about the influences of this original sin (the killing of the father figure) upon the later developments of totem worship, its evolution into a monotheism, and the enduring psychic guilt that mankind experiences. The basis of his formulation is the primacy of the paternal over the maternal. It is worth noting that according to his formulation, this guilt could theoretically only be experienced by the male members of humankind. If this original sin is to do with the murder of the primeval father figure by his sons in order for them to have access to the females of the tribe, then it would follow that this particular version of original sin would be a male preserve. There is scope, within Freud's formulation, to consider that the female members of the tribe were co-conspirators with the exiled males in some way—urging them on to kill the father figure, joining in, or doing nothing to try to stop it—but this guilt would be of a different order to that of the males.

Freud traced the emergence of a variety of god figures throughout history. He started from a maternal deity which shifts to a paternal deity which then shifts back to a maternal one before finally settling upon the primacy of the paternal. He doesn't really expand on the maternal deities.

In *Moses and Monotheism*, Freud writes:

> And here it seems I have reached the conclusion of my studies ... Jewish history is familiar to us for its dualities: two groups of people who came together to form the nation, two kingdoms into which this nation fell apart, two gods' names in the documentary sources of the Bible (Yahweh and Elohim) ... the foundation of two religions—the first repressed by the second, but nevertheless later emerging victoriously behind it, and two religious founders who are both called by the same name, Moses, and whose personalities we have to distinguish from each other ... All of these dualities are the necessary consequences of the first one; the fact that one portion of the people had an experience which must be regarded as traumatic and which the other portion escaped. (1939a, p. 52)

Freud, in this work, and his later additions to it, is intent on trying to find a way of explaining and corroborating his sense that the primitive history of mankind is somehow carried forward in the unconscious of man and still exerts an influence. Thus, his view of the original sin, being the slaying of the father figure by his sons, would be carried forward in the unconscious and exert its influence in the minds of modern man as guilt, as well as the need to put aside instincts with the development of the superego. This carrying forward of something that has been instrumental in formulating society and behaviour seems a reasonable thought to me, but I question both precisely *what* event has had this impact, and also the concept of original sin being this slaying of the primeval father. This formulation is from within the framework of paternal primacy and thus has the problem of immediately discounting the experiences and situations of half the population of the world.

Freud's highlighting of the duality of the Jewish religion seems to me to be a perceptive awareness of something that he framed in the paternal, instead of perhaps being able to go beyond. This duality seems to be precisely that which every creature on earth faces—the duality between the male and the female. Perhaps Freud's statement could be reconfigured as "Two groups came together, male and female, to create. Two kingdoms fell apart and two deities and religions (maternal and paternal) were created. All of these dualities came about due to the female having experienced a trauma the male escaped": the eternal struggle that has always been and seems to have settled into a primacy of male over female—to the extent that even in modern times, the psychology of the female is denied, denigrated, or classed as mysterious pathology.

In Freud's series of events, the sons kill the father and set up a brotherhood community in which the females are shared around. The guilt stays with them and they assuage this guilt by setting up a totem figure which they worship and from whom they seek protection. Each community would, thus, have an individual totem different to the next community. With exogamy now being preferred, these communities intermingle and one totem god becomes many. This is easily understood to be a root of polytheism, and the communities develop a whole pantheon of gods with different meanings and powers.

He goes on to explore the development from this position to that of monotheism with the formation of Judaism. He investigated Moses, Egyptian history (noting that the first recorded case of monotheism was the religion founded by Pharoah Akenaten, which didn't last very long), and the exodus of the slaves from Egypt. He places the "first" Moses as being aware of, and a spiritual leader in, Akenaten's religion; and, upon the failure of this to survive, Moses takes the slaves away from Egypt with a view to establishing his religion somewhere else. The years in the wilderness test Moses and he formulates the religion according to his temperament and needs. This exiled group of people then turn against their Moses and kill him—re-enacting the original sin of the primeval man. They meet another group who have as their god Yahweh, a volcano god. This is a local god and they are led by another figure who realises the need to try to incorporate the meaning and history of this new people into the existing one. He becomes the second Moses and takes on much of the tradition of the new group—such as circumcision. Yahweh gives way to the "one true God" and the Jewish religion is born.

One of the major differences between these monotheistic religions and the previous polytheistic ones is the prohibition on having images of the one true God. Also, the refutation of magic. Freud feels that these prohibitions were instrumental in creating a space for the intellect and imagination.[14] Man had to now have a sense of god and imagine him instead of having an image of him. Also, by the moving away from magical aspects, man had to reframe his sense of what a god was. A capacity to put to one side an immediate need for action, and to have a longer view of something promised at the end of a struggle. This is the beginning of a capacity to postpone gratification and to bear struggle. Even though the putting to one side of magic is part of this experience, nonetheless the creation myth itself that the religion is founded upon is very much magical; also it could be said that in moving away from having images of a god to needing to imagine him, the potential for challenge would decrease, while the potential for the god to be more powerful, frightening, and "everywhere" would increase.

These positive consequences of the development of monotheism (ability to delay gratification, to bear struggle, and to imagine a long-term aim) are all factors which I feel can rightly be

---

[14] In *Moses and Monotheism*, Freud links this shift from needing a visual god, to one who is an "idea" as an indication of the triumph of intellectuality over sensuality, that is, the abstract thought over the sensory perceptions. He also extrapolates this experience back to the formation of language and the "pride of [a] mankind" who could now have ideas, memories, and inferences in contrast to the lower psychical activity which had direct perceptions by the sense organs as its content (1939a, p. 113).

attributed to a maternal function—and they do (to me) seem to be the projection of something that is owned by the maternal function onto something that is created by man to assuage guilt in some way.

Original sin to Freud was this enduring guilt of the murder of the primeval father figure, carried forward and felt by all. Original sin according to Augustine was that of Adam and Eve in the Garden of Eden and their inherent flaws of disobedience and lust; these flaws being the original sin that we all have to accept is in us and that we need redemption from.

The mythology arising from the characters of Lilith and Eve has elaborated on the demonisation of a woman who might challenge a patriarchal system and the subordination of Eve to Adam. This sense of a woman who refuses to be considered less than a man, and her exile from a community, is perhaps a story that could run parallel to that of Freud's exiled sons who later kill their father. These sons are exiled, like Lilith, and also have a wish for equality.

The external danger, if you like (that is, outside the Garden of Eden, which I am suggesting is the "bubble" of the primal father and his harem of women), then becomes that of the murderousness of the exiled sons who wish to be considered equal to the primal father, and the reprisal of the exiled woman who wished to be considered equal to Adam. Eden, in this sense, becomes a place where a single male holds dominion over a group of females who are used, but protected, by him. The system relies upon this structure (or creation myth) prevailing and the power of the single male to maintain his position. The sons represent those other males who wish for equality, in the sense that they wish for females of their own. Lilith represents those females who wish for equality and the right to exert their own will over their own destiny. Both represent, in some way, a sense of individualism and socialism, as opposed to a dictatorship. The route for each version of self-expression (male and female) is different. The sons manage to overcome the father and create a position for themselves within a fraternity which keeps the primacy of the male over the female. But the exiled Lilith is demonised and made responsible for the deaths of babies.

Both Lilith and Eve find themselves in positions whereby they are made to bear the punishment, guilt, and sin of mankind, whilst also not being given the entitlement to a status of representation and awareness in the mind. Given the loneliness and demonisation of Lilith—someone who tried to stand up for her equality—Eve is given a terrible choice: the best she can hope for is to bear her burden and wait. (Interestingly, the bearing of the sin, guilt, and punishment of mankind, along with a need for patience, are all attributes given to Jesus.)

This suppression of equality is, for me, the original sin. The internal ramifications of inequality are colossal. The damage done to the female (Eve) parts of us is so profound and all-encompassing that the guilt which comes from this would be one of the biggest factors influencing behaviour. More so than the "instincts" that Freud talked about. He spoke of his structure of mind, instincts, and behaviours from within the Garden of Eden—from within the construct of male primacy. This structure necessitates the formation of the superego, rules, and obeying; whilst (as a consequence of exiling those who wish for equality) envy, murderousness, self-expression, and so on become another structure which exists as "sin" outside this Garden of Eden, but which envelops it. What lies *outside* the garden is only threatening and destructive as it holds all the envy and destructiveness of the prime occupant *in* the Garden of Eden. The drive of Lilith and the sons to be equal, because they *are* equal, is met by a creation myth which is designed to counter any attempt to re-establish an Adam and Eve equality. To exist within the paternal primacy structure necessitates the disavowal of the maternal and female.

Within our minds we have an Adam and an Eve, and *who* is given primacy is fundamentally important to how we behave. Without equality, mental anguish persists. Original sin, for me, then becomes the psychological murder of Lilith and Eve, and cannot occur without consequence.

Freud, again in *Moses and Monotheism*, stated that,

> Under the influence of external factors into which we need not enter here and which are also in part insufficiently known, it came about that the matriarchal social order was succeeded by the patriarchal one—which, of course, involved a revolution in the juridical conditions that had so far prevailed ... But this turning away from the mother to the father points in addition to a victory of intellectuality over sensuality. (1939a, p. 113)

He goes on to equate this step with a concurrent advancement of self-esteem and pride of man. In working backwards from the status of man at the moment, the sense and importance of woman would be like a void which could only be filled with further elaboration of man, as there would be no platform or awareness for woman to build from. The void would (by the processes of secondary Adam and the impact of the original sin) be filled with everything maternal becoming appropriated by the paternal (an example of this is the maternal function being appropriated by the mythology around Jesus and then deified).

Also, after describing the primacy of the primeval father, then the killing of him, and the development of totems, Freud supposes that a period of matriarchy evolved during which mother-goddesses appeared:

> At a point in this evolution which is not easily determined, great mother-goddesses appeared, probably even before the male gods, and afterwards persisted for a long time beside them. In the meantime a great social revolution had occurred. Matriarchy was succeeded by the re-establishment of a patriarchal order. The new fathers ... never achieved the omnipotence of the primal father; there were many of them, who lived together in associations larger than the horde had been ... It is likely that the mother-goddesses originated at the time of the curtailment of the matriarchy, as a compensation for the slight upon the mothers. The male deities appear first as sons besides the great mothers and only later clearly assume the features of father-figures. These male gods of polytheism reflect the conditions during the patriarchal age. (1939a, p. 83)

Thus, Freud's beginning, his "first thoughts", is as follows:

- A primal father figure who exiles sons and has a female horde for his own use.
- The banding together of these sons who then kill the father.
- The sons set up a fraternity for equality of access to the females. Totems are established which psychologically represent the killed primal father.
- A matriarchy ensues, which over time diminishes until patriarchy resumes its place.
- As a "compensation" to the loss of the matriarchy, mother goddesses are created.
- Son gods evolve which then leads to the establishment of father gods.
- This later leads to the formation of Judaism and monotheism: a "victory of the intellect over sensuality".

According to this construction, we are still within the age of patriarchy and father gods.

This "victory of the intellect over sensuality" is an interesting observation. It seems that Freud's use of the word sensuality (or at least the translator's use of the word) is not a concept that makes the general index and is only inferred from many entries regarding "sensory stimuli" and also "sensual excitement".

It might be worth looking at a definition of "sensuality":

1) The aspect of human nature concerned with the senses as opp. to the intellect or spirit; man's animal nature, esp. as the source of sensual appetites and desires.
2) The pursuit of, or excessive devotion to, physical pleasure or gratification of the senses; sensual self-indulgence. (*Shorter Oxford English Dictionary*, 2002, 2: p. 2756)

A definition of "sensual" is:

1) Of or pertaining to the senses or sensation, sensory; physical, bodily.
2) Of or depending on the senses only and not the intellect or spirit; appealing to or involving the appetites or desire; carnal, fleshly. Also (derog.), lewd, depraved.
3) Absorbed in material or temporal matters rather than intellectual and spiritual interests. (*Shorter Oxford English Dictionary*, 2002, 2: p. 2756)

Freud's exact phrase is:

> But this turning from the mother to the father points in addition to a victory of intellectuality over sensuality—that is, an advance in civilisation, since maternity is proved by the evidence of the senses while paternity is a hypothesis, based on an inference and a premise. Taking sides in this way with a thought-process in preference to a sense perception has proven to be a momentous step. (1939a, p. 114)

This association of sensuality with the maternal has enormous consequences. He seems to be saying that the maternal exists in the realm of the physical and sexual senses, is based upon gratification and pleasure, and that it is only by developing a capacity to "put this to one side" that thought and the intellect can grow. This, he says, is how civilisation advances. The inference that lingers is that therefore the maternal is not the realm of thought, intellect, and advancement, and all such advances are in the male dominion.

The sensual reception of the environment is achieved via the perceptual apparatus; this is a universal phenomenon equally experienced by both male and female. By being able to experience these sensations and "put them to one side" in order to have space for thought, advancement in civilisation and in the development of mind can occur. To suggest that these sensations are the realm of the maternal, and that the capacity to put them to one side are the realm of the paternal, does great damage to the status of women and the maternal function—especially when the capacity to put "sensuality" to one side has to be primarily a maternal process. It is only when Adam pleasure has taken over that the capacity to put sensuality to one side needs to become a paternal one. If secondary Adam creates his world according to an intolerance of pain in all its forms, then the centrality of pain and its vicissitudes being the foremost determining factor in the "health" of the individual is also put to one side when the paternal function takes over. Freud's two statements of categorical primacy—that of the pleasure principle and the paternal victory—are only applicable for an Adam-dominated mind. In this situation pleasure does become the orientating factor and the paternal has destroyed Eve.

Once the maternal function is demeaned, the paternal function not only puts to one side sensuality, but also pain. Pain, torment, turmoil, anxiety, dread, grief, fear, depression, sorrow, inadequacy, dependency, fragility, vulnerability, tumult … all become factors which need a maternal function to become assuaged, but all that is available in this structure is the paternal function which "puts them to one side".

This focus on sensuality is taken up again in the chapter on Bion's first thoughts.

It is straightforward to see that Freud's version of primitive communities and the killing of the primal father fits in well with his Oedipus complex. This became the focal point from which Freud viewed all development and disturbance—the central complex from which everything else was determined. He used his clinical observations and the myth of Oedipus to develop his thinking around this concept, but it would be interesting to explore the relationship between the two constructs—the primitive killing of the father and the complex that Freud developed from his work and the myth of Oedipus. Which came first in his mind? Did he always have a sense of the "beginning" as that outlined in *Moses and Monotheism*, and so interpreted his observations in the consulting room from the starting point of this belief; or did he develop this original construct having arrived at his Oedipus complex from his work?

Either way, there is a strong theoretical link between the two. If his creation myth was indeed that primitive scene, then he would be heavily influenced to interpret his observations accordingly. If his observations led him to the primitive scene, then we might be able to say that he was responding to a creation myth that he was unconsciously influenced by; or he had arrived at a universal truth which revealed a truth about the beginnings of mankind. However, what is apparent is that there is a strong link between what is thought of as a central complex of human behaviour and the extrapolated sense of what the corresponding beginning must be. It does thus become important to question creation myths, and discern whether they are having an unconscious influence upon our thinking, our behaviour, and our work. Creation myths provide a framework from which we all operate and often remain unconscious, as if they are such a given that they remain unknown and unthought.

Freud's Oedipus complex was adapted later in his life to try to account for the differences he found in how it was expressed in boys and girls. If the concept had been an irreducible universal truth, then adaptations and the later elaborations by others would not have been necessary. Freud thought he had reached a universal truth and so felt confident in the corresponding creation myth he developed as a result. Perhaps in the search for a universal truth and underlying nuclear concept from which we can understand development, behaviour, and even human life itself, if it only corresponds to half the population, then it cannot be the irreducible truth it is hoped to be. This then brings into question the primitive scene that is arrived at too.

What I wish to emphasise is the interrelatedness between a theory and an unconscious beginning. In the formulation of a theory, even if it is based in observation, there is always an invisible hand reaching back into the past which grabs another hand belonging to a particular version of a starting point. In this way, we can understand that Freud was operating from the starting point of the primacy of the paternal over the maternal and also the pleasure principle. From this position, his Oedipus complex does become a nuclear complex of the human mind. There is enough in Freud's Oedipus complex that is observable and pertinent to the human condition, so perhaps the mistake that Freud made was to consider it as being the nuclear complex. He thought he had arrived at something core and fundamental, but perhaps it was instead *part* of something bigger and yet more fundamental. He had put images, words, and meaning to part of the jigsaw puzzle, but had mistakenly thought it to be the whole picture. In a way, this could only have happened as he was fundamentally operating from this paternal primacy creation myth.

His acknowledgement about the insufficient knowledge and the uncertainty about how the periods of matriarchy came about have the sense of only being necessary to try to explain the presence of the mother goddesses in history—that is, an attempt to fit them in somehow, as he couldn't deny their existence, rather than really understand their development and importance. It seems a big oversight for Freud to have so little curiosity about something which is fundamentally about half of the experience of human kind. This lack of curiosity seems to me to be indicative of the position or frame or structure of mind he was operating from. He was, in an "a priori" manner, functioning from Adam. This means that he would have unreservedly been operating from certain givens … the biggest one being that patriarchy is the beginning and that the original sin would be the killing of the father.

CHAPTER 17

Klein's first thoughts

Original sin—not obvious, but perhaps could be said to be what is carried by the death instinct.
Instincts and processes—life and death (envy, destructiveness, and greed); projection, introjection, and splitting.
Solution—superego development, depressive position.
Central concepts—"good" and "bad" breast; paranoid–schizoid (P–S), and depressive positions.

* * *

Melanie Klein took a great deal from Freud's formulations and thinking and expanded them to incorporate her own ideas and observations from her experience of working with children.

She starts from the premise of a life and death instinct being in operation, which, like Freud, she believes is present from the beginning, and which then engages in battle. She—seemingly more so than Freud—equates the death instinct with aggression and destructive impulses.

An important addition to Freud's thinking was Klein's awareness of the processes involved in the mental life of the newborn baby. She tried to understand and put words to the condition of the infant mind, concentrating on the primitive forces at play. These were not only given prominence in her thinking, but were also shown to be an essential understanding of how interaction occurs and the deeper ramifications of disturbance at this level. The primal processes of projection and introjection, for Klein, worked alongside the primal instincts of the life and death instincts.

Thus, for Klein, the beginning involves an infant being born who is at the mercy of the life and death instincts, but has the processes of projection and introjection to try to manage this.

While Klein adopts Freud's ideas of the life and death instincts, she disagrees with the idea that no fear of death exists in the unconscious; for her the fear of death is the primordial fear and she believes the newborn infant to be in danger of being flooded by this terrible anxiety: "I hold that anxiety arises from the operation of the death instinct within the organism, is felt as a fear of annihilation (death) and takes the form of fear of persecution" (1946, p. 4). This is a deviation from Freud, who regarded the death instinct as "mute" and only able to be inferred as present from within the action of the life instinct.

For Klein, her theory of development starts with an unintegrated ego with a tendency towards integration and also a tendency towards disintegration. The ego's first act is the projection of the life and death instincts into the object. Klein uses the term projection, whereas Freud uses the term deflection. In a late paper (1958, p. 238) she elaborates on this difference and says that for her, projection involves both the attribution of death instinct to the object and also a conversion of the remaining death instinct into aggression that is directed towards the now persecutory object.

This then results in a splitting of the object into "good" and "bad", and as an object cannot be split without a corresponding split in the ego, there is a binary splitting process in the mind too. Klein saw this as a vital developmental step (1946, p. 6).

Towards the end of her life, her view of the death instinct developed to include a constitutional envy: "I consider that envy is an oral-sadistic and anal-sadistic expression of destructive impulses, operative from the beginning of life, and that it has a constitutional basis" (1957, p. 176). She felt that the relative strength of the destructive impulses in interaction with the libidinal impulses provided a constitutional basis for greed too.

In trying to bring her thinking into an original sin framework, it is the constitutional nature of how these impulses come together relatively that could be considered as such. She believes that we are born with an individual relativity and quality of the coming together of the impulses which impacts how we relate to the world and ourselves. While she is emphasising the individual manifestation of this constellation (genetically and environmentally), she nonetheless considers the battle to be part of the universal human experience.

Her sense of there being a constitutional greed, envy, and aggression, which form part of the death instinct, alongside the life instinct, can be thought of as her theoretical position from which a hand reaches back to grab another hand belonging to a particular creation myth.

Klein based her initial formulations from the premise of Freud's work on the life and death instincts and the Oedipus complex. Thus, to begin with, we can say she was, unconsciously or more consciously, being influenced by a version of a creation myth that was the same as Freud's.

For a variety of reasons, primarily her inability to satisfactorily fit her observations of children into Freud's theoretical frame, and also a strong motivation to alleviate the anxiety she saw in children, she then expanded and developed these theories and her own thinking. Klein's capacity to understand that what children were saying and how they behaved had a deeper meaning led her to question this "universal truth" status of the theories as they stood.

This led her to "moving" the start of the Oedipus complex from the three- to five-year-old child's relationship with his father, to the first manifestation of it being the newborn infant's primary relationship to his mother.

This expansion and revision of Freud's formulations led to the maternal aspect having more prominence. The questions that can then be asked are:

- Has Klein incorporated enough of the maternal and the feminine for her theories to be considered as "an irreducible universal truth"?
- Is she being influenced unconsciously by a spectre of a creation myth that is such a given it obscures something bigger?
- Do her concepts of the maternal come from within the paternal primacy position, or is she coming from a different starting point?

Klein certainly does bring in the influence and importance of the maternal and, as such, seems to develop a more comprehensive thinking than that of Freud, perhaps precisely because she had the advantage of starting from the strong position gained from the work of Freud.

Alongside her sense of the life and death instincts (envy, greed, and destructiveness), Klein also highlighted the primitive aspect of the processes of projection and introjection. She shows these processes operating within and for the instincts—hence projection and introjection occur within the action of the life instinct and the same for the death instinct. This leads to the splitting of the object and the splitting of the self. The good object is equated with the action of the life instinct and the bad object with the action of the death instinct. This can be summarised as follows:

- The life instinct causes the infant to seek out an object for sustenance and gratification. The object that meets this is experienced as a good object.
- Unsatisfactory experiences and the death instinct cause the infant to experience frustration, pain, and anxious dread, which is projected out and is felt to then reside in an external bad object.
- Continued good and bad experiences are taken back inside the infant by introjection and are felt to become part of themselves.
- The object becomes split into the good and the bad, and the inner world of the infant becomes split into a corresponding good and bad too. This is the "paranoid–schizoid position".
- The projected bad is felt to be caused by the infant's own instincts (greed, destructiveness, and envy) acting upon the object, and primitive guilt comes into being, enabling a "depressive position": the object is perceived as whole, loss and mourning are tolerated, and reparation can occur.
- This results in the oscillation between the depressive and paranoid–schizoid positions as described by Klein.

Klein's solution to the splitting and battles between the life and death instincts is the oscillation between a "depressive position" and the "paranoid–schizoid position". She sees the paranoid–schizoid position as being characteristic of early life and continuing to a greater or lesser extent throughout life. The main aspect of this position is the splitting of the object and self into good and bad, with little or no integration between them, as outlined above. She sees omnipotence and idealisation as identifiable traits marking this position—bad experiences being omnipotently denied wherever possible, and good experiences being idealised as a protection against the fear of the now persecuting breast. She sees this binary splitting as essential to eventual healthy development, as it enables the infant to take in and hold on to sufficient good experience to provide a central core around which to begin to integrate the contrasting aspects of the object and the contrasting aspects of the self (Bott Spillius et al., 2011, p. 63). The establishment of a good internal object is thought by Klein to be a prerequisite for the later working through of the depressive position.

The capacity to reach a depressive position is felt to be central. What characterises it is the realisation that hateful feelings and phantasies about the loved object are in fact felt towards the same object. In the earliest experiences of life, the main anxiety is concerned with the survival of the self; in the depressive position, anxiety is also felt on behalf of the subject. If this confluence of the loved and hated object can be borne, anxiety begins to centre on the welfare and survival of the other as a whole object, eventually giving rise to remorseful guilt and poignant sadness, linked to a deepening of love. With this also comes an urge to repair. Ego capacities enlarge and the world can be more realistically perceived. A consequence of this means that maturation is associated with loss and mourning—loss of the ideal object and mourning for the damage incurred (in phantasy) by the once hated, loved object. The inherent pain involved in this process can lead to a return to the paranoid–schizoid position. A person who is able to maintain a depressive position functioning can take personal responsibility and perceive themselves as separate to the object (Bott Spillius et al., 2011, p. 84).

All of this seems reasonable and understandable. I do not doubt the processes and overall sense of the experiences involved. The question that remains is whether this is the whole picture, or is there something else? If there is something, then the existence of another layer, or starting position, would have an impact on how these processes and experiences are perceived.

Perhaps looking at the solution might help us think about this question. Klein has highlighted the constitutional expression of life and death instincts via projection and then introjection; this leads to a splitting of object and self into good and bad (the paranoid–schizoid position); if the good, idealised experiences are adequate, then the ego is able to develop and begins to be able to bear the realisation that the hated object is also the loved object (the depressive position). This creates guilt and pain, and so is difficult to stay with and can lead to a return to the paranoid–schizoid position. This guilt and pain inherent in the depressive position varies according to the severity of the fantasised damage that has been incurred. Klein sees this as partly dependent upon actual experience and partly on the constitutional relative expression of the life and death instincts.

All of this can be thought to be an accurate construction of what I see as the psychology of secondary Adam. While guilt can be viewed as an essential component of both maturity and the bearing of pain, it is also, paradoxically, a factor in not being able to develop and to bear pain too. The nature of this guilt is of the fantasy of damage done—of having attacked, destroyed, scooped out, emptied, or bitten the bad breast. This fantasised attack emanates from a fear of dying and not having a need fulfilled. This fits well into how I have thought of secondary Adam—when he is in need and there isn't a good enough Eve available to meet his needs, then he creates a god and a devil—he creates good and bad. This tendency increases when his needs are consistently not met or if Eve (either the infant's own Eve inside his mind, or the Eve his primary carer represents) has been reduced in her efficacy somehow.

An acceptance of this situation as being the totality of early experience does necessitate a beginning or creation myth being in operation that is akin to "in the beginning was the word", or Genesis and Adam and Eve. How would a different creation myth as a starting point impact this? And from this, how would Eve exert herself in the mind of the early infant? Certainly in the sense of introjection processes, the capacity to take in is Eve. If Adam is about power, then a developed, mature Eve would be about strength. Adam is the representation I have given to the projective forces which operate and Eve is the representation of the introjective forces. Both are needed to enable the coupled unit to achieve a relative stability. Klein is also aware of this as she describes the relationship between projection and introjection. Gratification, avoidance of pain, the creation of gods, the demeaning and denigration of Eve, and the need for ever increasing rules and regulations are all characteristic of the Adam constellation—this can be equated with the paranoid–schizoid position. Thus, from a Kleinian perspective, Eve could potentially be equated with the depressive position—the tolerance of pain and awareness of reality. She also states that the oscillation between the two positions carries on, to a greater or lesser extent, throughout life. This also corresponds to what I have said about the battle between Adam and Eve. Is the distinction I am making between Adam and Eve, therefore, fundamentally the same or different to Klein's paranoid–schizoid and depressive positions?

I would say that they are different in important ways, but at first sight it is difficult to differentiate them. From Freud's life and death instincts to Klein's life and death instincts, from projection and introjection to paranoid–schizoid and depressive positions—all binary forces which oscillate with one another that can be thought of as Adam and Eve. If Eve doesn't have strength, Adam dominates (perhaps Eve could also be equated with "ego strength"?). When Adam is in ascendancy, then power, rules, superego, misogyny, religion, and gratification, all are dominant too. Eve is represented in the increasingly split-off aspects of the mind, and society. Pain is held by her in the mind, and as Adam's powers of action are all being utilised consciously in serving his ends, she is only able to "silently" express her condition. This becomes evident in the "repetition compulsion", in behaviour disturbance and what has been characterised as the pathologies. It is interesting that this expression is mostly a silent one—no words, but a suffering while waiting for conditions to change. Donna Savery (2018) has written about this in her book *Echoism*.

If religion and an Adam-based creation myth are integrally thought of as a given—a beginning which is seen to be fundamental and the start of life—then this position of Eve is her lot: a silent mother, a Madonna, or a whore to man.

In this society, the best to be hoped for is that Adam becomes aware of his guilt and pain and is able to bear the damage he has done (in fantasy and reality). He can only do this if he also feels that there is a forgiving object who has been able to receive his damage and still wishes to love him. While this is essentially the maternal containing function, in an Adam-dominant society, this becomes: Adam is able to bear his original sin, reach out for forgiveness, and feels that there is a forgiving god who can suffer for him too. In history, and in many societies, the object that is sought to bestow forgiveness is a god, or a brotherhood.

Adam's guilt becomes orientated around having transgressed against his god, his country, his society, or his father. This is obviously in the conscious realm, and perhaps the damage done to Eve might be considered to be unconscious guilt. The bringing of this unconscious guilt to a more conscious position involves the dismantling of religion, gods, and the paternal primacy. This feels deeply destabilising as it involves feeling the chaos and nothingness without a creation myth in place, as well as deep pain from the awareness of the damage done to Eve.

When religion, gods, and paternal primacy are in place, the fundamental damage done to Eve cannot be addressed. Instead, the damage is projected onto a male deity figure who serves as a substitute for Eve *within* the paternal primacy framework. This type of guilt and pain does not reinstate Eve to being equal to Adam.

This concept of damage/sin, guilt, and forgiveness is an age-old construct which is fundamental in most religions. It comes from the position of an Adam psychology being dominant and binaries of good and bad being the starting point. In this scenario, the paternal primacy societies can be said to be operating from the paranoid–schizoid position, and there are enormous obstacles for Eve to be heard.

The interrelation between damage, guilt, forgiveness, ego, superego, and bearing of pain is different for Adam than it is for Eve. Adam is mostly similar to what Klein has described. Eve (in being left holding the natural awareness) understands the only instinctive force that operates between particles, between cells, between substances, between creatures, and between minds: the fundamental need for a particle to reduce its level of tumult by coming together. Thus, for Eve, projection and introjection are natural and necessary. The need for these interactive processes never ceases. The location—either outside or inside the body—is the marker of development. Initially, for the tumult to be reduced in intensity, the maternal body and mind are needed; over time, the person is usually able to own these functions for themselves. For this to happen, there needs to be a functioning Eve part of the mind, which is able to come together equally with Adam in the service of stability and health. Klein also suggested this with her understanding that enough introjection needs to occur alongside the initial projections for the infant to begin to be able to develop a healthy mind.

Klein's starting point is the infant's psyche, which then becomes split. This leads to a potential ability to accept reality and bear pain, with the corresponding impact on how others are perceived by the infant. This suggests Klein views the primitive mind as having a unity at birth, which only later becomes split. In my description of Adam and Eve, there has never been a unity: the psyche is split to begin with and maintains that split throughout life. What can develop, with a good enough maternal function experience, is a capacity to organise the primary Adam and Eve couple within to function together, so that most experience is endured with a grasp of reality. The functional couple moves away from the mother–infant to that of Adam–Eve in the psyche in healthy development, until a situation arises which is beyond the Adam and Eve couple to contain. An external maternal containing function is then again needed.

What is common in all these situations is a coupling and the qualitative experience of it: how the sperm and egg come together; how the foetus and womb come together; how the baby is born (going from a coupled foetus and womb to a coupled baby and mother); how the coupled maternal object and baby come together; how the parents come together; how the family unit and society come together; and so on.

All these experiences coalesce to create a qualitative sense for the infant/child about the impact of pain, anxiety, and distress, and the permissibility, quality, and efficacy of coupling. That is, how Adam and Eve can come together in the mind, in the family and in society. Societies, especially religious ones, seem to propagate and perpetuate a denigrated and lessened position for Eve, and prohibit or infer a prohibition of penetration.

We cannot exist outside an interacting couple; we are never whole, in the sense of being one in our minds. We are always a couple, a couple comprising Adam and Eve which represents wholeness. Health entails them both interacting with equality.

Klein highlights the importance of the depressive position resulting in integration and being able to see the self and object as whole, as opposed to the splitting characteristic of the P–S position. In an Adam sense, this is true … good and bad are in the same object and in the self, and being able to be aware of this entails mourning, a wish to repair, and guilt. This then inhibits any future similar behaviour and both the ego and superego aid the mind in controlling this. This system suggests the unconscious (which is mostly Eve) is full of demons, monsters, sin, and destructive elements (Klein's destructiveness, envy, and greed) which can only be controlled or mitigated. This mitigation is achieved mostly by Adam's introjection of an idealised good experience (mostly equated with gratification—as opposed to a diminishing of tumult) and his projection of the destructiveness, which eventually results in the ego being strong enough to realise that the hated object is the same as the idealised one. The guilt, sadness, and wish to repair then creates a different sort of relationship.

If the starting point is actually an awareness of a couple (egg–sperm, foetus–womb, infant–mother, hunger–fullness, thirst–satiation, and so on) then the baby is born with that innate awareness of there being something "out there" to meet the tumult. This is similar to Klein's object relating, and I agree that infants are born with an innate object-seeking function. But I am emphasising the need for the infant to regain the coupled status both from within the womb and at conception, a regaining of Adam and Eve interacting with good enough equality. When any anxiety or pain is felt, the instinct, aim, or drive is to couple.

There is tumult for both the rudimentary Adam and Eve in the infant's psyche. Adam (in the nature of sperm) would be active in his wish to reduce his tumult; Eve (in the nature of the egg) would be waiting for something to come to her to reduce her tumult. They are both object seeking, but express it differently: for Eve waiting *is* object seeking! Adam would root around for the breast; Eve would be waiting for the breast to find her, an other who is aware of her need. Adam would be wishing to actively project his tumult into another to relieve it; Eve would be wishing to have something missing inside her filled, in order to relieve her tumult. Throughout life, every new situation will need an external Eve; someone who can provide a maternal containing function. If this Eve is missing, or demeaned, then the Adam part of the psyche will take over.

When a couple is able to be created—and the corresponding tumults eased—the joy that is felt is beyond the pleasure of gratification. Having a hunger met in a robotic manner can be gratification, but it does not release joy. Klein does go a long way in trying to describe this but the frame she puts it in seems deficient.

Klein suggests the death instinct comprises destructiveness, envy, and greed. As these forces are mostly unconscious, the implication is that the death instinct is equated with Eve. Eve's awareness of the universe, nature, and reality does give her the capacity of destruction over Adam's structure; he knew this in the Garden of Eden. Thus, the very acknowledgement of Eve comes with an associated danger and she would be felt by Adam as a great destructive force.

Freud's sense of the life and death instincts being something which moves towards integration and something towards disintegration, rather than destruction, seems closer to my sense of the forces at play. But there is a lack of distinction between what they mean to Adam, and then to Eve. They also mean different things to secondary Adam and secondary Eve.

For Adam, the life instinct involves action, penetration, projection, and a wish to couple (using projective processes). For Eve, the life instincts involve waiting, being penetrated, introjection, and a wish to couple (using introjective processes). For Eve (and a "failed" secondary Adam), the death instinct would involve a wish to return to a more primitive state. This is not a move towards death, but a move towards being in a more favourable state for coupling to occur. The fundamental need and drive is to couple, and if the mind is dominated by Adam or Eve, then a good enough coupling cannot exist. External factors need to be found to substitute for this lack, or, if conditions are comfortable, narcissism takes over. In occupying more of the unconscious compared to Adam, Eve can be left inadequately coupled, without expression and having to bear the suffering. She would then see death as a means to rectify this situation, as her "particles" can break up and seek other interactions. For Eve, disintegration and destruction can be something akin to life-seeking (in a particulate natural sense).

In this constellation of a dominant Adam—with Eve being mostly in the unconscious—death becomes only death for Adam and is mostly narcissistically felt. Death, in this form, is meaningless to Eve. She, conversely, potentially achieves life.

Klein's understanding of the life and death instincts does not include this. Instead, in reducing the death instinct to a destructive power which is constitutional, Adam and Eve are left without this essential frame.

This focus on the couple is vitally important. It shows the necessity of an equal and constant interaction throughout life.

Eve's need is to be penetrated (with curiosity, love, and care), whilst Adam's is to penetrate. When the penetrated position is thought to be unnatural or disagreeable, or demeaned, then Adam will quickly gain dominance over the psyche. Gods are created (in various forms) to compensate for the lack of Eve function, and society will reflect the structure of the psyche of the most powerful. This situation would be enforced through fear and quickly become an organising force within which everyone has a designated place and exact laws to fulfil.

This leaves the position of the object receiving Adam's projection of his destruction, envy, greed, and pain—the end position of the "straight line"—as abhorrent. Thus, misogyny is inevitable.

For both men and women who are operating from mostly an Adam psychology, the reality of nature, what is inside, pain, and who a person is (the qualitative and quantitative amalgamation of all pains, suffering, loves, and hates—the passions) becomes anathema to consciousness. Adam's action and power become invested in beauty, gratification, and the need to hide the "who". Eve's suffering, existence, and reality become something which is associated with ugliness, and her strength becomes invested in the compulsion to repeat and having to wait to find expression.

For Adam, anxiety is based on the nature and content of his projections which, to begin with (even if this beginning is only momentary) are benign. His projections then, in phantasy and reality (with aggression) increase in destructive content when he has created a heaven and a hell to manage his needs and pains. This omnipotent demiurge then follows all the psychological consequences, dilemmas, and problems that Klein maps out. Anxiety becomes awareness of reality, fear of the damage he feels has been caused, and associated guilt, fear of the loss of his demiurge status (narcissistic fall), and death.

Anxiety for Eve is being left with her own awareness of the unexpressed passions (pain, suffering, a need to couple, impotency, emptiness, despair, and meaninglessness) and the need to have "me-words" given to it. She has strength to be able to persist and wait in this position, but eventually she becomes hopeless and despairing before finally finding a different form in which she can seek the coupling she needs. This is the death instinct from Freud's description of it.

From an Eve perspective, the death instinct is not full of destruction, envy, and greed. It is full of a wish to couple for her pain to be expressed and known by another. An Adam solution to suffering (straight-line projection) does not satisfy Eve. It also eventually does not satisfy Adam, as it is only good for as long as it works. Adam's solution always requires a hierarchy, which necessitates somebody being at the end of the straight line. The world becomes occupied by those who are high enough on the hierarchy to be relatively pain-free and those who are not, who become the holders of the pain and suffering in the world.

If we take the beginnings, as described in creation myths, as having something important to say about the experience of being human, then it seems that both Freud and Klein are operating from a creation myth which starts from a male demiurge position. While Klein does take into consideration the maternal impact she does it more from the perspective of Adam.

Perhaps what becomes complicated in the beginnings that both Freud and Klein suggest is that the nature of the death instinct becomes confused with the nature of Eve. The (conscious or unconscious) fantasies that come about in the infant's mind are instrumental in the qualitative construction of the split into good and bad objects, and the primitive oedipal position that comes about. According to Klein this is different for males and females. Male infants want to protect their mother's insides (her womb or stomach) from their father's aggressive penis. But, as in Freud's Oedipus complex, this wish to castrate their father becomes turned against themselves and is felt as castration anxiety. Female infants, through envy of the mother's capacity to produce babies and receive the father's penis, want to rob the mother of these capacities. This also evokes a fear of retaliation, but instead of castration, they fear they themselves will be robbed of the capacity to produce babies. The boy's main anxiety is thus the castrating father, but the girl's main anxiety becomes a persecutory mother.

In making sexuality and pleasure into a central concept, Freud based his thinking on the assumption that the psychic structure had been built up from this centrality. These are central concepts for Adam, and so have relevance for all (in that Adam and Eve are in all minds), but Eve is not about this. Eve is about intimacy (in the sense of a coming together to alleviate pain and elicit joy) and pain. Adam will wish to ameliorate pain (in all its forms) by getting rid of it, and replacing it with pleasure (or more accurately an illusion that he can get rid of it and have gratification). The third position, or space that can open up which can be filled by thought, that results from this situation are words that come from an outside awareness, as that is where Adam has projected his "me". Eve will wish to ameliorate pain by utilising her introjective processes; she needs a penetrative maternal curiosity and function to be able to transform it to something less painful. The third position that results from this is based on thought and words that come from inside awareness. If Eve is not able to undergo this process enough, and her pain is too great, then the pain inside needs to be dealt with either psychosomatically, or perhaps ameliorated by depression or addiction.

Envy, aggression, and greed were thought to be the main factors involved in the death instinct according to Klein. If these are irreducible and therefore part of what it means to be human from conception on, then there has to also be a belief in a transcendent god and that the totality of the human psyche is that belonging to Adam. By describing the female Oedipus complex as that involving a girl's envy of her mother, Klein is attributing envy and greed (as a wish to take in everything) to the female aspect. If the "holy grail" of pain management is to achieve a productive coupling—one that creates the maternal third position of "me-words" and energy release—then attempts at pain management using just Adam or Eve are illusory, narcissistic, psychosomatic, addictive, and so on. As soon as this coupling does not occur well enough or often enough, envy, aggression, and greed occur. Envy of another who is deemed to have something desirable which is denied; aggression against another who denies the coupling, and greed to try to take in anything that might serve as the needed maternal curiosity. All these characteristics take on different meanings and relevance when looked at from the perspective of either Adam or Eve.

The primary position between Adam and Eve is one of circularity. Once this circularity has not been effective or the interim circularity between mother and child has not been good enough, either Adam or Eve or both will intensively utilise their powers in a bid to offset pain.

When circularity has not been possible or good enough, the secondary processes take over. Eve will try to take in everything to try to emulate the original process that was effective in dealing with pain (greed and aggression). Adam will try to forcibly make everyone around him feel his pain instead of him (aggression). Both will have a sense of envy when they feel another has a sanguinity that they don't. To my mind envy, greed, and aggression cannot occur without first having an awareness of a more or less calm state of being—the primary position of circularity between Adam and Eve. This also contextualises what object seeking might be—it is seeking the lost other. To seek an object, there must be an innate awareness of having lost it. From the moment of conception the embryo and the rudimentary mind are constantly in a circular Adam and Eve relationship. At birth, in infancy, childhood, and during trauma, this circularity is lost and another needs to be found in order to have an external circularity before it can be owned by the mind.

If envy, greed, aggression, and the death instinct are primary processes (that is, they are innate and present from the very beginning) then the understanding that they are intensified projective and introjective forces gets lost, as does the level of psychic pain that is associated with it. Perhaps, rather than stating these characteristics as being primary and constitutional, they might be better described as being a tendency. If there is only an Adam aspect of mind, then they do become primary, but as soon as Eve is considered, these traits need to be rethought.

There is a secondary gain from thinking that these aspects of human behaviour are innate, that is, there is a point at which curiosity, thought, and awareness stops. If they are innate, then thinking can stop at their identification and the naming of them will suffice in employing a controlling or reining in superego aspect which can rectify the situation. The penetrative process that is being sought by both Adam and Eve can be denied, denigrated, and thought of as pathological. The outcome of this scenario is a transcendent god and a virgin birth.

I feel there is only one innate aspect or instinct—the need to be in a more or less equal Adam and Eve couple in body and mind. Everything else is a consequence of this either being met or not met.

As Klein used Freud to build on, so Winnicott and Bion used both Freud and Klein, and the sense of something not being quite right or missing led them both to push the boundaries of the known further.

CHAPTER 18

Winnicott's first thoughts

Original sin—if you like, could be thought to be the failure of the "maternal facilitating environment" to facilitate the emergence of the self. This then locates the sin in the environment and not the infant—this is a fundamental departure from Freud and Klein.
Instincts—Winnicott did not accept the concept of the death instinct, and saw aggression as being only present when the infant was able to distinguish self from not self.
Processes—holding, primary maternal preoccupation.
Solutions—the emergence of the self.
Central concepts—holding, maternal facilitating environment, "good enough" mother.

* * *

From Freud, who based his premise of psychoanalysis on sexuality, pleasure, Eros and death instincts, and the Oedipus complex with the father, to Klein who looked at the infant's inner world in relation to the mother (specifically with regard to envy, greed, and aggression), and then to Winnicott—a paradigm shift has occurred. Winnicott saw the mother–infant relationship as *the* basis of the psychoanalytic situation. He rarely linked what he saw in the psychoanalytic relationship to the erotic, which was a great departure from Freud. For Winnicott, it was the infant's early dependent vulnerability in a two-person relationship with mother (not the Oedipus complex—a three-person relationship) that was the focus.

Winnicott (1971, p. 70) rejected Freud's concept of the death instinct which he saw "as the reassertion of the principle of Original Sin"; he also rejected Klein's view that life begins with an envy of the breast which gives rise to urges to destroy it. He believed that "aggression" originates in the prenatal activity of the infant, where aggressiveness is almost indistinguishable from activity. He traced the roots of aggression to prenatal life, and saw, in the muscular movements that meet opposition, the earliest manifestation of pleasurable aggression. The foetus, in this experience, is not aware of his aggression—he uses his motility to move and meets the limits of his universe when he encounters the womb wall.

As Winnicott writes:

> The main idea behind this study of aggression is that if society is in danger, it is not because of man's aggressiveness but because of the repression of personal aggressiveness in individuals … In a total psychology, being-stolen-from is the same as stealing, and is equally aggressive. Being weak is as aggressive as the attack of the strong on the weak. Murder and suicide are fundamentally the same thing. Perhaps most difficult of all, possession is as aggressive as is greedy acquisition; indeed acquisition and possession form a psychological unit, either is incomplete without the other. This is not saying that acquiring and possessing are good or bad. (1975, p. 204)

This is a complicated picture being described by Winnicott, and for me, one which fits in well with my thinking on Adam and Eve. Winnicott does not see a baby as an individual at birth; he can only conceptualise a mother–baby unit resulting in his famous comment, "There is no such thing as a baby" (1975, p. 99). From my argument, this is synonymous with, "There is no such thing as Adam without Eve and vice versa," although, of course, in narcissistic structures of mind they each feel they can exist without each other.

If this relationship between Adam and Eve is known instinctively, then the capacity for these processes to be working in dynamic tension enables a calmness and stability to be achieved. Within the womb, this is more or less achieved without significant impingement; it is only at birth that this process is disrupted. This established-since-conception (or established since our-speck met other-speck) instinctive interaction between Adam and Eve is not mature enough to enable the infant to survive alone post-birth.

When the impingement of birth occurs, the infant is in need of an environmental provision in order to achieve a level of calm and stability again. The mother needs to be able to "step into" this relationship between the infant's rudimentary Adam and Eve dynamic and provide what the infant is unable to provide himself.

Winnicott states that "aggression is a part of the primitive expression of love" (1975, p. 205). I think it might be helpful to try to differentiate between what I feel Winnicott is trying to describe here, and a later "aggression" that perhaps is more easily associated with the word being used. He is stating that he feels the very nature of what might be described as aggression in the beginning of life cannot really be aggression in line with a later sense of what it is considered to be; that is, in this early experience, what is seen is "life itself"—the movement, motility, and muscularity of the infant being exercised. As Winnicott writes, "A baby chews the nipple with his gums; it cannot be assumed that he is meaning to destroy or hurt. At origin aggressiveness is almost synonymous with activity" (1975, p. 204). He further emphasises this in a footnote: "I would now link this idea [aggression] with that of motility" (p. 204).

This idea mirrors my thinking about the sperm and the egg—motility and nourishment and Adam and Eve. Adam has projective processes and motility at his disposal; Eve has introjective processes and nourishment at hers. The foetus moving in the womb is utilising his Adam capacities and thus could be said to be acting instinctively. However, this cannot be thought of as aggression until, in a way, he *means* it. In the womb, Adam has a "head start" on Eve in becoming aware of himself through this movement, perhaps that is why projective forces are more easily identified and are the first to be used.

At birth, the mother needs to become an auxiliary participant in this dynamic; without it, the infant is not able to survive. His own rudimentary Adam and Eve are not sufficiently equipped to provide everything the infant needs: Adam has not mastered motility to search for food and Eve does not have enough nourishment (which here equates to robustness, stamina, perseverance, capacity to tolerate impingements, reserves, fullness, and so on) to sustain herself. Impingements and traumas are not able to be processed internally—when feeling anxiety or dread, Adam will project out these feelings, and Eve will introject anything that enables her to feel full or robust. Both of these processes are responses to the same anxiety and their presence signifies *life* and a need to find another to recreate the dynamic tension that enables stability and calm.

At this stage, this is *not* aggression. Instead, it is object seeking due to a catastrophic failure of their own rudimentary Adam and Eve dynamic.

I believe this is similar to what Winnicott was saying in the quote above—"[I]n a total psychology, being-stolen-from is the same as stealing, and is equally aggressive. Being weak is as aggressive as the attack of the strong on the weak." In the circumstance of having just been born, the infant cannot be said to be acting as an individual who responds to another individual. Instead, the mother and baby "unit" *is* the individual, and, in as much as they are also representing the needed dynamic tension between Adam and Eve, it is the relationship between the two aspects that is the important experience. At times the mother needs to be an Adam and at times she needs to be an Eve—she needs to be aware of the oscillating insufficiencies of the infant's own Adam–Eve dynamic and step in accordingly. In this light, Winnicott's statement above becomes clearer. It is the "in between" that is important—Adam and Eve at one and the same time are being-stolen-from and stealing in order to create a whole which is in balance.

"Possession is as aggressive as greedy acquisition"—both Adam and Eve feel that the other can provide them with something they need.[15] When in need, the processes that are available

[15] Although Winnicott himself felt that the infant was not born with an awareness of the other, he felt that projections occurred, but with no sense of there being an objective-object that might receive them; instead, a subjective-object is in place which is external, but not experienced as such by the infant. In this context, for Winnicott, the object does

to both step up in intensity, as the need to find another feels more and more desperate. This, in the beginning, is fundamentally an instinctive and natural phenomenon and is not aggression in the more usual definition of the word. Perhaps in retaining the word "aggression" in this description, Winnicott may have been wishing to directly challenge the concept of the death instinct and to counter the widely accepted view of destructiveness being inherent. It does, however, confuse the situation and perhaps a different word for this stage of experience might be preferential. In the manner in which he is describing this stage, it might be better to call it a "life force". I think this describes well the essential character of it, as well as it being "forceful". It is a forceful expression of the processes available to both the Adam and Eve aspects of the infant in the service of life itself.

Introjection has been thought of mainly in terms of introjecting the good or bad objects. This is thought to be an essential part of development. The mother's capacity (or not) is taken in by the infant and becomes part of the infant's sense of himself and others. A vigorous or desperate "taking in" at the breast becomes aggression or greed in Kleinian thinking, which is then thought of as being innate. In order for it to become aggression and greed, the infant does need to become aware of the other (whether that be a whole object or breast, blanket, food, etc.). When initially faced with anxiety, hunger, impingement, trauma, and so on, the infant will utilise the Adam and Eve aspects within his body and rudimentary mind in order to achieve some relative stabilisation. If the existing Adam–Eve dynamic available to the infant has not sufficed, then an external source of these functions is needed.

The mother, in her capacity of being an auxiliary Adam, will move the infant to safety and move towards him to give him food and warmth. In her capacity of being an auxiliary Eve, she will receive the infant's projections and enable him to feel robust, whilst encouraging a sense of being able to tolerate external impingements, as well as filling the infant with something that feels sustaining.

For Winnicott, the infant's ego was not able to emerge until sufficient holding and primary maternal preoccupation had occurred. In his paper, "The Theory of the Parent–Infant Relationship", he argues that satisfactory parental care can be classified into three overlapping stages:

---

become other but is not able to be experienced as being a completely differentiated other. I am suggesting that there is an innate awareness of another, otherwise projection and introjection would not occur in the first place; also both Adam and Eve have been interacting with each other since conception, and so this awareness is innately known. Perhaps Winnicott was trying to describe the impossibility for an infant to survive physically and psychologically without an external function serving to minimise the shock of this breakdown in circularity at birth. The subjective-object then becomes something which remedies this, but nonetheless it is still an object being used in a circular manner. I think when he differentiates between a pure male element and a pure female element he does isolate these aspects and infers otherness to the opposite elements, but he attributes objective-object relating to be at the point of psychic awareness of inner and outer. Again, though, I would say that Adam and Eve have an innate awareness of inner and outer from the particulate to the complex.

(a) Holding.
(b) Mother and infant living together. Here the father's function (of dealing with the environment for the mother) is not known to the infant.
(c) Father, mother, and infant, all three living together.

> The term "holding" is … not only the actual physical holding of the infant, but also the total environmental provision prior to the concept of *living with*. (1965, p. 43)

During the holding phase, Winnicott goes on to state, the aim is for the "psyche to achieve an indwelling in the soma" and for the infant to become a person, or individual in his own right (p. 44). The basis of this indwelling is

> a linkage of motor and sensory and functional experiences with the infant's new state of being a person. As a further development there comes into existence … a limiting membrane, which … (in health) is equated with the surface of the skin, and has a position between the infant's "me" and his "not-me" … the infant comes to have an inside and an outside, and a body-scheme. In this way meaning comes to the function of intake and output; moreover, it gradually becomes meaningful to postulate a personal or inner psychic reality for the infant … other processes are [also] initiated; the most important is the dawn of intelligence and the beginning of a mind as something distinct from the psyche. From this follows … the secondary processes and symbol functioning, and the organisation of a personal psychic content … At the same time there starts in the infant a joining up of two roots of impulsive behaviour. The term "fusion" indicates the position process whereby diffuse elements that belong to movement and muscle erotism become (in health) fused with the orgiastic functioning of the erotogenic zones … without a good enough holding, these stages cannot be attained … (p. 45)

Winnicott sees the holding phase as reducing the number of impingements, which causes the infant to react with a resultant annihilation of personal being. He means by this that "annihilation anxiety" is felt by the infant when his sense of "being" has been interrupted. He sees the early life of the infant as an oscillation between these two states—"being" and "not-being" or annihilation. Under favourable conditions, the infant establishes a continuity of existence and then begins to develop the sophistications which make it possible for impingements to be gathered into the area of omnipotence, that is, for the infant himself to be able to manage them.

In this paper, Winnicott also states:

> The alternative to being is reacting, and reacting interrupts being and annihilates … At this stage the word death has no possible application, and this makes the term death instinct unacceptable in describing the root of destructiveness. Death has no meaning until the arrival of hate and of the concept of the whole human person. When a whole human person can be hated, death [and maiming] has a meaning. (1965, p. 47)

This obviously is a complete departure from Freud and Klein who both base their sense of this early experience upon the existence of the death instinct and either an impetus towards a simpler, inorganic state, or an innate destructiveness (composed of greed, envy, and aggression).

In the context of this book, Winnicott seems to be placing original sin in the external environment which does not allow for a "continuity of being". This failure of the environment then becomes the factor which pushes the infant into a state of annihilation anxiety and all the secondary processes of destructiveness, envy, greed, or, if extreme, even more psychotic aspects ensue.

Returning to Winnicott's statement that "acquisition and possession form a psychological unit", it seems that a phrase I heard during a radio drama might shed some light on what I feel he means by this, as well as a distinction I am trying to make. The phrase was "there is no such thing as ownership in the world, only exchange". In my thinking, it is the secondary aspects of Adam and Eve that try to own, while the primary aspects are aware of the process of exchange. This fits well with my thoughts about the vicissitudes of penetration and how the quality of each of the three penetrations I have outlined form the fantasies and phantasies which then formulate a person's personal creation myth, character, and behaviour. Everything in nature, from atoms to zebras, undergoes this exchange. Everything interacts in this process of exchange in some form or other, and this process is, to my mind, the very meaning and purpose of life.

We interact continuously with our environment by a process of exchange—taking in oxygen and expelling carbon dioxide, which is then taken in by plants; taking in food and expelling faeces which then is taken in by other organisms, and so on. We do not own the oxygen or the food or the particles we are made of, we use them during the process of exchange within nature. This exchange process is fundamental to life and health—without it, we would not exist.

This philosophical concept of interaction, exchange, and perpetual movement is also vitally important to the development of the "me, myself, and I" of a person. Ownership counters this—it implies a stagnation and a closed system.[16] The secondary aspects of Adam and Eve are about ownership, in which penetrative processes and their importance are negated.

I think the importance of this can be seen in the experience of a patient who had been through the system in terms of being under psychiatric care, hospital care, and with psychologists who wished to diagnose him. After many years of this, he knew that he was depressed, anxious, and perhaps had some sort of personality disorder. He had the names for things which others had applied to him, giving him ownership of these labels. He did not have any idea of how he felt or who he was, other than that he was very tired and had no reason to live. I had the vivid image of him in a very crowded room, but all alone, whilst everyone talked *about him*.

He said that he'd been told he had mood swings, and could apply that label to certain situations, but he could not tell me how that felt. When I said that perhaps we might try to

---

[16] This is can also be demonstrated in physics by the law of conservation, in which energy within a closed system remains constant, although it may change form—this might give an understanding to how anxiety and trauma can be changed to a psychosomatic presentation and so on.

not resort to these names, but try to discover how he felt, he looked surprised and elated. He then said, very tentatively, that actually he felt he was many people—a hospital patient, partner, worker, son—but at the same time, he was no one. To my mind, he had experienced the system as forcing an ownership of himself upon himself, while not providing him with the exchange processes he was in desperate need of. As a result, he not only had no idea who he was, but also felt he did not exist. The naming of things and labelling can instantly become an ownership which tacitly denies exchange. It can be secondary Adam, which therefore inherently denies Eve.

The interaction with this patient seems to demonstrate a "me" or self that is not known, and instead is experienced as non-existing. His ego was functioning in that he was a worker, a partner, and a son, but his "me" and "myself" had no existence, and his ego was very tired of trying to negotiate this tumult within him when he had no recourse to the exchange mechanism that is essential for meaning and life. The system had effectively rendered him a closed system with no hope of the energies and tumults inside him being known by an other. The system had also foisted upon him an ownership of these traits—leaving him solely responsible for the management and reduction of the energies within him, while not recognising that this was impossible as they had also left him as a closed system. This seemed to me to be a situation which understandably was full of despair and hopelessness. Unfortunately, I was not able to help this patient; his fear, mistrust, and disturbance along with the extent of his need and deficit in the area of holding, as described by Winnicott (1965, p. 44), was too great. But I think that even an acknowledgement of this serves him better than the other scenario in which his real experience and needs are denied, and he is forced into ownership.

Winnicott's statement that acquisition and possession form a psychological unit can then be understood as possession being Adam's solution when in isolation and acquisition being Eve's. Adam possesses and appropriates; Eve acquires, hoards, and takes in. These characteristics are present when Adam and Eve do not operate well enough within the circular exchange mechanism. The psychological unit instead shifts to a relationship between the secondary aspects of each—acquisition and possession. Winnicott also emphasises that "being weak is as aggressive as the attack of the strong on the weak", and that "being-stolen-from is the same as stealing". When thinking about these in the light of possession and exchange, they become easier to understand. Adam would steal (by appropriation), whilst Eve would be stolen from. It is when the exchange mechanisms break down that the unit separates into possessor/acquirer, depleter/depleted, attacker/attacked, and so on.

Perhaps in this light, the mother and baby unit that Winnicott describes can only become the mother and baby that Klein describes (the good and bad breast) when this inherent exchange has broken down. Adam and Eve would first need to have an awareness of relative stability and exchange before knowing that it was missing and utilising their own processes to try to rectify it. This primary Adam and Eve relationship is what the mother needs to try to emulate with her holding and maternal preoccupation. With the inevitable failures inherent in this, the infant (depending upon the quality of this care) is able to develop a capacity to tolerate these impingements and have an awareness of himself and the other.

The understanding of aggression and destructiveness, for Winnicott, also becomes a complicated picture with a considerable moving away from Freud's and Klein's thinking. He explores these themes in his paper, "The Use of an Object":

> It will be seen that, although destruction is the word I am using, this actual destruction belongs to the object's failure to survive. Without this failure, destruction remains potential. The word "destruction" is needed, not because of the baby's impulse to "destroy", but because of the object's liability not to survive, which also means to suffer change in quality, in attitude. (1971, p. 93)

He goes on to say that in orthodox theory, aggression is thought to be a reaction to reality. This, in simple terms, becomes: the infant does not receive what he wishes, becomes aware of a reality which does not meet his idealised fantasies, and so reacts with aggression. For Winnicott, the perspective shifts and he suggests that it "is the destructive drive that creates the quality of externality" (1971, p. 93). Thus, for orthodox theory, reality causes aggression; but for Winnicott, aggression causes reality.

This, in my argument, becomes the situation whereby the destructive drive is equated to the coupling drive, and is the foundation of being able to make sense of, experience, and allow reality.

In locating the "sin" of destructiveness as being inside the infant, and belonging to him, Freud and Klein can only interpret aggressiveness as being a reaction to reality. In shifting the perspective to the environment, Winnicott is saying that it is the *interpretation* of the infant's behaviour that renders it aggressive and destructive, or not. If the object *feels* attacked by the infant, then it becomes aggression *for* the object. In that the infant is behaving in a manner which is seeking coupling, whilst also utilising projective and introjective processes this behaviour has no aggression or destructiveness. For Winnicott:

> Annihilation means "no hope"; cathexis withers up because no result completes the reflex to produce conditioning. On the other hand, attack in anger relative to the encounter with the reality principle is a more sophisticated concept, postdating the destruction that I postulate here. There is no anger in the destruction of the object to which I am referring, though there could be said to be joy at the object's survival. From this moment, or arising out of this phase, the object is in fantasy always being destroyed. This quality of "always being destroyed" makes the reality of the surviving object felt as such, strengthens the feeling tone, and contributes to object-constancy. The object can now be used. (1971, p. 93)

Winnicott is suggesting that being in connection with an object, in order to provide the necessities of physical and psychic life, is essential and natural. This process at the beginning of life has become confused with the destructiveness and aggression that more rightfully belongs to a later stage. This confusion places the site of this destructiveness within the infant, whereas it is actually a failure of the object to function as an object for the infant. In stating this, Winnicott is shifting the unconscious creation myth that is in operation from an Adam-based myth to a more nature-based one. He is saying that the connection between an infant and his object is *always* going to involve the tumult of the infant being placed in the object. This, in being felt to be intolerable and unsurvivable to the infant, becomes, in fantasy, the placing of something unsurvivable into the object, and thus the object is potentially destroyed. There is no anger in this, as Winnicott says, because it is something that our-speck and other-speck have been involved in for eternity. The joy that can come about when the object survives is the joy of being in connection, the joy of having tumult assuaged, and the joy of having found existence and thought. Once this object has been found, then, and only then, can this function be developed within the infant. In fact, Winnicott says, it is absence of this aggression and destructiveness which is the more worrying clinical phenomenon, as this indicates "no-hope" and no object use.

The projective and introjective processes are essential, natural, continuously needed throughout life, an instinctive drive that never goes away, and something that is the essence of meaning. Any factor—an experience, a trauma, a fantasy—that causes an excitation in any way (trauma, bodily urges, needs, fear, anxiety, and so on) has to undergo this exchange mechanism in order for it to become part of the known "me" of a person, and so also then be able to be incorporated into the ego's remit—that is, to be able to become tolerated, endured, borne, and less demanding upon the individual. The excitation then becomes manageable and less urgently seeks an other as a suitable exchange partner.

If the creation myth that someone is operating from involves a magical creation element—one which denies nature—then the ego (I mean by this, the "myself" aspect I have already referred to—that which is the product of the "me" and the "I" coming together to have a sense of self and efficacy, and is able to function in the world at large) would be seen as almost creating itself. The penetrative exchange needs would be negated and viewed as pathology or attack.

For a realistic "myself" to exist, this process needs to provide us with our "me" words, our sense of *who* we are. Without it, we are just left with *what* we are, the "I". The patient described above has had few opportunities for his "me" to be known and received by an other, and therefore has no meaning or wish to live.

So, this question of *how* a "myself" becomes, seems to be of vital importance. A "myself" which is mostly "I" (built on a secondary Adam structuring of the world) is left with a hollow sense of who he is and (without success or power) has no meaning in life. He will also not know himself in an Eve sense; he will be heavily invested in gratification, avoidance of pain, and exhibit either an unconscious misogyny or a more overt hatred of women. A woman with a dominant secondary Adam aspect will also be heavily invested in gratification, avoidance of pain, and seeking power, and is likely to exhibit unconscious self-hatred. The fundamental aspect of this position is a repudiation of nature and of the importance of penetrative processes, that is, the importance of Eve. To move from ownership to exchange involves a dismantling of the prevailing creation myth, a forbearance of pain, an understanding of the need of Eve, and also a capacity to tolerate the inherent guilt about how secondary Adam has treated Eve.

In "Creativity and Its Origins" (1971, p. 82), Winnicott explores the difference between a breast that "*is*"[17] for the infant and a situation counter to this whereby the breast is unable to be experienced as such. A breast that "is" enables the infant to "be"; this creates an experience when baby and mother are not yet separated out in the infant's rudimentary mind. Winnicott states clearly that he views this capacity of the breast (mother) to be a purely female element:

> I have arrived at a position in which I say that object-relating in terms of this pure female element has nothing to do with the drive (or instinct). Object-relating backed by instinct drive belongs to the male element in the personality uncontaminated by the female element … it is necessary to separate out (not boys from girls but) the uncontaminated boy element from the uncontaminated girl element. The classical statement in regard to … oral sadism, anal stages, etc., arises out of a consideration of the life of the pure male element. Studies of identification based on introjection or incorporation are studies of the experience of the already mixed male and female elements. Study of the pure female element leads us elsewhere … to BEING, and this forms the only basis for self-discovery and a sense of existing (and then on to the capacity to develop an inside, to be a container, to have a capacity to use the mechanisms of projection and introjection and to relate to the world in terms of introjection and projection …) … when the girl element in the boy or girl or patient finds the breast it is the self that has been found. (1971, p. 82)

Obviously, this is very similar to my thinking around Adam and Eve. Winnicott calls Adam the pure male element; and Eve, the pure female element. So far, it seems that the point I have arrived at, after following our-speck, can be said to fit well into the frame (and therefore creation myth) of Winnicott. His differentiation of the pure female and male elements, along with an acknowledgement of their existence in *all* infants seems very important.

Where I might (slightly) disagree with him is his clear statement that the pure female element is not to be confused with the drive or instinct involved in object-relating. This he sees as part of the pure male element. If he means that drive to relate to another to gratify a sexual or pleasurable urge, then I can agree. But object-relating can be thought about in another way: the seeking of another to couple with, to assuage unthinkable anxiety. For this, I see both the pure female and pure male elements participating in this equally, albeit in very different ways.

From my perspective, Adam and Eve exist from conception (even pre-conception). As such, they are in a dynamic tension throughout all stages of growth; and it is this dynamic tension

---

[17] By this I understand Winnicott to mean a capacity to "be something" about which the question "Who does it belong to?" need not be asked. It makes it possible for the infant to consider the breast as an extension of himself in order for the circularity of Adam–Eve interaction to be maintained. Perhaps this stage enables the infant to become aware of the possibility of being able to experience this outside the womb, and therefore, eventually, be able to feel safe and enable the interaction within himself. If this does not occur, then the male elements take over in the mind of the infant, as the breast was not able to "be" (without "doing") and so the infant will find no circularity of being in the external world.

that is the precursor to object-relating after birth. Both Adam and Eve are involved in this and seek it. Adam is active, Eve is still and waits. I see all (later) sexual and pleasurable instincts as secondary to this first instinct to couple in this way. In many ways it might be said that sexual instincts are a sublimated aspect of this primary, unitary drive to be in circularity with another.

Adam's role in this is obvious—he moves, he seeks, he makes noises, he projects—Eve's role is more difficult to describe. She needs a penetrative action, but this action is of a maternal curiosity. The mother's mind penetrates with curiosity and provides "me-words" in order for Eve to begin to exist. Eve's object-seeking behaviour is, by necessity, a stillness or silence and waiting. Her own Adam cannot help her in this, as it is only when Adam has stopped making his noise that she can be distinguished.

It seems the battle between the secondary and primary aspects of Adam and Eve, or the concept of ownership and exchange, or narcissism and altruism, are all based upon the phantasies regarding the penetrative processes—which "who" comes about and who might "own" creation. Self-hatred for Adam could easily be understood as arising from a scenario when he has not felt able to be received by an Eve. Self-hatred for Eve would be a situation when she has waited and received no penetrative maternal curiosity. It would be felt as an abhorrence, or as though the "who" of that person is anathema to the other, and it signifies failure of both Adam and Eve. In the experience of the infant, Adam's projections have failed to elicit a circularity of being which is fundamental to Eve's existence. Eve waits and if the waiting fails too, then that is a psychic catastrophe.

It is my understanding that the "Winnicottian baby" emerges without form. He is without any instinctive awareness of the other and his tumult arising from the perceptual experience of birth and loss of the womb is full of annihilation anxiety, chaos, and nothingness. Winnicott emphasises the importance of holding and primary maternal preoccupation at this stage. Holding both physically and psychically—the physical holding provides a boundary from which the infant can begin to bodily orientate himself in relation to not-him. He is able to discover and feel his own body and differentiate that from the other; he is able to psychically represent the inside-him and the outside-him. From being held psychically by the primary maternal preoccupation of a parent, he is also then able to represent the other as a recipient of his tumult. From this, he says, the gradual awareness of the other develops, going from relating to the other, finding the other, destroying the other, and (as long as both have survived) the capacity to productively use the other.

Through holding, the infant is given the space and time to emerge. What this emergence might be is bound up with experience, the other, phantasy, and the resulting ego that all these factors combine to create. The ego of the infant is that which negotiates between all the competing elements that demand attention—the tumults, the fears, the sensations, the external restraints and constraints, as well as the needs. In my understanding of his thinking, he sees this emergence as mostly coming from the infant, with the maternal object providing the facilitating environment which enables him to differentiate himself from the other and then begin to formulate his ego.

In comparing this sense of beginning to that of Klein, it is immediately apparent that, while Klein emphasises a death instinct and Winnicott emphasises an annihilation anxiety, they differ in how the baby experiences this and how a solution is arrived at. For Klein, the baby splits (by projection and introjection) the object into the good and bad breast, which then results in a corresponding split in the mind. This then allows the good breast to be unencumbered by the bad experience and so can be introjected to build ego strength and this leads on to a superego and so on. For Winnicott, the holding and primary maternal preoccupation of the maternal figure allows the baby to be able to represent an inner and outer. This then allows a concept of a delineation between self and other to develop. The self can then emerge into a facilitating environment and become known. For Klein, the initial projections are object seeking, but for Winnicott, the anxiety is felt by the baby, but the baby does not have an object-seeking drive. The projections, for Winnicott, emanate from the baby, but the baby has no sense of the other. Winnicott's baby only becomes aware of the other by the physical holding of the maternal figure. Thus, the physical holding experience becomes able to be represented in the mind and the sense of an other to receive projections becomes possible.

What does this difference in beginning mean? For Klein, the baby is born with an inherent sense of the other and expects the projections to find an object into which they can reside. For Winnicott, the baby is not born with this inherent sense of the other, but this needs to be facilitated by the maternal holding function. Both babies are thought to have anxieties—for Klein these are based upon the death drive which is comprised of constitutional destructiveness, envy, and greed; for Winnicott these are based upon a fear of annihilation (or a "discontinuity in being"). For Klein, therefore, the beginning is one in which the starting point is an acceptance of a destructive aspect of self. For Winnicott, the beginning is one which allows for a sense of fear, but doesn't accept a destructive aspect of self.

So, in tracing the development of psychoanalytic thinking from Freud through to Winnicott, the progression can be thought about as an expanding awareness of the psychology of secondary Adam, from within the frame of "paternal primacy" to a growing unease that, while pertinent to many aspects of clinical phenomena, the formulations do not account for all. Klein is able to introduce a maternal importance and observations that take into account her view of the earliest experience. Winnicott is able to further elaborate on the maternal, and begins to consider a self that might be able to emerge or not—depending upon the environment the infant is in. The progression is one of an increasing awareness and attributable importance of the maternal impact on the infant. The psychology is expanding to try to include all clinical phenomena. The difficulties inherent in each, so far, could be thought of as follows:

Freud does not explore enough of the maternal and his theories are constructed from a "paternal primacy" creation myth.

Klein does include a stronger maternal element, but she considers the counterpoint to the life force to be an inherent destructiveness, envy, and greed. She also seems to be coming from a starting point of paternal primacy (in that she follows Freud closely and her solution to this tension between the life and death aspects is a superego and the depressive position with its inherent guilt).

Winnicott follows Klein and places the maternal as central in the development of infants, but doesn't agree with the "counter force" of the life instinct being comprised of destructiveness, greed, and envy. He sees the infant as being "non-object seeking" initially and feels that the infant's self is able to emerge in a facilitating environment. Therefore, he does not see the starting position as a coupled Adam and Eve, capable of knowing the other exists, and also therefore sees the infant as being a whole whose self can emerge in the right conditions … a seeming prioritising of projection processes over introjective ones as being the factor involved in emergence. The self emerges in favourable conditions, like the tentacles of a sea anemone when the surrounding waters are safe. The water is only important in that it is safe or not—it doesn't have to have an active penetrative action upon the anemone. Winnicott's primary maternal preoccupation and facilitating environment becomes a relatively non-penetrative process.

Winnicott, compared to Freud and Klein, isn't so easy to fit into a word creation myth, nor is it easy to say he is operating from a paternal primacy beginning. The inherent split that exists in every cell and in the mind—that between Adam and Eve—is represented in his model, with the pure male and female elements. He has also formulated a beginning in chaos by highlighting a "nothingness", he understands how relevant the mother's capacity to provide a good enough experience and environment is, but what seems lacking is the extent of the dynamic nature of the mother–infant dyad (interestingly, Klein does describe this, but attributes what is secondary—for me—to something primary). Where his theories fall down (in my thinking), aspects of Bion's work compensate, in that Bion elaborates on the container–contained experience.

It seems therefore, that while Winnicott has moved away from a word creation myth and paternal primacy towards a maternal primacy, especially with regard to psychic health, his solutions indicate that his concept of the beginning doesn't take into account the coming together of the egg and sperm and the inherent cell memory that could be carried over. He also seems to lack the maternal potency that is needed to facilitate the emergence of self. As such perhaps he is (unconsciously) still operating from a passive female position, even though he has raised her from void (in the Freudian beginning scenario) to having a status.

This is also, interestingly, highly related to what might be considered to be the contents of the "unconscious". For Freud and Klein, the unconscious becomes occupied primarily by Eve, as she is not represented enough in their models. Her processes then become thought of as the instincts, pathologies, destructiveness, greed, or envies. For Winnicott, in having more of a representation of her in his model, the unconscious becomes a different place. It is occupied mostly by repressed or raw experiences which have yet to receive representation.

It feels to me that Winnicott places the onus and impetus for the development of ego and thinking in the mind of the infant; it feels as though he says it self-generates within the frame of being held. Whereas, Bion seems to place this onus *in between* the infant and the other and the next chapter investigates my thoughts regarding aspects of his work.

CHAPTER 19

Bion's first thoughts

Original sin—thinks more of an original guilt, or the fact of being born.
Instincts—life and death.
Processes—projection and introjection; container–contained.
Solution—to enable thought from O; no memory, no desire.
Central concept—container–contained.

* * *

It could be said that original sin, for Bion, seemingly, is simply being born—from the moment when Psyche and Soma have to split and tension arises. He also mentions many times in his writings that, for him, original sin is more an original guilt which seems to be something humans are born with:

> B: Religious people talk about "original sin"; Freud talks about "free floating guilt". It has a long history—long before anybody managed to attach an articulate label to it. So you can be reasonably sure that whether you are an analysand or analyst you will be a prey to feelings of guilt …
> O: It is like the crime of being born human.
> B: Or potentially "civilised". (1977a, pp. 308–309)

And:

> Our primitive, primordial impulses don't appreciate being invaded by stuff from up here (the brain). It is like being the original possessor of the personality or character; things like primitive guilt—or original sin as religious people call it … (1977b, p. 58)

From this, it can be inferred that Bion believed in an original guilt that seemed to be part of what it means to be a civilised human. My interpretation of this is that he felt there was something about being civilised that created a need for each human to carry a preponderance of guilt, regardless of the reality of the experience of that human. He equated this guilt to an exacting morality or conscience which paralysed the character of the human. In my reading of Bion, it seems that the source of this guilt was being born. In *The Dawn of Oblivion* (1979) he writes the following:

> *EM* Your fetal membranes, as you call them, are a nuisance as it is impossible to break through them. I cannot reach you because of them. Who or What are you?
> *TERM* I knew till you butted in. I am mind and my mental membranes make me able to reach far beyond my feet. How and What and Who used to help.
> *EM* Now you have muddled me. I shall be body; for ever I shall gird at your mind.
> *MIND* Hullo! Where have you sprung from?
> *BODY* What—you again? I am Body; you can call me Soma if you like. Who are you?
> *MIND* Call me Psyche—Psyche-Soma.
> *BODY* Soma-Psyche.
> *MIND* We must be related.
> *BODY* Never—not if I can help it.
> *MIND* Oh, come. Not as bad as that, is it?
> *BODY* Worse. You got us into this air. Luckily I brought some liquid with me. What are you doing?
> …
> *BODY* Typical of Mind—all words and no content. Where did you find them?
> *MIND* Borrowed from the future—you are borrowing them from me; do you get them through the diaphragm?
> *BODY* They penetrate it. But the meaning does not get through. Where did you get your pains from?
> *MIND* Borrowed from the past. The meaning does not get through the barrier though. Funny—the meaning does not get through whether it is from you to me, or from me to you.
> *BODY* It is the meaning of pain that I am sending to you; the words get through—which I have not sent—but the meaning is lost… (pp. 433–434)

In this, Bion is very creatively trying to demonstrate the difficulties that both Mind and Body experience upon birth. There is a confusion of tongues and only retrospectively can Mind put words to the pains that Body has. Bion is trying to show the impossibility of words being found that could hold the experience. This antagonism between Body and Mind seems to be the source of Bion's sense of original guilt: Body and Mind both feeling misunderstood and guilty for the manner in which one treats the other. It seems it is this very act of not feeling known by the other which creates the guilt which Bion sees as original. If one aspect dominates, the other is lost. This separation between Mind and Body he locates at birth.

He is also showing the ineffectiveness of words to convey even an adequate approximation to the experience. The words that Mind chooses do not satisfy the needs of Body, and vice versa. This seems to correspond well to the relationship I describe between Adam and Eve in this book. It might be considered that I am equating Adam with Bion's Mind, and Eve with Bion's Body; however, I do not think that it fits as neatly as that. I am seeing Adam as the psychology of projection and Eve as the psychology of introjection, and, as such, both are present in Mind *and* Body.

Adam and Eve within the Body become the physical processes of ingestion/excretion, inhalation/exhalation, vision/hallucination, hearing/auditory hallucination, and sexually penetrating/penetrated. Adam and Eve within the Mind become the mental representations of all of these physical processes, especially in respect to discomfort, anxiety, pain, dread, and tension.

Just like all particles which have an excess of tension, there is a need to find another which can correspond in some way to reduce that tension. If discomfort is present, then the infantile mind and body cannot initially reduce it alone. The infant is in need of another to correspond with. If this is good enough, then tensions are reduced and the infant can, over time, incorporate this into his mind and body, until the next tension arises that cannot be reduced alone. The body and mind of another is needed again.

As Adam and Eve are therefore present in both, it cannot be said that Body and Mind are one or the other—they are both. The word that may possibly arise from an experience in both Body and Mind is therefore potentially able to be from either Adam or Eve. This is where I am differing from Bion. He feels that Body is, in a way, anathema to Mind, and we can only infer through inadequate retrospective-yet-future saturated language an approximation of what each other feels. He says that we can only achieve this by moving towards O:

> Psychoanalytic events cannot be stated directly, indubitably, or incorrigibly any more than can those of other scientific research. I shall use the sign O to denote that which is the ultimate reality represented by terms such as ultimate reality, absolute truth, the god-head, the infinite, the thing-in-itself. O does not fall in the domain of knowledge or learning save incidentally; it can be "become" but it cannot be "known". It is darkness and formlessness but it enters the domain K [knowledge] when it has evolved to a point where it can be known, through knowledge gained by experience, and formulated in terms derived from sensuous experience. (1970, p. 242)

For Bion, O is that state of being akin to the chaos within creation myths—without light or form. He seems to be inferring that all language and knowledge originating from outside this realm is inadequate in its attempt to represent what might be inside it. It can only become "known" by allowing it to "become" and experiencing it in a sensuous way. From my perspective, this can be represented as: Adam language and knowledge cannot symbolise, convey, or understand Eve.

Bion feels that in order to try to reach O, the analyst needs to put to one side memory, desire, and understanding in order to allow the experience of an "at-one-ness" with a patient (or infant).

> … if his mind is preoccupied with what is or is not said, or with what he does or does not hope, it must mean that he cannot allow the experience to obtrude, particularly that aspect of it which is more than the sound of the patient's voice or the sight of his postures. What sounds the patient makes, or what spectacle he presents, relates to O only in so far as O has evolved into the K domain. (1970, p. 255)

This, of course, might be considered the same reverie or maternal preoccupation that Winnicott describes. Both Bion and Winnicott seem to have taken a similar hermeneutic loop process and arrived at a new understanding with their own conceptualisation of beginnings. They both were able to evaluate and re-evaluate theories already learnt, and the realisations they gained enabled them to formulate their own new creation myth.

From my hermeneutic loop, I can look at Bion's work and see that my own thinking has also arrived at many similar places to his. Of course, I cannot say that I haven't been influenced in this by having been aware of some of his work (as well as Freud's, Klein's, and Winnicott's), but I can say that in having tried to start from a beginning, rather than look at theory and assimilate it without question, I have realised my own realisations in my own way. I can find many of my realisations already present in the works of the four psychoanalysts I include in this book, mainly in the works of Winnicott and Bion, but there are important differences too.

The first difference in Bion's work is that I see words as coming from two opposing thinkers in Adam and Eve, which are present in both Mind and Body; Bion (in my reading of him) places this opposition between Mind and Body. I see the opposition arising from words which originate from either inside or outside—that is, from an inward-looking or outward-looking perspective. Eve (in this case the maternal object) is able to formulate the unformed by using words that belong to both her and the infant; in doing so she is providing a living narration. Adam uses words that belong to him (Adam) to give a narrative to the infant, especially in regard to what is outside.

This living narration belongs to the "me" of the person—the suffering, pain, discomfort, anxiety, dread, and despair which needs to be told in a joined couple (the at-one-ness from Bion and the maternal preoccupation of Winnicott). It is a word that comes about from a maternal third position and bestows strength, resilience, stamina, patience, and forbearance. It cannot be arrived at from Adam.

The narrative given by Adam is the "I" of the person—the sense of the self in relation to hierarchy, good and bad, the position in society, and so on. These are words which, if they come from an Adam who is not coupled well enough with Eve, can cause the development of a very onerous and severe superego, moral conscience, guilt, envy, and aggression. These words, from a benign Adam, can bestow a sense of duty, of right and wrong, and self-control.

When Adam and Eve are working well enough together in the mind of a parent or analyst, words from both positions are able to be used by the mother, father, or analyst. The resulting infant or patient will then begin to be able to formulate his "myself". This is a combination of both the living narration and narrative which gives the infant a sense of who they are inside and outside.

Another point of departure from Bion is that I see guilt as secondary. For me, the primary Adam and Eve processes prior to birth (and in the initial period post-birth that Winnicott describes as holding) operate without guilt. Guilt comes about as Adam has a head start on Eve in his capacity to project (he has been able to move in the womb and so has a rudimentary sense of him/not him. Eve has not been able to experience full/not full and so does not have a sense of her/not her as much as Adam). This head start enables him to utilise his capacities sooner than Eve when faced with distress. Projection to evacuate occurs before a psychic capacity to introject can grow. In this way, Adam can be more powerful than Eve. To my mind, this is the cause of primitive guilt. It is primitive as it has its origin in the very early stages of post-birth life, but it is not primary which would be having been in existence since conception. It is a paradox that the more a society is Adam-dominated (creation myths which situate the source of creation with a male entity and deny or denigrate Eve), the more primitive guilt will be present. It is only when Adam and Eve are able to operate with relative equality that guilt is negligible.

The solution to this original guilt (sin) for Bion is allowing thought to "be": to enable the thought to have a contained experience and to give a space for expression of the thought that hasn't happened. To be able to achieve this, "no memory and no desire" is put forward by Bion as a way to put to one side the intellect, jargon, memory, and desire, and to see what emerges.

A memory of something existing before Adam is absolutely essential in being able to allow the giving up of Adam memory and desire. When Adam is the predominant presence in the conscious mind, then the damage that has been done to Eve feels catastrophic. It feels as though she has been completely killed off and so in *this* mind, it would feel like complete nothingness would open up if Adam memory and desire were to be taken away. This is why Bion talks about the "faith" needed to be able to achieve this:

> It may be wondered what state of mind is welcome if desires and memories are not. A term that would express approximately what I need is "faith"—faith that there is an ultimate reality and truth—the unknown, unknowable, "formless infinite". This must be believed of every object of which the personality can be aware: the evolution of ultimate reality (signified by O) has issued in objects of which the individual can be aware. The objects of

> awareness are aspects of the "evolved" O, and are such that the sensuously derived mental functions are adequate to apprehend them. For them faith is not required; for O it is. (1970, pp. 246–247)

For me, it is not faith but the memory, desire, and awareness of Eve. The state of mind described by Bion as "no memory, no desire" is only achievable if Eve has been remembered and desired. In a universe that Adam has taken for his own, the lack of Eve leaves him terrified of a nothingness when his structure (creation myth) fails. To my mind, nameless dread, unconscious guilt, original sin, and terror of nothingness all come about due to the damage in actuality done to the Eve part of the mind. It is only when Adam and Eve are able to be coupled together in relative equality, that all these dreads are assuaged—or do not become actualised in the first place.

Bion, throughout his "Commentary" in *Second Thoughts*, uses the term "sensuously" or "sensuous":

> An attempt is made to represent the experience in terms of sensuous experience—C category terms. Description of such terms avoids the danger of manipulation of jargon but it introduces dangers which are as great though different. First the terms cannot represent the psychoanalytic experience which they purport to describe, but only a sensuous experience of physical fact supposedly analogous to the mental experience (18–20) are a transformation of an emotional experience into a verbal formulation of a sensuous experience. (1967, p. 130)

He is trying to describe how important he feels this sensuous experience is and how it is only through trying to put words to this (without jargon and relying on intellect), that transformation can occur. However, he is also stating that even these words are inadequate at representing the actuality of the emotional experience.

A definition of "sensuous":

1. Of or pertaining to the senses or sensation; derived from or affecting the senses.
2. Of, derived from, or affecting the senses aesthetically rather than sensually; readily affected by the senses; keenly responsive to the pleasures of sensation.
(*Shorter Oxford English Dictionary*, 2002, 2, p. 2756)

As previously stated on p. 153, a definition of "sensuality" is:

1. The aspect of human nature concerned with the senses as opp. to the intellect or spirit; man's animal nature, esp. as the source of sensual appetites and desires. Now *rare*, Absorption in material things rather than intellectual or spiritual matters.
2. The pursuit of, or excessive devotion to, physical pleasure or gratification of the senses; sensual self-indulgence. Sexual activity or excess lustfulness.
(*Shorter Oxford English Dictionary*, 2002, 2, p. 2756)

Freud's use of the word sensuality, I feel, has a direct connection with Bion's later use of sensuous and sensuously. Freud was highlighting a developmental progression he saw as a victory of the paternal over the maternal, intellect over sensuality. By this categorisation he was using his own intellect and thinking to persist in the victory of the paternal over the maternal. He effectively was enabling the persistence of that victory, whilst also enabling himself to not have to give thought to the maternal. In reducing the maternal to sensuality, Freud is also attaching the instincts (in his formulation of them) to the maternal. The Oedipus complex is a consequence of this starting position. The maternal is therefore, for Freud, comprised of sensual, bodily feelings and responses, which give pleasure and gratification, primarily sexual. Thought cannot exist unless these phenomena are somehow repudiated, and thought, therefore, is a paternal preserve. This was taken to extremes in the Greek civilisation (Langdon-Davies, 1938, pp. 89–98), where thought was owned by man, and where, in his pride at his own creations (which he was able to exercise without woman), he essentially pushed woman to almost non-existence.

In looking at civilisations and advancements in thinking, Freud took his understanding to be that sensuality was female and thought was male. Bion, in his work, has recognised the importance of trying to put words to the sensuous. However, in the general index of his complete works, even though in his commentary he repeatedly emphasised the importance of the sensuous experience, there is only one entry of "sensuous space". This is in his *Memoir of a Dream* (1975, p. 159). It seems that while the word is used a great deal, it doesn't really "become" in its own right—it doesn't cross the threshold between phenomenon and name. Perhaps this is illustrative of the point he is making about how difficult it is to find words which can convey meaning from the sensuous; but also perhaps he has an awareness of wishing to keep this phenomenon away from Adam and his tendency to change living words into dead metaphors.

In changing the word "sensuality" to "sensuous", he has removed the emphasis on sexuality. He is shifting the sphere of pleasure and pain so that it is not only to be regarded in sexual terms (that is, a psychology based on sexuality), but also in other bodily and sensual ways. Sensuous becomes that which is brought into awareness via the senses. In investigating this sensuous realm, he is also trying to find a way of putting words to the experience and "being" of it.

This putting of words to the sensuous counters Freud's conclusion that the "victory of the intellect over sensuality" is the development that enables thought. In order to put words to something, thought must be involved; however, the specific nature of the thought involved is different. This indicates a distinct departure from Freud. Freud felt that sensuality was the realm of the pleasure–pain principle and was a system in which thought was not available.

For Freud, it seems that we all have a body within which the instincts operate and these are impacted by a constitutional factor and experience. The instincts' interaction can manifest in disturbance and sexuality is the primary basis of behaviour and neuroses. The primacy of the paternal over the maternal is a solution which advances society as well as man. If man can put his sensuality to one side, especially that part expressed towards his mother, then he can think and advance. Man's oedipal conflict becomes the central drama upon which development is based. In this way, a body and its mind can be thought of as needing to be controlled and made impermeable. This may arise from infancy whereby, in relationship with the maternal, bodies are "leaky" … and "things" (feelings, wishes, urges) try to escape to find gratification. With the paternal victory over the maternal, bodies become close to impermeable, and, thus, thought takes the place of urges and wishes.

Bion's sensuousness—that experience relating to the senses—suggests that "thought" was able to be applied to this state of being. His O, or absolute truth and reality, is described as ultimately unknowable, but for an analyst to effect transformation within a patient, faith in O is required. See, for instance, Bion's various descriptions of O in *Attention and Interpretation*:

> It is darkness and formlessness but it enters the domain K when it has evolved to a point where it can be known, through knowledge gained by experience, and formulated in terms derived from sensuous experience; its existence is conjectured phenomenologically. (1970, p. 242)

> The psychoanalyst can know what the patient says, does and appears to be, but cannot know the O of which the patient is an evolution: he can only "be" it. He knows phenomena by virtue of his senses but, since his concern is with O, events must be regarded as possessing either the defects of irrelevancies obstructing, or the merits of pointers initiating the process of "becoming" O. (1970, p. 243)

> The psychoanalyst and his analysand are alike dependent on the senses, but psychic qualities, with which psychoanalysis deals, are not perceived by the senses, but, as Freud says, by some mental counterpart of the sense organs—a function that he attributed to consciousness. Without wishing to discard this possibility I prefer to consider it an open question and substitute a more general postulate which I represent by O … the more "real" the psychoanalyst is, the more he can be at one with the reality of the patient. Conversely, the more he depends on actual events, the more he relies on thinking that depends on a background of sense impression. (1970, p. 244)

Bion goes on (p. 244) to describe his view of the relationship between container (♀) and contained (♂). Freud theorised that the primitive phase was dominated by the pleasure principle and therefore does not involve memory, as memory would need the capacity of thought to be able to become laid down. From this position, it is the use of projective identification that enables a prototype of thought and therefore memory to develop. Bion saw the interaction between the mouth and the breast to be the first projective identification that takes place, and this process has to "fulfil the duties of thought until thought can take over" (1970, p. 244). The infant projects his unpleasure into a container, who may or may not get rid of it, and who may or may not transform it into something more tolerable. This experience is experienced by the infant and becomes part of his "memory without words", or "an unborn thought". This remains held in the body until another thought process can be applied which transforms this memory without words into words.

I wonder what these "duties" of thought might be? To my mind, the duty of thought is one of promoting a capacity of resilience, tolerance, forbearance, and self-knowledge (knowledge of "me" leading to a "myself"). This is only possible if an infant has had a good enough experience within a container–contained relationship. In a way, perhaps Bion was saying that projective identification acts as a transitional object until the capacity of thought-attached-to-a-word production can be established within the mind.

It seems to me that K represents the thought that originates in Adam. Adam psychology is about projection and Eve psychology is about introjection. The two are in opposition to one another and do represent the two modes of being as described by Bion: that which is in contact with K and the oversaturated words arising from external sources, and that which is moving towards O and words arising from the internal. He says that memory and desire need to be put away in order to be able to approach O.

The functions and processes associated with Adam and Eve in the womb are represented psychically as an innate awareness of these processes. The automatic functioning of these necessitates a functioning of the whole body according to these foundations. Birth causes a trauma to this system as suddenly the smooth running of Adam and Eve is thrown into disarray.

Once born, the infant is subject to the vagaries of the physical world, as well as the vagaries of care. As the infant is not equipped to manage well he is excruciatingly dependent upon being cared for. For Adam and Eve to operate in relative equality, the mother (or substitute) needs to be an auxiliary "Adam and Eve constellation"; however, as the infant is more proficient in projection (Adam), it is the Eve aspect of the constellation that could become neglected. If you like, an ideal situation might be that mother is able to supplement this process well enough in order for the infant to learn from experience that pain, anxiety, and disruption can be borne by him.

Failure in this phase leaves the infant with his dread and anxiety unchanged. Therefore, he needs something to remove awareness of this anxiety or dread (neurosis), or he succumbs with nothing in place to hold him together (psychosis). To put it another way, neurosis is disturbance *within* the prevailing creation myth within a society, and psychosis is disturbance *outside* the prevailing creation myth or not having a creation myth at all. This succumbing, to my mind, is either the failure of a creation myth to contain, or the infant never having been able to incorporate a myth into his psyche. The prevailing myth is most suited to those who are most comfortable in it or who can position themselves high enough on the hierarchy which the myth creates. This type of myth is inadequate in the face of real dread and anxiety. To be able to emerge in any form from under mother's care, a good enough creation myth has to be in operation. Perhaps humans are unique in the animal world in having a prevailing creation myth which is so at odds with a significant proportion of their "being".

In thinking about what happens when particles come together, there is a third particle always involved which carries the energy that leaves the united couple (see p. 215). In the mother–infant couple the third element becomes the word or idea that is able to be thought. If this word comes from the secondary Adam aspect of the mother's mind it does not suffice. The imposition of an Adam-based creation myth into the mother/infant couple forces the infant's "in need of containment experience" to be pushed into the unconscious and defences put in place so it remains in a position in the mind which does not threaten the creation myth in operation. If the dread and anxiety prove too great, the myth can no longer function as a structure to orientate oneself within and from, and the mind disintegrates due to having no viable structure to hold it together.

If the word or idea originates from Eve, then it can suffice in this energy release. This word is alive and belongs to both the infant and the mother (Bion's "at-one-ness"). This word, unlike those that originate from Adam, does not rely on externally orientated observations but on an inner sense. It draws on Eve's deep memory of someone being curious about her, of having been held, contained, and having had these energy-releasing words applied to herself. It is a sensuous awareness; a psyche–soma knowledge that all particles have interacted in this way for all of time. This is the innate knowledge that we all carry. There is no other animal on Earth that uses symbols as humans do—we place ourselves *above* nature and create myths full of words and symbols from Adam.

The creation myth the infant carries into later childhood and adulthood is crucial in two ways: first, without one, the infant cannot emerge out of dependency, and, second, the content of the myth. The nature of the word, and where it comes from, become pivotal in the type of creation myth established.

Freud's "victory of the intellect over sensuality" necessitates a religious creation myth, paternal primacy, and ultimately misogyny. Yet, Bion seems to challenge this by understanding that there is something important about allowing the sensuous nature of experience to "become" in the consulting room: to enable O to become. This is a word which comes from inside and a "maternal third thinking" which allows a nature-based creation myth and also allows Adam and Eve to work together.

It is the *narration* of anxiety, dread, and pain which allows the "me" to become, and, until the "me" can become, it is doomed to keep trying. An Adam-based creation myth gives form to an "I" which can only survive if the person this particular "I" belongs to is powerful or comfortable.

In this sense, the absolute truth and reality of O is the memory and desire of each particle to come together in the service of stability and regulation, like our-speck and other-speck. When this is frustrated, or not available, then the absence of the *narration* that "me" needs creates an "I" which uses a *narrative* to maintain position. Bion knows that the type of thinking available in most situations is from an external origin and involves K. The memory and desire that this focuses on impedes being able to be with the patient in terms of O.

Optimum mental health involves Adam and Eve processes working in tandem to create a "myself". With "myself", Eve's "me" and Adam's "I" come together, this "myself" knows in an inner way the pains, traumas, and anxieties that have been experienced ("me")—giving a sense of existence, while being able to hold on to a sense of "I"—being *some* thing in action, rather than *no* thing. "Myself" necessitates a creation myth which is close to nature and reality, as, without this, "I" takes over.

When Adam's "I" predominates, religion and law take over from altruism and being. Knowledge is all important and hierarchies prevail. The thirdness produced, the thought from Knowledge, involves the external, and hence reason and order. However, this reason and order is hierarchical—slavery and the subjugation of women prevails. Adam is all about the external. He thinks prohibitions—he comes in between the mother and the baby in order to protect his own right to gratification. Without Eve, he is tormented by guilt and needs to create an ever increasing sense of "I" to try to push his guilt away. All words created come from the external and the senses are reined in to service the "I". The senses will see, hear, taste, and smell only what is needed to justify and confirm the "I" and the creation myth that is being used.

Throughout Bion's writing, it seems that the existence of the death instinct is a given. He seems to follow Klein's sense of this in that he sees primary forces of guilt, aggression, and envy in operation. The problem with this, from my perspective, is that as soon as you state or believe that these are primary—that is, that they are innate, part of who we are from conception, something inside us that is irreducible and can only be controlled—the consequences of having this belief are profound. The only creation myth which can be used as a structure becomes a secondary Adam one. This belief in primary aggression and the death instinct is, therefore, deeply misogynistic.

Perhaps by maintaining a belief in the death instinct, Bion is able to consider his O in unknowable and mysterious terms. He cannot go beyond "something" as he has planted his feet firmly in a particular position which has no representation beyond, except in the existence of an unconscious religious creator. If there is a belief in the death instinct, then (according to my argument) there must also be a belief in a male deity who has created. This is a magical creation, based outside nature, and therefore O has to remain mysterious and unknowable.

I am not saying that everything *can* become known! As when God said to Job ...:

> Who are you to question my wisdom
> with your ignorant and empty words? ...
> ... Were you there when I made the world? ...
> Who decided how large it would be?
> ... Job, have you ever in all your life
> commanded a day to dawn?
> ... Was it you, Job, who made horses so strong?
> ... Look at the monster Behemoth;
> I created him and I created you ...
> [The Behemoth is] [t]he most amazing of all my creatures!
> Only his Creator can defeat him. (Job 38–40; Gibson, 1981, pp. 822–825)

He has a point: all of these things are unknowable from an Adam perspective. No person can ever know them as Adam can know things. And, whilst a male deity creation myth is in operation, knowledge is able only to be thought of in this way. Perhaps this diatribe from God to

Job can be thought of as a father telling his son that he will always be more powerful as he was there at his creation. It is a diatribe which perpetuates the primacy of the father. It is all about power and owning creation (especially with regard to keeping woman in a lower place compared to man). Within these parameters, all of the knowledge God owns cannot be known by Job. It needs to remain a mystery. If Job becomes aware of the nature and reality of creation, the primacy of the father will collapse. Terminology such as "mysterious" and "unknowable" perpetuates a patriarchal system.

Of course, no human being can know the beginning of the universe and life from an Adam perspective—he wasn't there, and so hasn't witnessed it. However, in realising the nature of the universe—we are born of our parents, we need others, we are going to die, we are particulate and behave according to the nature of all particles—we can become aware of the nature of how things interact and how things are created. If we believe in a creator god, then how things are created has to remain a mystery. If we are aware of how things interact, curiosity about insides is possible and the Eve in us all is able to reveal to us her awareness. The ultimate connection between our-speck and other-speck is all we really need to know. Everything else in the world is the direct result of that interaction. If we understand at an Eve level the nature of interaction and connectivity, then our particles which *were* present at the dawn of time can lend us their wisdom. We don't need to know in an Adam sense—that is an impossibility. We could never find the external words to describe everything that has occurred over time—Adam would need to see it to be able to apply words to these events. We need to put Adam to one side and allow more of Eve's inner words to be put to the experiences that all our particles *already* know about.

I am not saying that this is completely possible, but I am saying that it is not a mystery and we do already "know". It is the accessing of it that is the issue. O, therefore, for me, is something already known inside, which we have available to us, but Adam and "I" get in the way. If we are operating from an Adam-based creation myth, then we will never be able to get close to O. To be able to have a sense of O, and be able to move towards it, necessarily involves the acceptance of the true nature of how things come together and interact, the place of humans within nature, and also the equality in creation of Adam and Eve.

The "at-one-ness" that Bion talks about, in the context of this book, becomes the connection with another in almost a merged manner. It is allowing the self to be in another self and to not need to put boundaries in place. They are two "me"s joined together, without feeling the need to instate the "I". Two Eves together with no need for Adam's actions to create boundaries and hierarchies. Asking Adam to become dormant for a while, whilst Eve "does her thing". The knowledge, memory, and desire that Eve carries are vital in being able to utilise this experience; without these there would be *no* structure and *no* "thing"—that truly would be terrifying. It is only when there is a representation of Eve and nature in the mind that nothingness can become "somethingness"; until then the fear of nothingness is actually the fear that belongs to Adam after he has destroyed Eve.

In terms of Adam and Eve, the more a thinker operates from the Adam part of his mind, the more the theories resulting would be dominated by names, labels, right/wrong, good/bad, primary aggression and envy, and a stagnation in developing the theory beyond what has been stated. The more a thinker operates from the Eve part of his mind, the less the theories would be named, labelled, and dominated by aggression/envy. These theories would move freely and evolve. A structure would operate on a bigger scale, which not only tolerates the unknown, but has a space for it—just like Mendleev and his periodic table.

Given the more defensive nature of Adam compared to Eve, Eve's thinking is anathema to Adam (although, as previously stated, Eve is able to be aware of Adam). I think this is shown by a patient whom I saw for analysis. He had great difficulty in tolerating any aspect of Eve, either within himself or in me. He was preoccupied with action, masculinity, and trying to destroy any feeling part of himself. He was seemingly all Adam, and his mantra was to reinforce his masculinity when anything came along that felt overwhelming. After much work, he had begun to discover, tolerate, and enjoy his curiosity about himself and me, but was surprised one session to realise that he was unable, in his role as a manager, to be both curious and managerial at the same time. Adam and Eve were so separate, he could not envisage a way to bring them into relationship within himself, but he was nonetheless now able to be curious, whereas before he could not.

Bion, like Winnicott, goes far in his thinking and formulations of the beginning and it seems that the two together represent much of what I am trying to say. Where I think I am left frustrated is the lack of representation of Eve—or, if she is referred to, it is in a passive or mysterious way. Bion felt that there was an original guilt that seemed to become present after birth; the consequence of this belief is an acceptance of paternal (Adam) primacy, as it is Adam who would feel this guilt. It seems to be saying that the nature of us all is inherently guilty and therefore the psychic constructs that are present to assuage or manage this guilt are also inherent. There is nothing to be done about Adam's dominance as it is our nature!

I wonder if thinking of these aspects of the mind, behaviour, and character as primary or original (that is, envy, aggression, destructiveness, greed, guilt, and so on) is in fact a defence in itself—a defence against seeing the world as particulate, natural, all-connected, and that humans are a part of nature like all other living things. All these seemingly original characteristics come about from the failure or breakdown of an Adam and Eve relationship, whether that is within the mind, between baby and mother, or between patient and analyst. These failures are, of course, inevitable. But to view the resulting greed or aggression as original by necessity sets up a resulting creation myth which is Adam-based and has a paternal primacy. This, again, maintains misogyny and hierarchical thinking. Perhaps Bion, in his acceptance of an original guilt and also the maintenance of the death instinct, was defending against the bigger awareness of not only what has been done to Eve, but also that Eve is the source of thinking—it is the penetrated object that does the work and gives the space to think, and is thus the source of creation. This awareness of penetration being at the heart of thought and life is anathema to Adam and "I". Adam wishes to be a closed system which denies penetration, but still own creation for himself. Maintaining original sin (guilt, greed, aggression, destructiveness, envy) actually provides a structure whereby penetration can be viewed as pathological and thus not necessary. This reduces Eve to a silent existence in the unconscious. The outcome can be thought of as creating a system which sustains, perpetuates, and promotes suffering.

CHAPTER 20

Gathered thoughts

One day it thundered and lightened.
Two women, fairly frightened,
Sank to their knees, transformed, transfixed,
At the feet of the man who sat betwixt;
And "Mercy!" cried each—"if I tell the truth
Of a passage in my youth!"
Said This: "Do you mind the morning
I met your love with scorning? As the worst of the venom left my lips,
I thought, 'If, despite this lie he strips
The mask from my soul with a kiss—I crawl
His slave,—soul, body, and all!'"
Said That: "We stood to be married;
The priest, or some-one, tarried;
'If Paradise-door prove locked?' smiled you.
I thought, as I nodded, smiling too,
'Did one, that's away, arrive—nor late
Nor soon should unlock Hell's gate!'"
It ceased to lighten and thunder.
Up started both in wonder,
Looked round and saw that the sky was clear,
Then laughed "Confess you believed us, Dear!"
"I saw through the joke!" the man replied
They re-seated themselves beside.

—"Adam, Lilith and Eve", Robert Browning (1957, pp. 627–628)

This poem investigates the relationship between truth, fear, Adam, Eve, and Lilith. Eve and Lilith both feel paradise to be a hell, but are trapped. When there is a storm, they fear their lack of integrity is going to be punished, so they admit the truth. Adam is not afraid, as he, like the men in the Arunta tribe with their bullroarers, is the author of his creation. When the storm eases, another fear takes over, that of being punished for having told the truth. Adam is happy to see it all as a joke and the women resume their places either side of Adam. Adam's construct of his paradise and god prevails; but for Eve and Lilith there is no integrity and deep longings for intimacy and true love are never met. Perhaps *this* Adam can only be in relationship with either Eve or Lilith—a woman who has to perpetually wait to be truly loved or a woman who feels trapped in hell.

In looking at all four analysts, it is easy to observe a movement towards identifying and shaping Eve. Freud, by necessity, had more of secondary Adam's psychology available to him, with the unconscious (in Freudian terms) having to hold Eve and her importance. What wasn't possible to be thought of (in regard to Eve and the original sin, from my perspective, of having killed her), not only in societies at large, but also within each psyche, was needed to be considered as a malignant or mysterious force. She, or the unconscious, became that which held aggression, need, sexuality, envy, guilt, sensuality, pain, and so on. The accepted (or acceptable) conscious mind was the intellect, thought, action, gratification, reason, religion, belief, and so on. This was associated more with the masculine.

As this uneven coming together of Adam and Eve was skewed towards Adam, the consequence of this discrepancy is profound: Eve's efficacy is significantly reduced; her specific functions which are necessary to life, health, and a balanced mind are projected elsewhere; a god is needed to take care of creation and account for the distance between illusion and reality; Eve's functions need to be appropriated into the illusion—the maternal aspects of Jesus; women are curtailed in society as they need to be seen as diminished and the awareness carried by them is feared.

Freud was still operating from within this framework when he started his work. Towards the end of his life, he was trying to think beyond this, especially with regard to beginnings and the psyche of primitive man. He shone a considerable light on the psychology of Adam and understood that the unconscious held something that was difficult for the Adam mind to be aware of.

For Freud, it seems that a person had a body within which the instincts operated. These were impacted by constitutional factors and experience. He saw the interaction between these instincts as the cause of disturbance. Hence, sexuality was seen as the primary basis of behaviour and the neuroses. This is a focus on the vicissitudes of penetration involving the primal scene—the coming together of the mother and father during intercourse and the inherent pleasures involved. The other vicissitudes involving conception and the maternal function are neglected.

Klein took Freud's work and whilst agreeing with most, from her studies with children, she began to expand and adapt the original thinking. Most notably, she brought in an awareness of the importance of the maternal experience during early infancy and elucidated the tumults of the infant mind. If you like, she went deeper into the Adam psychology and revealed a fuller awareness of the forces at play. Maybe, it could even be thought that she pinpointed the moment that the Adam and diminished Eve couple (in the psyche) was born—when frustration or anxiety was first felt to be too much. Her sense that splitting then occurs and the good breast and bad breast come into being, is, I think, easily understood and seen in clinical work and infant observations.

Klein was able to shift her gaze from the primal scene to also include aspects of the vicissitudes of penetration between mother and infant. There seems to be an assumption present in her thinking that, at first, there is a unified psyche for the foetus in the womb. I would say that no such unity has ever existed. The psyche, body, and mind are, from conception to death, split into Adam and Eve. Health is intimately related to the relative equality of each in dynamic tension with one another. Klein's solution is for the infant to increasingly become aware of the wholeness of the object and in doing so, become able to bear the guilt associated with having hated the same person they also loved. This forbearance is a sign of the depressive position.

Winnicott and Bion both start to sense that something fundamental is missing in these descriptions of the proto-mind. Some aspect of the maternal function, essential to who we become, did not have enough representation in Freud or Klein.

Winnicott focused on the emergence of the fragile ego and the external environment that might facilitate this. He differentiated between pure male and female elements and understood that there is a mixing and balance needed between them. In the context of this book, this might be equated with the reinstating of the more or less equal space that Adam and Eve occupy in the represented mind (in that they have a presence in his model). Adam needs to move and discharge waste, Eve needs to sustain and take in the essential requirements. (In a way, if they didn't have equality, then it could be said that either the body would swell up and explode, or starve and wither—perhaps these scenarios are ultimately the outcomes of secondary Adam and secondary Eve narcissisms!)

When these physical processes are working well, when the body is in relative calm, it provides an opportunity for thought and therefore learning too. A learning based on discovery is one that uses all the perceptual apparatus and arrives at something using both Adam and Eve. This might be an awareness of something painful or joyful. A learning based on just secondary Adam or Eve is one which originates in the mind, as a creation and illusion. It negates the perceptual apparatus and is a path which ends at a rigid dogma needing to be upheld by power.

The role of the mother or maternal carer is to become a structure which enables the newborn infant to manage the world of trauma that opens up upon birth, in a manner which can provide what the mind and body of the infant can't. A good enough experience in being physically provided for enables the infant to become aware of different states of being.

Winnicott understands the importance of the maternal state of mind and holding capacity. He says that maternal holding enables the infant to be able to distinguish between self and "not self". She holds the infant, provides safety, and serves as a buffer between the external world and the mother–baby dyad, until the infant is robust enough to emerge from under her care.

This formation of a robust enough ego is similar to Géza Róheim's (1971, pp. 122–132) view of the formation of culture. He states that culture is a direct result of the extended period of maternal care needed by human infants which results in the eventual traumatic loss of mother needing to be sublimated into forming a culture, in a way which other animals don't. Thus, for him, the arts and other manifestations of human intellectual achievement are a direct consequence of needing to sublimate the trauma of the loss of mother.

Bion takes this maternal function further and talks about the dynamic between the baby and the mother—the container–contained model. He was a contemporary of Winnicott and they both seemed to independently arrive at this aspect of the mothe–baby relationship. They both seemed to recognise the need to start from a beginning and to put to one side what might have been learnt before. Bion was more focused on the space between mother and baby, and something psychologically interactive occurring between. He also tried to represent (in that it was able to have a place in a model or creation myth) the process of thought production.

Perhaps we can see in looking at Freud, Klein, Winnicott, and Bion that they each elaborate and represent some aspect of a structure, but their structures are not, in themselves, the whole. Freud represents the sexual aspects of behaviour and the mind; Klein represents the aggressive and destructive aspects of behaviour and the mind (secondary Adam); Winnicott represents the environmental needs for the self to emerge, and the focus on the mother–baby dyad; and Bion represents something of the nature of what goes on between a maternal carer and the infant to allow the infant to think (thought being only possible once an infant has undergone adequate container–contained processes).

In terms of each representing the totality of nature, penetration, and the maternal body, Winnicott and Bion are closer to it than Freud and Klein. Freud sees the aim as being the triumph of the intellect over the sensual, essentially the separation of Adam from Eve. This situation would sustain a secondary Adam mentality. Klein sees the aim as being the acquisition and awareness of guilt about what might have been done in fantasy to the mother's body. If guilt can be felt, then reparation and the depressive position can be reached. This can lead to an evangelistic mentality along with loving wishes, but nonetheless, because of the belief in the primary nature of the death instinct (destructiveness, aggression, and envy) this still sustains a secondary Adam dominance in the mind. Winnicott's aim is for the infant's ego to be able to emerge. It is not formed and needs to "become". There are factors which facilitate this process and he prioritises the holding element of maternal care. Bion's aim is for the genesis of thought. He understands the nature of the container–contained model in transforming a raw sensation into a feeling and then a thought.

This progression can be compared to the progression of the Egyptian creation myths. Freud would perhaps be from Thebes, in that he was starting from a male primacy and this primacy is viewed as all powerful. Klein would perhaps be from Heliopolis, as she had a place and an awareness of a maternal element, but it becomes appropriated by the male in her model. Bion would perhaps be from Memphis, as the thought was revered above the product of creativity, and the maternal aspects were not identified as such. He could also be said to have visited Hermopolis a great deal, as he was aware of something with energy needing to occur between the container and the contained, and attributed this to the mother. Winnicott (more difficult to categorise) would be perhaps from Hermopolis, in that he was aware of the pure male and female elements which can become mixed, and also the environment needing to be right for this to happen. In this progressive uncovering of the maternal and female elements, the four analysts are working counter to the myth-makers of Egypt who were intent on progressively covering up all things maternal and female.

Using Browning's poem, Freud's structure perpetuates Adam's relationship to Eve, and she can only wait for recognition. Klein's structure identifies Lilith and gives her form, but she is still in relationship to a powerful god-creating Adam. Both Winnicott's and Bion's structures dismantle the walls of Adam's Eden and understand the environmental influences that can create a hell for both Eve and Lilith. They also raise both Eve and Lilith to a more equal position with Adam.

Part IV

Reformulation

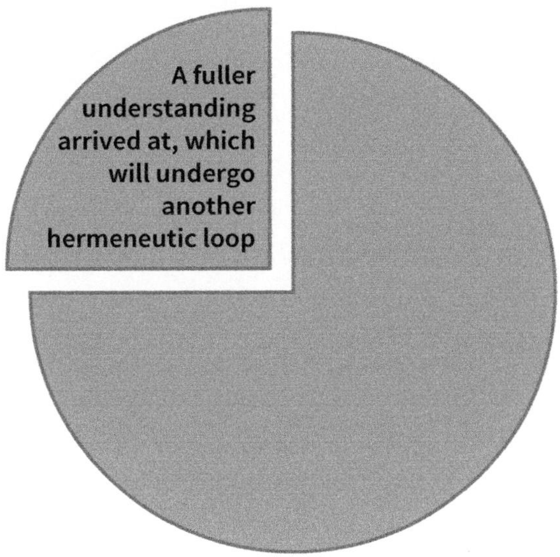

Formulation

And the Lord said to her, Two nations are in thy womb, and two manner of people shall be separated from thy bowels; and the one people shall be stronger than the other people; and the elder shall serve the younger.

—Genesis 25: 22–23

CHAPTER 21

Modus vivendi

Most people in the world are born into families which have a generational identity within one religion or another. They seem to remain in this status of identification even when they are not actively practising the particular religion, such as when a person born into a family who identify as Church of England, often without thinking, will fill in forms and put C of E as their stated religion. It becomes a part of their identity even when, in a conscious way, they have shrugged off the day-to-day meaning of it.

What does it mean to retain, as part of one's identity, something which in all other respects is rejected? What is actually being retained? And, can this particular process shed any light on the path that an analyst might choose? It is interesting that during training a candidate is not only exposed to theory which differs in fundamentally important aspects, but also comes across the teachers, practitioners, and theorists from each of these positions. Each candidate arrives (depending on the training) ripe to take in the learning from each of these theorists, and is tasked to find where he/she belongs.

This is very different to being born into a family which either consciously or unconsciously operates from the basis of one of the major religions, and for generations has been immersed in a society which functions according to the conscious and unconscious tenets that this involves. However, perhaps this process of something persisting from the religion, even when consciously rejected, can be similarly seen in psychoanalysis, not only in the relationship to theory, but also in the deeper relationship to a particular creation myth.

What does a religion still provide when it has consciously been deemed no longer relevant to day-to-day life? On one hand, it has been rendered unnecessary—a god no longer has dominion over the life situation—but on the other, it provides a sense of identity and belonging. Something is retained which describes, identifies, and orientates an aspect of fundamental experience and, from this perspective, the sense of belonging renders something which feels stabilising. However, at a deeper level, perhaps what is retained is the very causal anxiety which initiates the instigation of a religion in the first place. If a fundamental anxiety initiates the formation of religion, it follows that the development of the capacity of the conscious logical mind in the fields of reason, intelligence, cause and effect, perception, thinking, and so on, alongside a relative status of comfort, can reach a point of conscious rejection of a religion.

This conscious rejection, however, still has not addressed or resolved the fundamental anxiety which initiated the religion in the first place. It seems to me that the phenomenon of not living an overtly religious life, while still retaining an identity within the religion—or calling upon the religion when challenging times occur—is indicative of this divide between that which instigates a religion (unconscious) and the aware mind (conscious).

I believe that this fundamental anxiety and subsequent creation of structures which provide a stabilising effect is shown by looking at the different types of creation myths that can be found throughout the world. It also leads, generally, to certain "ways of being" or "modus vivendi", in the world.

Definitions of modus vivendi include:

1) [=mode of living] a way of living or coping: *esp.* a working arrangement between parties in dispute or disagreement which enables them to carry on pending a settlement.

(*Shorter Oxford English Dictionary*, 2002, 1: p. 1808)

Modus vivendi then becomes the manner in which a person engages with and lives his life, as a result of the settlement arrived at between opposing forces or parties which have differing influences on the person. From the focus of this book, this can be translated as the state of existence arrived at as a result of all of the vicissitudes of relationship between Adam and Eve, both internally and externally.

This can be generalised into three different ways of being: operating from either a mostly circular, or a mostly straight-line perspective, or something in between. These three ways of life can also been seen as being broadly three different ways in which a practitioner might practise. This is regardless of whether they have identified themselves as Freudian, Winnicottian, Kleinian, independent, or other. The external structure from which they operate, or from which they mainly draw their theories, doesn't matter as much as the way their unconscious relationship to that structure manifests itself.

The unconscious creation myth each person brings to the way they function in life is the crucial factor in how they present themselves to the world, how they view others, and how they organise the world in which they live. This is the formulation of a "way of living" from the "working arrangement between parties", which allows (them) to carry on working together in some sort of peace.

If the particular creation myth an analyst has, as their fundamental blueprint of life, is the major influence in how they approach their work, then it is important this is identified and understood. As the factors involved are primitive and all pervasive, it becomes a difficult process to actually see what is happening. It is like trying to see the meaning of the coordinated dance of a million beings while dancing and actually being one of those beings.

At the point when secondary Adam is unable to bear his pain (for whatever reason), he initiates a process which results in the creation of a god that makes him special, superior, and all powerful. This process inevitably leads to the necessity of the disavowal of nature and the natural order of things. This needs to be reinforced and the magical creation of the universe ensues.

This magical and supernatural creation process is intimately entangled in our psyches. Nature becomes subverted and a god that supernaturally creates everything is put in its place. This god is seen as transcendent and the all-powerful source of everything. His word is then thought of as the beginning of time and creation. What came before becomes either nothingness or full of chaos, which is experienced as terrifying due to the unconscious awareness of having destroyed Eve.

The setting up of this type of creation myth therefore has destroyed the very aspect of life that brings form to nothingness and is able to bear chaos. If Adam is then faced with the loss of the narcissistic self—the self that has dominion over the animals, is special to god, and is top of a hierarchy—he is brought face to face with the destruction of his illusion and the destruction of Eve. This feels truly terrifying as, subjectively, he is left completely alone in an unformed and chaotic universe. Adam creates religion in response to his fundamental anxiety in how to manage pain and chaos; when his logical mind and standard of life allows him to consciously shrug off this religion, he still identifies with it as he has not overcome the fundamental anxiety which originally instigated the religion. Thus, a person who consciously considers themselves to be areligious, can, nonetheless, be operating in a way which is fundamentally from a position of a god having created the universe.

If a total unconscious (or conscious) belief in an Adam creation myth is one extreme of a way of being, then a total refutation (conscious and unconscious) of religion and a belief in nature is another. That leaves an "in between", which I will describe later.

To be able to describe the impact of an unconscious belief in an Adam-based creation myth upon an analyst it is necessary to go back to the Garden of Eden and think about the potential state of mind of Adam. (Secondary) Adam has created God to help him make sense of a chaotic and frightening experience. In doing so, he feels he has swapped chaos for order; fear for safety; inferiority (no-thing-ness) for superiority (some-thing-ness); envy for arrogance; and he can feel he owns creativity for himself.

All of this feels relativity stable and safe compared to the overwhelming turbulence that he felt before. This stability is gained from a magical means (especially the magical use of words); a splitting of good and bad; a creation of an all-powerful deity; and a rationale by which he does not have to use his body in the way the natural world would require.

(Secondary) Adam also becomes heavily invested in this process, as, once embarked upon, it is very difficult to stop. He has to elaborate and reconstruct everything in order to fit into this way of being, and the damage he does on the way to Eve, and other creatures, ensures that his guilt keeps him invested in his creation.

In his elaboration, confabulation, investment, and reinforcement of this position, he creates laws, doctrines, tenets, edicts, and scriptures by which life has to be lived. These laws need to be forced upon a greater and greater number of people, as any difference or threat to the structure of Adam's genesis feels catastrophic to him (shown by the Crusades, the Missions, the pogroms and purges, the Holocaust, and so on). If everyone behaves, thinks, feels, and looks the same as him, he never has to consider what he is doing and dismantle the magical construct he has put in place (or feel the painful feelings that caused it in the first place).

This need for an external structure to be in place that safeguards against pain and chaos is easily understandable. For this structure to persist through generations is also understandable, as these are universal dilemmas and reactions to pain.

However, there is a cost to this structural, magical state of mind. As the external god becomes more and more imbued with responsibility, goodness, creation, law, and so on, the internal becomes deprived of these. People living according to this construct depend upon religious law, regulations, and order. If not religious in the obvious sense, it becomes religious in the sense that the structure occupies the same space as a religion might in the person's mind. Thinking, testing, discovering, freedom, and nature become more unavailable and the function that physically and psychically is more attributable to Eve is despised. The fruits of this structure are misogyny, stagnation, unthinking, and fear of losing the safety that it seemingly provides.

When, as practitioners, we take a theory and become beholden to it—revering it above all others; anxious to implement all aspects of it; use it in a totalitarian way and feel vehemence when other theories are spoken about—then it has become a religion in the same manner as described above. Thinking stops, discovery stops, and fear of words and woman (really what she represents as Eve) takes over. This description is an extreme one, but it serves to highlight a tendency of being which is easily slipped into.

This position is a defence against chaos, pain, and our natural need for the container–contained process to assuage our pain. This involves the body and mind being available, open, and potentially flooded by the unbearable chaos and pain that belong to others. This essential use of the body is bypassed in the structure created by Adam and allows him to impose regulations to ensure it is denigrated. This is the basic, fundamental source of misogyny and allows a disavowal of what is inside to take place. Secondary Adam, under the influence of his structure of being, can never know himself, other than in his capacity to follow the rules or not. He is either a good person who lives according to the religious/societal rules or he is not. The pain he is familiar with is guilt—primitive guilt associated with what he has done to Eve and the more obvious (to him) guilt of not being able to live according to the doctrines his structure requires. While this guilt is a challenge, it feels preferable to the chaos, pain, and needing to know the inside that Eve represents.

A practitioner operating from this position will choose a theory that feels closest to a structure that denies Eve and treat it as "gospel", trying to persuade others to join him, denigrating other thinking, and staying stagnant in his own thinking.

Words become magical in that a statement of a fact becomes the "mode of transformation", just like when Adam created a god who was able to say, "Let there be a firmament" and there was a firmament. The statement itself is seen to be the source of creation, and it becomes so in the room too. Another consequence of this system is the creation of a punitive function. If the laws and regulations are not adhered to, then a punishing aspect comes into being—fuelled by guilt, this becomes a superego. Within this system, this, combined with the magical status of the statement and word, gives rise to the seeming shift in behaviour—a more powerful exterior which through the application of a superego, rules, and guilt makes the person adapt in behaviour. However, the relationship to what is actually inside the person has not become known or developed. A consequence of this process for the patient is shame—a primitive shame inherent in not having the inner world of the patient received by another.

As this manner of living or way of life is essentially operating from a position of Adam being all powerful and filling the mind, then what would be considered to be at the bottom (the base of the unconscious) of this starting point would be destructiveness, envy, and greed. This is then thought to be something that we are born with and becomes the platform from which everything else is thought to have been built. Eve's destruction *is* the starting point for secondary Adam's new world order and, as such, destruction becomes thought of as the original sin which is preferred to be viewed as something innate within us, rather than become aware of our connections with nature and Eve.

Adam's "new world order" involves everything he needs to do *after* he has destroyed Eve. He needs to rename, rebuild, and recreate himself, all with magic, as he has destroyed his place in nature and in relation to Eve.

Perhaps original sin or original guilt is a misnomer. It is only able to be thought of as original if you position the starting point as being the word and the destruction of Eve. Thus, a belief in the death instinct and the innate aspects of envy, greed, and aggression necessarily means that an Adam creation myth is in operation. It is a very human construct which comes about because of our removal of ourselves from nature; this is not a consequence of birth, but rather a consequence of something that happens *between* Adam and Eve—between the egg and the sperm, between the mother and baby, between the mother and father, and between the Adam and Eve aspects of the mind. If there isn't an oscillating equality *between* all of these aspects, then nature is disavowed, Eve is destroyed, and Adam's word becomes the beginning.

Destructiveness, then, can be seen as innate as it represents something present at *this particular* construct of the beginning. Secondary Adam, in this beginning, projects out his own destruction of Eve and fears it coming back to him via a penetrative process, so he defends himself from this. Making destructiveness original is part of this defence too.

An analyst operating from this position will see the "thread that needs a narration", or the projective aspects of their patients as "trying to get inside" the analyst, and will see it as destructive. After all, the very thing that this aspect needs is a penetrative process in order to be known, and the very thing this particular analyst will not be able to countenance is any penetrative process.

The ultimate consequences of this system are guilt, shame, and an increased need for external structures to hold the patient. Along with this is a naming of the patient with the labels of original sin/guilt/destructiveness/envy as no representation of a time before secondary Adam dominance can be tolerated. Perhaps analysis interminable!?

The process employed is one of the analyst providing a *narrative* according to the theory/religion/thinking that is the external system that holds the analyst. This narrative becomes the analyst standing back and telling the patient what he thinks is going on. The actual Eve narration that needs to be told would be neglected in favour of the secondary Adam narrative.

We collect words like a naturalist—putting them in museums to study them.

—H. G. Wells

From this perspective the process for this analyst would be like the naturalist collecting words and names and staying apart. He would not use his body and would not provide a *narration* for the patient. This appears to work when the patient and the analyst are both operating from a secondary Adam world view (or the same creation myth). This employs a reinforcing of a superego-like solution and feels satisfying as it colludes with a joint defence against a perceived chaos and phobia of penetration and using the body or "going inside".

Winnicott's holding and Bion's container–contained are those processes by which an analyst can work with the unknown, sitting with the chaos, pain, and discomfort of not knowing and trying to employ an Eve-thinking mind. If this is achieved, containment takes place and an Eve word is able to be found which provides the narration that is needed.

If a secondary Adam mind is applied, containment does not take place. The analyst uses words to label the patient and, in experiencing an unavailable analyst, the patient can only resort to intensifying his projections, or reining them in with his superego.

My memory of being surrounded by derelict buildings and feeling shame about my wish to return and build a house for myself would be interpreted, in this context, as the destructiveness inherent in me and a wish to rebuild through guilt and reparation. Perhaps the memory itself would be considered by the analyst as a representation of this destructiveness and used to imply a tendency to destroy the good in my life—especially that good which the analyst feels to be the basis of his own creation myth. The creation myth or structure the analyst orientates himself with would become the only "house" able to exist between us, leaving me no possibility of building my own, through a living narration becoming available. My shame would possibly be left un-interpreted or subsumed under the label of guilt.

* * *

To be a zoologist is an opposite process to that of the naturalist—experiencing words in the wild. The analyst would collect experiences (not labels from theory) and take them inside and then provide a *narration* for the patient. This analyst would contextualise and comprehend the experience rendering names and labels unnecessary. The analyst is open to the use of her body and this reinforces a feeling for the patient of having been taken in, made sense of, and survived. This has the impact of dissolving the need for an excessive superego, and enables a freer and more spontaneous patient.

This way of being is to do more with the psychology of primary Adam and Eve, and a circularity between them. This entails an awareness of the natural order of things, how interactions require the use of bodies as well as minds, and an awareness and forbearance of pain and suffering (not only the guilt associated with secondary Adam). For a practitioner coming from this position, the main focus of work will be holding and the container–contained process and being with the patient.

A narration of the patient's inner world becomes available as the analyst is able to represent it from the basis of having experience of it.

An outcome of living according to a more natural creation myth is that shame and guilt ebb away, revealing a sense of having been known and accepted. For the patient who is with an analyst operating from this way of being, there is potential for a reduction of the impact of the superego, a reduction of reliance on external structures, and a concurrent freedom of expression. Although, of course, the pain released is difficult, it *can only* be borne with another; if this doesn't occur, lifelong defences and external structures will be needed. The analyst's ability to access her Eve, and thus the capacity to take in and create different words, becomes the essential experience.

The process that occurs here is one of *narration.* The analyst provides a living narration that brings life and form to the patient's inner world; it is dependent upon a maternal function and does not call upon an external structure to provide words.

From this position, my experience of the derelict buildings, the wish to rebuild, and my shame would be discovered within the work with the analyst. The narration would evolve over time for a deep understanding of my experience to "become". The analyst would arrive upon an awareness of my lack of "house", hopefully be able to allow this uncomfortable feeling to "be", and then be able to find words from an Eve aspect within. My shame would be understood as the shamefulness inherent in the situation of not having been taken in, and in not having a "house" that served as my home. The ruins would be the symbol of a catastrophe that had happened within my mind that mirrored a wider family catastrophe. My wish to rebuild would be seen as a healthy movement towards connection and the need to formulate a structure that would serve as a functioning creation myth.[18]

---

[18] An aside: The nature and origin of the word is important in how a mind develops, and so if the predominant use of words in a society is from a secondary Adam position, then that society will be hierarchical and patriarchal. Symbolisation initially takes place to convey something deeply meaningful from Eve, but then the word dies when secondary Adam takes over its use. This leads to a separation from the word and its inner meaning as soon as it is named in the Adam realm. Thus, language can inherently take away the need to tolerate pain. In the beginning was the word and the word became God as it was felt to take away pain.

* * *

Generally, most people do not wish to cause pain or difficulty for others. They are naturally benevolent in that they love and wish to be loved. The secondary Adam system reduces a person to hierarchical thinking, split between good and bad, and a reliance on naming instead of experiencing. From this position, a person may operate in it for cruel and narcissistic reasons, but they may also operate in it from a position of love. In this situation, a person would take their external structure, words, and need for magical thinking, and have a wish to approach others with love. The thinking might be along the lines of "I have achieved a status quo with my difficulties and feel happy, therefore I wish others to achieve this too"; or "I believe in something external, greater than me, and as that source has created the universe, I love all of what he has created."

An analyst operating from this position will be evangelistic in method. Wishing almost to hear the confessions of his patients in order for him to feel able to encourage the patient to join the thinking the analyst is committed to. Analysis is seen as a cure-all, external structure by which a patient can achieve redemption and join a club of missionaries who have gone out in the world to gain more adherents. This not only has the impact of removing the threat of non-believers but also enables the analyst to feel like the disciple of Freud, or Klein, or Bion, and so on. Thinking, however, is stagnant, and difference is deemed a threat that needs to be "loved" into non-existence.

Here, my derelict house and wish-to-build scenario might be greeted with warmth and acceptance, but I would be strongly persuaded that there was an alternative, better house elsewhere. I would just need to renounce all wishes to build my own, acknowledge this new house as being "all things to all", and join. The analyst's creation myth would be like a club that would be available to me as long as I had faith in its magical attributes. I would then have access to being happy. It would be magical as it bypasses the maternal function and is focused on an externally based love, rather than situating the transformative act as taking place within the maternal body. In this scenario, my shame would be seen, but it would be in the context of me being shameful in the eyes of a sinless and pure greater being.

* * *

If the external world is not balanced enough between male and female, then the mind, in its mirroring of society, would also favour one or the other. In a highly misogynistic society, Adam dominates in the psyche, and the Eve function would need to become appropriated within the created external structure. In this society, which is fundamentally hierarchical, other prejudices will also be endemic.

Drapetomania is a term coined by the American physician Samuel Cartwright, which described what was deemed to be the mental illness which caused enslaved Africans to flee captivity. It derives from the Greek *drapetus*—a runaway (slave), and *mania*—madness or frenzy.

Cartwright looked to the Bible in order to validate his theory. He said that the Bible calls for a slave to be submissive to his master, and that, in doing so, the slave will have no desire to run away.

In "Diseases and Peculiarities of the Negro Race" (1852), Cartwright describes the disorder as being well known to plantation owners and overseers. He stated that the malady was a consequence of masters becoming too familiar with slaves, treating them as equals.

In the case of slaves becoming depressed, angry, and dissatisfied with no apparent cause—a warning sign of imminent flight—Cartwright prescribed whipping as a preventative measure. As a remedy for this disease, doctors also made running a physical impossibility by prescribing the removal of both big toes.

What is interesting for the topic of this book is how easily "woman" could be substituted for "slave", the sense of there being people who are superior and those who are inferior, and religion used to vindicate and corroborate this state of mind.

The dynamics of the inferior–superior dichotomy are well known and not my main focus. The aspect of it which I find interesting is the bigger frame which the religion provides—that is, the creation myth which enables the beliefs and structures of mind to have existence. The submissive and dominant, inferior and superior, and slave and master scenario—all can be seen to originate in the Garden of Eden myth, the main crux of which is Adam's fear and envy of Eve, and his intolerance in bearing his own pain. He then creates a system within which he makes Eve inferior to himself, a god who considers him special, and a world which he has dominion over.

Drapetomania then would be a disease as each creature in this system is deemed to have been created by God for Adam, and, therefore, implicit in this should be a knowledge of *their* position in the order of things. A wish to run away is thus a disease as theoretically, within this system, it should not exist. As it does exist—slaves and women have always rebelled against their enslavement—this is anathema to the system that has been created by Adam as it is a profound threat to the very idea of God; either His creation is flawed and He is not all-powerful, or He is not the author of creation.

Thankfully, Cartwright's view of the superiority of white over black is being dismantled over time and most people now would be outraged at his statements. We know that it is wrong to enslave a group of people because of the colour of their skin. What is far more insidious and harder to comprehend is how much of a given the status of women in society is. If all "-isms" can be said to have their roots in the first "-ism" of the first hierarchy becoming established, then that first one is between man and woman, Adam and Eve. It is an age-old hierarchy that has been in place since man first looked at woman and wanted to own creativity for himself. I wonder if societies, as a whole, were to remedy the inequality between Adam and Eve, and therefore man and woman, then racism could really become a thing of the (very shameful) past too.

The slave's wish to run away, to have freedom, equality, and to exert his right to own himself, is also Eve's fight for existence and equality (in the later myths, represented by the figure of Lilith). The quests for individuality, efficacy, and existence of those who are deemed inferior have, thus, been viewed as a disease and a threat to the very foundation of the religion Adam has created. But existence, equality, and efficacy, in terms of Adam, would be to see the exterior trappings of equal status conferred on those who were deemed less than, and rules and regulations put in place for it to be policed. In terms of Eve, existence, equality, and efficacy, however, have a different meaning. Existence would mean having the "me" of the person known and acknowledged; equality would mean elevating the "me" to that of the "I"; efficacy would mean allowing and enabling pain and suffering to not only be held, but to also undergo an active maternal function process which creates a maternal third position. This is the source of creation and thinking.

If what Freud and Klein described was all there is, then misogyny, religion, patriarchal societies, and racism are the consequence. Perhaps the best that can be hoped for from an Adam-only mind is Klein's depressive position. As a result, the content of the unconscious (that which cannot be countenanced) is theorised to be destructiveness, demons, fears, aggressions, and passions, and a superego is needed to rein in these forces. No other force or method can suffice. This splitting of the mind effectively into a conscious, unconscious, and superego has all the resonance of a religion. As Klein observed, if the object becomes split, so does the mind—if the mind becomes split, so does the object. Religion, with its sense of god being transcendent, seems to be a direct, evolved copy of the mind of secondary Adam.

If theories in psychoanalysis do not evolve to incorporate a structure of mind that represents more of Eve, then we, as psychoanalysts, are also doomed to be stuck in a vicious circle of secondary Adam. We will only have words and theory available to us that are Adam's, and the creation myth that we are operating from will be limited and religion-based (even if we think otherwise), and our own (unconscious) solution will be the same as the patient's. Any progress and development that occurs, in spite of this system being present, is appropriated by the system and thought of as the unknowable, mysterious impact of this thing (religion) we call psychoanalysis. A persistence in this view colludes with a denigration of Eve and perpetuates misogyny.

Perhaps the holding on to concepts like the death instinct, even when there is a conscious moving away from the religious associations to original sin, is due to the causal anxiety which instigates religion to begin with. This anxiety is to do with the true nature of being, relationship, and the circularity of life. The idea of the death instinct, or original sin, serves as a position beyond which feeling and being doesn't need to go; thought itself can stop at this point and the causal anxiety need not ever be addressed. In going beyond this position, the orientating factor of life shifts from pleasure-seeking to pain-management and from Adam being the essential force to that of the capacity of Eve.

CHAPTER 22

An elemental structure

> *So, how do we get atoms? You need a third particle: another electron, another proton, or a photon. If you've got three bodies, you can have two of them stick together, lowering their total energy, and the third one carries off the extra energy. This is a simple idea, but it has a lot of implications. It's why we can date the formation of atoms to a very specific moment in the history of the universe: you need the temperature and density of particles to be just right: high enough that you get three particles coming together to allow electrons to get stuck to atoms, but not so high that the newly formed atoms get knocked apart again.*
>
> —Chad Orzel (2020)

From my engagement in this personal hermeneutic loop, it seems that I have arrived at a particular understanding of how I see the mind. It is highly likely that it will undergo many more permutations, and also contain inaccuracies and misunderstandings. It can also be said to be greatly similar to other understandings of the mind—perhaps just a different way of saying essentially the same thing said by others previously. Bearing this in mind, the fundamental structure that I've arrived at, from a position of discovery, becomes, therefore, my own creation myth. The relevance to me is obvious, and in setting it out in this book, it becomes something which has shifted from discomfort and chaotic feelings, to thoughts, to ideas and words, and then to the written form. This transition can be one which is thought to perpetuate a particular structure and to justify a particular way of being, leading to stagnation. However, I hope that I have conveyed something different—a more dynamic, ever-changing something which, with curiosity about insides, becomes open to constant re-formulation.

I have come to see the mind as only being whole when Adam and Eve are able to be in an oscillating, more or less equal dynamic tension with each other. The primary aspects of each involve the innate awareness that each cell has of the circular processes of introjection and projection. This is both an internal and external need. There is a constant ebb and flow between an organism's cells internally, and externally between the whole organism and the environment. When the introjective forces (Eve) and projective forces (Adam) are working well together, the organism attains a relative calm, or equilibrium.

Bodily, this is essential to be able to feed, remain safe, and stay alive. Food and oxygen are taken in, waste materials are expelled; individual organ cells are connected and interact with each other to attain their relative calm via these same processes. This is known innately by every particle in the body. A state of distress for a body (or cell) might be hunger or dehydration—it would then engage in a circular relationship with the environment, whether internally or externally, to alleviate this.

This capacity to engage in the environment, both internally and externally, in order to alleviate pain and discomfort, is what I see as Adam and Eve working together in dynamic tension, as opposed to the isolated functioning present in secondary Adam and Eve. This is a primary process as it has been present since conception, but can become lost and regained to varying extents throughout life. It is a capacity to engage in a circular way. The body, since conception, has known this process, and the vicissitudes of all the three penetrations (egg by the sperm, mother by the father, and baby and maternal object) indicate how the transition from the womb to being a young child is experienced psychically.

When this transition has been good enough, the child has a sense of being able to utilise these processes in a stabilising manner. He can feel fear, project this fear, and take action to seek another for protection; he can also be receptive to the fear being transformed by the other providing a living narration of his experience. These words, from a maternal third position, fill him up, and he knows he is connected and not alone. The process is one of a maternal curiosity about the inside of the child, and then a filling with maternal words or an awareness of a togetherness. This filling enables the child to know he has been taken in by the other, rather than the shameful position of having his projections dissipate to nothing. The filling also provides an internal structure which strengthens the child's capacity to make sense of himself and the world. This is a working primary Adam and Eve relationship, and is based on circularity. Before the child is able to position this circularity within himself, he is dependent on an external capacity to provide it for him.

The potential for secondary Adam and Eve to fully develop comes after the trauma of birth. If the maternal function that has been provided is good enough, and the traumas which have been experienced are not too great, then an oscillating, but mostly balanced state becomes predominant.

When situations arise which are beyond the infant psyche or the highly traumatised mind to deal with, then the infant's Eve capacity isn't strong enough to manage. She cannot give form to the formless, and secondary Adam (S-Adam) takes over almost completely,

Primary Adam/"what"/"I"	**Primary Eve/"who"/"me"**
Action; can think, which leads to thoughts, ideas, and words; under stress, wishes to be inside or to get rid of the discomfort; can protect, complement, and fulfil—therefore can give ease and joy. Uses projection to join with Eve.	Being; can think, which leads to thoughts, images, ideas, and words; under stress, wishes to be filled with something which can provide an inner structure; can operate an Eve function of containment—therefore can give great joy and ease. Uses introjection to join with Adam.
Secondary Adam features	**Secondary Eve features**
Adam narcissism; sadism; misogyny; appropriation; religion and creation of gods; prioritisation of gratification involving projection; perversions.	Eve narcissism; masochism; androgyny; eating disorders; addictions based in the body; abstinence; prioritisation of gratification involving introjection.
Unconscious Adam/anxieties	**Unconscious Eve/anxieties**
Full of guilt, aggression, envy, and fear of having damaged by being inside; fear of nothingness as Eve has been destroyed. Afraid of being in position of being penetrated as he has a terror of insides.	Anxiety of not having trauma, pain, and suffering expressed (existential anxiety) and contained (anxiety about not having been taken in); fear of emptiness; fear of violent and straight-line penetrations. Shame.

and immediately. Hence, Klein's observations of the splitting in infants and the S-Adam aggression displayed. If there is a functioning environmental Eve, then at some point the infant will be able to feel filled up by these maternal provisions, and space will be created for thought to emerge. In effect, the infant's Eve gains a structure and reduces the need for Adam to take over.

If the environmental provision is not good enough, pain or chaos becomes projected onto any object that is available to take it. It is dependent upon the instigation of hierarchies—the structure necessary for straight-line projections—and as long as the person feels high enough in this hierarchy to be able to continue to project, it will proceed. It fails when the person finds himself at the bottom of this hierarchy. Eve, in this situation, will wish to take in to solve the trauma, she will hungrily take in anything that she feels will fill the empty space that is felt to be the cause of the anxiety or pain. When Eve takes over, Adam has already failed, and it is at this point that drug, alcohol, or food solutions may be sought.

If sexuality and pleasure are seen as the fundamental organising factors of the mind, then every experience would need to be interpreted in this way. From this position, destructiveness, envy, and greed become constitutional, and Eve is mostly relegated to the unconscious. If, instead, pain (chaos, anxiety, and distress), and how it is solved, is seen as the fundamental organising factor, then the myriad of solutions that are available offer a different perspective. When pain is thought to be the organising factor, destructiveness, envy, and greed are not constitutional, and the seeking of another for a maternal function experience is natural and outside the sexual arena.

Bion and Winnicott both became aware of something missing in the structure of mind described by Freud and Klein. They each attempted to address this and developed their own models. They were both able to go a long way towards putting words to that something, and shifted the inherent creation myth within the theory of mind from being Adam-based to more nature-based. In having more of a position for Eve, they can be said to be supporting Pelagius more than Augustine.

Physical holding is an Adam developmentally important factor; he is able to exercise his action and mobility and discover where he ends and the other begins. Eve needs the reverie and maternal preoccupation leading to a maternal third word or idea in order for her to be filled. This feeling of fullness is obtained by meaningful words or an "at-one-ness" connection being given to her inner world—in doing so, it becomes furnished. Without these words or ideas she is left empty and has little meaning in life. These words need to be relevant to her—the narration of who she is—and be good enough, not leaving her stuffed, or filled with nothingness.

For circularity (and not straight lines) to be the predominant mechanism for managing trauma, an experience of a maternal function is necessary. This involves the capacity to provide an inner sense of togetherness for the infant, and, ultimately, words. This becomes possible when the maternal object has been able to generate a third position within herself, away from the cycle of binary transference of chaos. She is able to order the chaos and give it form, and, in doing so, manages to convey a level of connectivity *at the point of the chaos*. This is felt by the infant and makes what is chaotic, traumatic, and painful less so.

The maternal third is vital to the process of becoming who we are. It precedes the paternal third position and is also necessary to have occurred well enough before the paternal third position can be experienced in a non-persecutory manner. It is the fundamental basis of all thought and being.

The container–contained process and that of primary maternal preoccupation go some way to describe it, but each of these processes omits the status of the actual position. They infer a process by which something is taken in by the maternal or containing object, and that it is a dynamic process. What then happens to the something is dependent upon the capacity of the containing or maternal object. In a system where the object has no words, or is overwhelmed with anxiety, or collapses under the something (whether this is in phantasy or reality, it doesn't really matter), the dynamic process remains a binary one in which the something is constantly exchanged with a collapsing object in a Sisyphean tragedy. Here, the something that is in need of undergoing a particular process remains unaltered and is experienced as a torturous pain, which becomes more and more monstrous in quality the more it is met with a collapsing object. Trauma and pain beget more trauma and pain.

The maternal third position is the capacity of the maternal or containing object to establish a third perspective of the pain—not just the binary dynamic of shifting pain from one body to another. This third position has the sense of the pain being enveloped within the maternal body, and instead of overwhelming the object, it becomes bounded and curiosity can prevail. This process creates a third dimension away from the binary experience and thus allows the subject to have the experience of his pain as not being destructive, and instead it is alleviated. The containing process, without this third position being achieved, is passive and is not actually containment. The maternal third position, in contrast, is a highly active process and demonstrated by curiosity being present. If the maternal or containing mind can remain curious after taking in the something, then the third position of alleviation of pain, having words being found, survival of the object, and a sense of self coherence is found. The word produced in this process becomes the third particle carrying off the energy of trauma in Chad Orzel's description above.

This third position is the necessary position for thought to be possible and for a sense of who we are to begin. If the maternal third position is not able to be found or achieved, then the subject is reduced to using the paternal third for his sense of safety and, instead of "who", "what" he is becomes dominant. He will become dependent upon external structures (like religion, narcissism, hierarchies …) to feel safe and judge himself externally by what status he has, and by what he feels he is. This is a fragile and precarious state of being.

When the psyche is out of balance, then what Eve represents becomes unrepresented, not only with regard to her functions, but also the pain that is left, in effect, uncontained. Theories of mind from this situation will also omit representation of Eve. Her essential functions have to be appropriated by Adam, but the pain will not be adequately contained in the structure Adam sets up. It will constantly try to find expression and containment (the repetition compulsion), and the original sin—that is, the unconscious guilt associated with the metaphoric killing of Eve—will add to the counter force to deny expression.

Each part of the mind needs a thirdness to be able to think. Adam achieves this via the oedipal situation. For a boy, his Adam and Eve aspects of mind have wishes and urges towards mother, and father is experienced as a powerful obstacle. In realising his powerlessness in relation to his father, he has to put his wishes to one side which creates space for thought. This thought has its foundations in an external reference to father, and can become orientated around reason, intellect, and action. It is also at the root of the development of religion, rules, and the superego. Therefore, for this type of thought to come about, an external father and a hierarchical reference are needed.

This thirdness is not only internal (between wish–prohibition–thought); it is external—child–mother–father and person–religion–law.

For Eve thought to come about, an active maternal function is needed. It becomes active in the sense of going inside the infant or traumatised other, with curiosity, to "get" the "no thing", and for meaningful words or ideas to be applied. The thirdness here is the creation of "some thing" from the "no thing"—the mother and baby couple interact to form a word, or idea, that belongs to both, but is needed by the infant to enhance the strength of his own Eve. This has the impact of filling his Eve with a structure. The "no thing", felt to be chaotic and overwhelming, has become "some thing". The inner world of the infant has been received by another and has been transformed into a third position. The infant can then feel *qualitatively* that he is not abhorrent, and that his inner world is survivable.

Adam thought is brought about by an external powerful prohibition. Eve thought is brought about by an internal awareness. Guilt, superego formation, religion, and rules can be the outcome of an overly prioritised paternal third process; and shame can be the outcome of a maternal third process which has not been experienced well enough.

Freud's victory of the intellect over sensuality, or the victory of the paternal over the maternal, would leave an empty inner world—all "I" and no "me". It also suggests that the person has no capacity to manage his desires and passions without a prohibition from father.

Words are creative forces ... they enabled man (Adam) to own creativity, and deny nature. Thus, when Adam is thought to own creativity, his words become the beginning of the universe. When Eve is thought to be the source of creativity, her words can become a different sense of what the beginning is. Either the beginning is outside the body with the external word, or inside the body with the internal word. Therefore, it can also be said that the beginning belongs to either Adam or Eve. Augustine believed that the external word was the source of the beginning, and Pelagius believed that we each had a light inside that was the source of the beginning.

The debate at the Council of Lod between Pelagius and Augustine is indicative of the enduring battles between these two positions. Psychoanalysis also has this battle. Theories based on the beginning being Adam's word are represented by Freud and Klein, and the light has been represented most by Bion and Winnicott (in this book), although they can both also be thought of as appropriating or absorbing Eve into Adam to a certain extent. This tendency of Adam to appropriate and absorb in order to maintain his hierarchical position is one of his most enduring behaviours. The failure of this system is that, whilst it can be seen to be having a positive impact on society becoming more aware and altruistic, it does so in a way which Adam owns, instead of it being seen as Eve. He widens his knowledge base, instead of allowing awareness and equality to be. The sense of being seen to do the right thing takes over from actually feeling it naturally and unambiguously as coming from an aspect within, and Eve can still be demeaned.

* * *

Jacob

In a dream I was picking at a spot on my outer thigh and started squeezing it. The stuff that came out was black, but it went on and on—like a parasitic worm or something—I kept on pulling and soon had a long length of it dangling from my hand. I then realised that it was the inner bit of a Bic pen, the tube with the ink and the metal nib and I understood that I'd swallowed a Bic pen and it had travelled through me to my thigh, from where I was able to get it out. When I woke, I realised that I use a Bic pen to write down my dreams and also my thoughts about here—but it's not like any writing I've done before, which has mainly been about cataloguing things.

CHAPTER 23

Narcissism

The pursuit of ownership of what might be considered more positive traits—power, intelligence, beauty, status, and so on—is essentially the process of one type of narcissism. This becomes the overvaluing of secondary Adam and ownership, at the expense of Eve and exchange. Pain and difficult feelings outside this positive construct are projected onto something, or into someone, with whom no subsequent relationship is wanted. This is a scapegoat figure and is always present in this type of narcissistic system—someone who has to be the recipient of pain with no recourse to the exchange mechanisms that could alleviate it, the object or person at the bottom of the inevitable hierarchy present.

Another type of narcissism can be described as the situation of the person who is the scapegoat, unable to effect any change for themselves. In the context of a straight-line creation myth, wherein Adam projection is revered, these two types of narcissism could be said to describe the end points of this straight line—the projector not wanting to experience exchange, and the projection sponge who is unable to utilise any projective processes herself. Here, the potential of exchange has also become unavailable.

Narcissism, and the multitude of theories that have arisen about it, is an area full of thoughts, clinical experiences, and insights. An online search gives an idea of the vast array of labels and types, both in terms of clinical terminology as well as popular psychology. Many psychoanalytic theories on narcissism involve identification of a binary, interrelated system—for example, libidinal and destructive narcissism (Rosenfeld, 1965) which distinguishes between normal and pathological projective processes, or thin- and thick-skinned narcissism (Rosenfeld, 2002), which describes a vulnerable and a grandiose type. It is interesting that, from the basis of this book, one cannot exist without the other.

There is not much that can said about narcissism which hasn't been said, in various forms, before, but I think framing it in terms of Adam and Eve might be useful. From this context, the starting point is important and I will try to outline the story of Narcissus in the rough format of a psychological investigation.

Past history and present circumstances

Anecdotal reports and known lineages indicate that both Narcissus and Echo come from dysfunctional backgrounds with incestuous relationships being the norm.

Given the history of his family, it is likely that Narcissus' mother (Liriope, a fresh-water nymph) attempted to seduce him, particularly as his father (Cephissus, a river god) was mostly absent. This scenario would have felt highly threatening to Narcissus, with no parent to reflect back to him the individuality and separate identity he sought. With this threat to his existence, he seems to have chosen to turn his gaze inward and to "love" himself. The extent of his inward gaze is in direct correlation to the absence of a real reflecting person (mother) in his life. This led him to wander alone, unable to relate to others, as the only available relating he sensed was engulfing, suffocating, and likely to annihilate his existence, both psychically and bodily. In this "solution" he maintained his separateness and difference. As he had not experienced a good enough maternal relationship, he was unable to process or tolerate painful feelings about his terrors of engulfment and isolation. He could only countenance his more positive attributes, mistakenly believing this was what "good" mothers do.

Little is known of Echo's background, but it is not unlikely that she was also the product of incestuous relations. She spent a lot of time with the couple Zeus and Hera and would often divert Hera's attention with her talkativeness to enable Zeus to covertly engage in sexual activity with her nymph sisters. Upon Hera realising this, Echo was banished and cursed: from that day, Echo was only able to repeat the last words of what anyone said to her. This loss of speech was a result of a psychological catastrophe arising from the dynamic between herself, Zeus, and Hera. Its attribution to Hera's magic, rather than the reality of the situation, is an indication that there had been no maternal functioning available in this "family"; in blaming Echo, who symbolises the child in the incestuous relationship, Hera distorted reality. Thus, Echo was both the voice that prevented recognition of reality and the child to blame to avoid the reality of her husband's betrayal and possible incest. In this way, Echo moved from being an accessory involved in the denial of reality, to the body that is blamed and receives the projections of all involved.

Echo was probably very aware of the likely catastrophe that would come about if the truth were to become known—banishment and blame. This indicates that her collusion with Zeus was a "solution" to try to keep some semblance of having "parents" in her inner world. Once this fear was realised, her desires, wishes, and needs were never able to be spoken, as, with this, she had lost her projective capacities and sense that there would be anyone available for her.

The meeting

When Narcissus and Echo met, it was the disastrous coming together of two solutions to the incestuous situation.

First (Narcissus), in which he refused to be seduced by his mother and turned inwards in order to preserve and nurture his difference and identity. In doing so, he became alone, parentless, and unable to relate to others.

Second (Echo), in which she became involved in the incestuous seduction in order to try to retain her parents and ability to relate. When the truth became known and the bubble of illusion burst, she was left alone, parentless, and unable to relate. Her identity, voice, and existence became so tentative, it was only able to be discovered by another's perception of it.

When Echo saw Narcissus, she saw someone who was not only beautiful, but who also seemed to have held onto his identity and love of himself. Given her own lack in these aspects, it is not surprising that she would have found Narcissus attractive and compelling. She started to follow him and, given his extreme inward preoccupations, Narcissus surprisingly began to sense this. At some point after becoming aware of someone being there, Narcissus called out:

"Is anyone there?"

Echo responded in the only way she could:

"Is anyone there?"

Narcissus called, "Come here."

Echo: "Come here."

Narcissus: "We must come together."

Echo: "… come together."

At this Echo became overwhelmed by her desire to be known and heard, and ran to Narcissus—taking his words as an invitation. She embraced him and thought that she'd found someone who wanted to know her. He was appalled and pushed her away saying, "Hands off! May I die before you enjoy my body."

In her shame and humiliation, Echo ran into the woods and remained there for the rest of her life—only being known in the rare occurrence of her echo.

Narcissus carried on his journey and returned to his inward introspection. He came across a pond and caught sight of his own reflection in it. He was so captivated by this that he remained there for the rest of his life. Both Echo and Narcissus faded away in their own identity crises and drastic solutions to them.

The forces, fears, fantasies, and phantasies at play

Both Echo and Narcissus were in need of a good enough, benign maternal functioning object who could take their identities into her body and reflect back something which gave a sense of who they were—that they were lovable and wanted in their separateness and difference.

Echo, in wanting that from Narcissus, felt overwhelmed when that seemed possible—"... we must come together". She approached him with that wish and rushed towards him in her excitement. Narcissus, when he sensed that someone was following him, was interested and called out. He also had a wish for someone to be able to reflect a true picture of himself back to him. While Echo remained a voice he was interested, could tolerate her presence, and maintain his outward looking. It might even be said that he had a sense of knowing that something needed to "come together" for him to move forwards. But when Echo ran to him and embraced him, his fear of being engulfed bodily, and hence his precarious identity being annihilated, overwhelmed him.

When Echo presented her body, he panicked and felt her to be the seductive mother he was fleeing from. His "... may I die before you enjoy my body" sounds like the very statement he would wish to say to his seductive mother—his experience being of annihilation instead of a benign maternal function. In light of this, his fears caused him to repel Echo.

In being so profoundly rejected, Echo was left with no alternative other than to fade away to nothing. She had dared show herself and had hoped for so much, but had been powerfully rejected, leaving her feeling she dare not show herself ever again.

Conclusion

In the case of Narcissus, it seems he was able to tolerate the presence of Echo only if she were disembodied. In this way, he seemed to just about have the capacity to be aware of another—even if that other could only reflect his own words. At this level, he also has an awareness of his need to "come together" with someone, but as soon as the awareness becomes "embodied", he panics at the fear of an engulfment by a maternal object, and reverts back to his defensive position. For a different outcome, he would need to meet someone able to put aside their own body and needs; someone who could identify the voice within him that is aware of his need for others. Hopefully, in experiencing someone walking alongside this voice, trust could be built that the other's body and needs will not engulf him.

In the case of Echo, she had thought that she had found someone by whom she could show herself, be known, and loved for who she was. Upon rejection, and also horror at the thought that his assumption was that she wanted his body, she was left to fade away in shame and humiliation. For a different outcome, Echo would need to meet someone perceptive enough to know she is there and who could give her words to enable her to own herself. If the words given match sufficiently to how she is feeling and to her identity, she will show herself, but as soon as that is corrupted or misinterpreted, she will hide again.

Thus, Narcissus can be said to project all his pain and discomfort, while keeping hold of his inflated pleasure and wanted attributes; but in being unable to take anything in, he has retreated to a position of not interacting with others. Echo receives all the discomforts and pains of others; but in being unable to utilise projection, she is also unable to initiate interaction.

Both positions are a result of trauma, existential anxieties, and the absence of an effective maternal functioning object. Narcissus left his parental relationships before seduction occurred, and created a situation within which he felt able to protect his identity and existence. Echo remained in her "parental" relationships and became the victim of seduction. In remaining, she felt she might be able to keep an illusion of having parents. Both were faced with decisions reminiscent of *The Emperor's New Clothes* and the trolley problem. It could be said that Narcissus chose to save himself and let the five people (in this case, his parents and the outer world) die. Echo chose to save the five and let herself die.

* * *

Linking the above understanding of the experiences of Narcissus and Echo with the themes outlined in Parts I and II, narcissism can be thought of as an outcome of the vicissitudes of introjective and projective forces. Therefore, the three scenarios that can be the active sites of narcissism are in relation to:

- The qualitative sense that is made of the primal scene—how the mother and father come together within the family—as well as the sense that is made of the relationship between man and woman in the wider society.
- The sense that is made of the interaction between the infant and the maternal object—how the infant imagines his inner world has been received by his mother and the qualitative sense of the contents he has been left with.
- The sense that is made of creation—the coming together of the sperm and egg and either the illusionary idea that either can exist without the other, or the traumatic outcome of an environmental curtailment of the use of projective or introjective capacities.

If the interaction between the male and the female in the wider society and the family isn't balanced, a person would only have their maternal relationship as a potential good enough exchange process to fall back on. When this isn't good enough, as for Narcissus and Echo, they are left living their lives as though no penetration and exchange has occurred—effectively the sperm and the egg existing without the other.

Following this line of thought, there is then a masculine narcissism related to a sperm under the illusion that he can exist without the egg; and feminine narcissism which is related to the illusion that she can exist without the sperm. These illusions can be found within many magical creation myths which describe the beginning as being either a wholly male or wholly female event.

If we return to the Narcissus and Echo investigation above, then Zeus and Cephissus are showing traits of a masculine (Adam) narcissism. They are gods, in a patriarchal society, and so are at the top in the hierarchy of projections. They seek women for sexual pleasure only. They have no wish to think about the pain of others, nor do they wish to know their own. They allow bodily and psychological penetrations, but limit it to just their own projections. It might be said that their own experience of society, family, and maternal relationships has not given them any indication that exchange and equality between the male and female aspects is possible. It is their high position in the hierarchy that enables them to display this type of Adam narcissism.

Liriope (in my description of her) is also displaying traits of an Adam narcissism. Narcissus' recoil from the bodily embrace of Echo suggests that Liriope had been active in her seduction of him. In this situation, there would be a prioritising of her pleasure over the awareness of the pain she would cause. Perhaps she is repeating her own experience of being seduced by her father; or, perhaps, in having a child, she has found a body she can project into, so she is no longer the bottom of the hierarchy. She (like Zeus and Cephissus) is part of a patriarchal society and family and has not experienced a good enough maternal relationship.

Narcissus and Echo both occupy the position of the end of a projection straight line. They both also represent a situation in which there is no maternal function present (both having mothers who were too damaged to be able to fulfil this role). Narcissus' solution was to save himself at the expense of killing off the wider world; whilst Echo could be said to have kept the illusion of her parents, at her own expense.

Given the failure of society, family, and maternal relationship to provide enough of a balanced exchange between the projective and introjective aspects (Adam and Eve), they have no representation in their minds of this. The only representation available for them is the isolated sperm and egg.

Narcissus becomes like the sperm, all mobility and projective penetrative potential. He wanders about and projects his psychic pain, but has no representation in his mind of there being an egg to receive it. This creates an emptiness within him that can only be filled by taking something in via the only working introjective capacities left—sight and hearing. He hears Echo, but becomes so frightened he retreats even further to having just sight as an introjective aspect. This is felt to be having something rather than nothing, and he is trapped with his reflection until he withers and dies. Narcissus could be said to be focused on gratification and projective forces, with no sense of any nourishment inside him. He hungrily drinks in his own reflection which has to suffice for all of his identity, existential, and bodily needs.

Echo becomes like the egg, all nourishment and introjective penetrative potential. She is full of the psychic pain inherent in being the end point of a projective straight line, and has had the illusion of her parents shattered. In not having any opportunity for the exchange processes needed in healthy development, she is left waiting for a benign, maternal penetrative action of curiosity. She has no projective capacity, other than reflecting back the words others have projected into her—these words do not belong to her, but she has none of her own. She does, however, have the egg's capacity of nourishment. She is able to exist in this state for a long time. Waiting.

Narcissus, thus, represents an extreme position of Adam narcissism, and Echo represents that of Eve.

* * *

Jacob

I had two bits of dream last night, one of which disturbed me—I was in a room in a hotel with a woman I knew to be my partner, we started to make love—have intercourse—I was on top of her and I was tenderly stroking her face and neck, everything felt right for us to have sex and I was looking at her face—I didn't recognise who she was, and I notice a distinctive mole on her chin, I ask her about it, but then I wake up. I was thinking about this when I woke and I knew instantly that she was me ... the fact that she has this mole meant immediately that she was me and I was looking in a mirror while having sex.

I stroked her face, I think I do feel that as a growing caring attitude I have towards me ... a curiosity and tenderness ... I do believe it to be me, it was not my sister ...

Analyst: There seem to be many levels to that experience—a growing curiosity and care towards part of you that has felt opaque and a protective experience in which it feels safer to relate to yourself in here rather than allow me to have an emotional intercourse with you.

[*Pause*] But I think it is because of you ... I wouldn't be able to be curious about that part of me without you ... so it's like ... oh ... I'm searching for a word ... what is it ... it's like a love triangle ... your presence here is enabling me to be able to relate to me and without your presence I wouldn't be able to.

CHAPTER 24

Threads

(All identifying aspects have been altered, obscured, or omitted)

Jacob

For Jacob, the battle for supremacy between himself and his sister was life and death. Throughout the work with him his mind produced a wealth of dreams which tracked the ongoing vagaries of his inner relationship with a killed-off aspect of himself. He could speak of this from his memories of being a child with a sister whom he felt was opaque and unfathomable, and also through his relationship with his cats.

He had created a world of fantasy for himself to live in, which enabled him to feel safe and invulnerable, as long as he was able to stay there. He used magical thinking to change potentially chaotic and disordered situations into ones which felt to be under his control.

In being faced with a crisis of identity at a young age, he was able to hold on to himself, but at the cost of having destroyed the world around him. He was presented with the catastrophic choice faced by Narcissus, the boy in *The Emperor's New Clothes*, and the trolley problem. This sealed off position left him feeling triumphant but deeply sad as he began to realise the extent of the prison he had placed himself in. This sadness became increasingly available to him in the work, and he was in touch with a deep grief regarding his loneliness and pain. His capacity to see me as someone he could be with to help him oscillated with his anger at an increasing awareness of his need too.

> The other day when I was angry with you, it was probably more anger at me for being enthralled to you ... needing to be here and it feeling like a weakness ... I came and spoke about it here ... I do find I talk a lot here, more than I've ever done before ... but I guess what you said about the "script" ... I do have a script ... and that infers too that

> it has a purpose … has been constructed by me to suit me … and that what might have actually happened has been lost … I seem to wear glasses that have a picture of my making on the inside and that I look out through that picture …

If a creation myth was thought about for Jacob, it would be one which denied all penetrations and gave the power of creation to a word and a god. He could change the nature of his experience by changing the meaning of a word to a different version. This word and the power it had became a "god" which was able to manage his anxieties and pain, instead of a maternal function.

He had felt that his mother wasn't interested in him, unless he allowed her to completely take over his mind, and this was something he greatly feared about me too. My constant curiosity about both him and his "sister" (or cats) allowed him to be able to begin to be curious about previously unavailable aspects of himself.

> It's as though I developed into a mirror image of her (mother)… she was impenetrable, cold, and unable to think about all of those feelings in that room, but at the same time she felt so overpowering … as though she could completely annihilate me with her thoughts and personality … in a bid to retain ME … a sense of ME existing … I retreated into a mirror image of her … seemingly impenetrable, unaffected by things … it was a bitter stand-off in which we were both angry … I kept on thinking that it would be okay when I leave, but I didn't reckon on it becoming an ingrained habit … that I'd never be free … I'm like a cartoon character that ran off a cliff and has been running ever since as I've never become aware of there not being ground … like in the cartoons, they only fall on becoming aware …

The first phase of our relationship involved Jacob telling me about his life, and, when I was able to have some space to speak of my thoughts and observations, he invariably responded with "No … that's not right." Over time, he began to be interested in what I was saying and allow himself to begin to consider what I had said. After a great deal of care spent in identifying both him and his sister—and, in a way, both of them beginning to trust me—he was able to say:

> I am beginning to realise that I can't analyse myself—even if I would want to … I can't do it alone and that I do need another … you … to help me … that what goes on between you and me and other people isn't necessarily what I make of it … and that it is very lonely trying to do so … [*pause*] … I have been startled by that realisation …

He began to be able to feel compassion towards a part of himself which he had boxed away, and he also began to be able to see a third position in his relationships which didn't have to be condemnatory or judgemental. This third position presented him with a great deal of confusion and disorientation. He had a dream which illustrated this:

> I was playing cards with my sister and father … when I looked at my hand I ended up getting very confused and bewildered as to what to do with them … I knew that I had to group these cards in threes—three kings, or queens, and so on—but each time I tried to figure out what to do, I got confused and couldn't do anything … I had a good hand and I knew that there was a way in which I could put down all the cards in a particular order, but I couldn't figure it out … I then woke up … I have played this game before and liked it, but usually I like playing with just one person as it becomes something else entirely with three or more …

In thinking about this, he was able to expand on a particular third position and characterise an aspect of himself which mostly sabotages connections. He used this aspect to interrupt or render any meaningful relationship impossible by applying words which condemned and measured the other. This third perspective was from an external source which became like a persecuting, godlike judge whose intent was to keep him isolated. In having identified both him and his sister within himself, we were also able to start to find a different third position—one in which he began to have words for his feelings of loneliness, fear, and grief. These words came from an internal source.

This curiosity about another aspect of himself featured heavily in many dreams:

> I was in a room which I didn't recognise, but I knew it was my sister's. There was a desk with lots of files, CDs, and a computer. I had an urge to look on the computer to try and find out about my sister—what she might be thinking and feeling … as I did so, I realised that the computer had been rigged to stop people accessing it—it was alarmed. In my panic, I realised the solution would be to turn the computer off—the dream then shifted to a restaurant and I came across an old friend … I was talking to him and I realised that my sister was also with me. As I talked to my friend, I was hoping that he would see that I was with my sister and that both of our heads were very close together—almost touching and merging and I wanted my friend to see them as the same, but different … to notice … I woke then and that feeling—to be close to my sister but different—shocked me.

Jacob had only had words belonging to an Adam aspect of himself to apply to his experiences and feelings. Words which originated from an external structure of measurement, judgement, and fear. As these words had been able to allow him to feel better in some circumstances, they had become his method of managing his pain. They became godlike and magical in this capacity. It seemed that, in not having had a continuous good enough experience of having his projections returned to him in a benign and formative way, his inner world had become impoverished of his pain, feelings, and selfhood (his "me").

Because his projections had been left in the external world, his creation myth inevitably was based on a straight-line hierarchy. The god which was able to alleviate his confusion and pain became a transcendent word which, in being situated outside himself, also became the point of creation or beginning. A time before this, when chaos and pain were more available to him, became a disordered universe which needed to be denied into non-existence. In relying so completely upon this magical word, or external third position, to manage his pain, he had a need to rewrite his beginning. He "began" when he destroyed his sister (the feeling aspect of himself) and mother, and gave up on having a maternal function available for him. In a way, this point in time represented both the destruction of his inner Eve and any Eve in the outer world. In a straight-line, hierarchical creation-myth construct there is always a transcendent god figure and a hell. The maternal function has been destroyed and paternal primacy takes over. This hell is the end point of the straight line where all the projections end up—a place full of pain, suffering, chaos, and (as pain is felt to be caused by disobeying god) sin.

In order to be able to start to allow another third—a different type of word coming from an inner awareness—a maternal function is needed. This gives form to the formless, and, when good enough, can take away the need for a transcendent god to be created to try to manage pain. This is circularity, and with this in place the mental structure of a hell dissolves.

The capacity to use a maternal function and experience it as the process that alleviates pain enables a different beginning to be countenanced. Time now begins with chaos and disorder, and proceeds to become ordered using a circular maternal function. The third position that results is an awareness of inside, an awareness of the importance of penetrations, and an awareness of the natural world. Jacob, when using an external magical word to order his universe, found himself above the natural world; but when, on occasions, he was able to use a different third—my maternal curiosity which augmented his own—he found himself *in* the natural world.

> I had a dream, I was with my sister for some reason, I don't know why, but we were working together, cooperating, there is something about it that seems important … I was then looking from a room into a bay … a cove … I saw a huge sea creature come up to the surface … it was a humpback whale or something, it was huge and beautiful … there was a woman swimming and it looked like the whale might swim into her—but I knew the whale wasn't dangerous, and as it approached the whale arched over her … it felt like it was a very primitive creature and when I woke I was surprised at the fact I knew it wasn't dangerous—it would have been terrifying to me many years ago.

Emotional pain in all its forms was mostly unavailable to Jacob when he was essentially operating from an Adam-based creation myth—the external thirdness of a magical word and transcendent god—but when he was able to shift his perspective (and location of thirdness), he was able to bear some pain:

> I want to say something that has totally taken me by surprise … I was watching something on TV last night and it was something which I have seen before … at the end,

> I knew what was coming, but this time I found it unutterably sad and I just cried and cried …

We continued with the session during which he was able to connect with a vulnerable aspect of himself, and when I said "Time" he got off the couch and said:

> I have watched a different programme on TV many times and the last scene involves two people saying to each other "See you next time" … I find that unutterably sad too … very, very sad … [*While he was saying this, his face crumpled and he started crying*] … well … bye, thank you.

Jacob had lived most of his life imprisoned in the fortress he had made for himself after destroying the Eve aspect, both in his inner and external worlds. This growing capacity to bear pain reinstated Eve (the penetrated object) as the alleviator of pain. Words could be found to describe and give form to this pain and he was able (at times) to feel a very important connection with me.

This connection also felt intolerable at times, and his oscillation between utilising his "special powers" to control and not feel, and then being more in touch with his terrifying inner world, were shown in a particularly vivid dream:

> The dream was in two parts, the first was a rehearsal and the second was the actual performance. In the rehearsal I was a superhuman trying to defeat a villain and the way I did that was by wearing a striped top … there was something about the stripes and the optical illusion they created that would incapacitate the villain and defeat him. In the rehearsal it all worked smoothly … but then in the actual performance the stripes didn't work … perhaps they weren't defined enough … but anyway, the villain, who was like a devil and had an aura of absolute, powerful dread about him, got hold of me and started to beat me up. Punching me, kicking me, throwing me … there were henchmen who were stabbing me over and over and I was eviscerated … I was still alive when my eye was gouged out and held up in front of my other eye … I couldn't decide if it was to show me my evisceration or for me to see my death … I then woke up.

After telling me this dream he said that his fantasies of being a superhuman go back as far as he can remember, and that they worked in the rehearsal. He said that he was struck by the way time felt to him in the dream, as though it was just happening and that it was everyday … that the torture and evisceration was just so ordinary and everyday.

I responded to this by saying that he felt his super powers did not work with me, but that in having a different kind of relationship every day in our sessions felt like a kind of torture which left him feeling eviscerated. I said that real emotional contact terrified him as he felt it will either end in his or my destruction.

He paused for a while and responded by saying that he wasn't conscious of that, but it was certainly how he felt with his mother. He remembered as a child feeling absolutely certain that he would either die from cancer or suicide … he had an "absolute wish" just to "not be" … to "be nothing" … to not exist. The next few sessions focused a great deal on the sense of there being something inside him that held pain and when his mind failed in some way, he was left with a body full of pain and horror. I became someone who had taken away his superhuman powers and was exposing the horror of what he felt was inside. I was the person who was holding up his eye to himself.

During one session when he arrived with a sense of having little to say, we were able to consider his extreme sense of loneliness when he was with people and his longing to be on his own. This awareness was a very painful one for him.

> I do feel lonely when I am with other people … that resonates very deeply with me … when I'm with people I can operate from a social mask for a while, they don't seem to notice, but then I seek to be alone … in fact I yearn for it … my feeling of having nothing to say might be me insulating myself from not having been here on the weekend … and also the long summer break coming up … like putting on warm clothes in preparation before going out into cold weather …

I responded by saying that I thought the breaks were feeling very painful for him. He replied that he thought it would be easier for him in many ways—he paused for a while, and then said in a very quiet and halting manner that he felt despair and nothingness if he thought about it.

The work with Jacob came to a premature and unfortunate end. After a long summer break, despite having done much work regarding the impact of the break, he felt he did not want to return. He said that he had realised over the break that he had become attached to me and he felt he needed to focus on his own capacities. It was very sad to abruptly end in this way, and I was left keenly feeling the sense of abandonment and pain present in his inner world.

The good, the bad, and the ugly

My first meeting with Elisa was notable as she had brought her own big box of tissues, and because of the impact she had on me. She became pleasurably animated while talking about her father, as though he were a cuddly teddy bear, almost in the same breath as telling me that he had regularly beaten her.

At the end of the session, I accompanied her to the top of the stairs where she hesitated and grabbed the handrail. She said that she got vertigo on stairs.

My thoughts after this initial session left me wondering where the truth was—was her father a cuddly teddy bear, or a cruel and aggressive man? What were her expectations from the work? These seemed both enormous (bringing a box of tissues suggested she felt her feelings would somehow be elicited within the session) and futile, as she would have to be self-sufficient and would not be able to take anything that would be as effective as herself in dealing with what spilled out of her. Inherent in this was the recognition of great pain and need, but also a concurrent expectation of being too much, too big, and having to deal with things herself. The experience left me feeling small and she loomed large in an overpowering and threatening manner.

In response to a traumatic childhood, Elisa had seemingly developed a character which was overpowering, physical, and focused on achievement, perfection, and rules. She was overweight and had created a buffer of fat which would protect her from the blows from her father. She felt that she would somehow succumb to them if she were to lose weight. Her relationships were focused on her being "perfect", and if they failed, it was because she wasn't perfect enough.

In many ways, it could be thought that Elisa had developed a secondary Adam character which created an illusion of power and hierarchy while denigrating or destroying her Eve.

The first stage of the work involved a prolonged phase of her boasting to me. It seemed that session after session she would tell me how indispensable and needed she was and how people envied her. During this stage, she continued to show a great respect for her father, but her attitude towards her mother was derogatory. She wanted to impress me with her accomplishments, skills, and knowledge, and wanted me to see her as perfect. It seemed she had a great deal to prove and was desperate for someone to be proud of her.

We spoke about her need to seem perfect for me and she said that she wanted to become her ideal—she wanted the perfect flat, the perfect job, and the perfect relationship. She told me that she had often been intrigued by the god Janus, who had two faces, and who she felt represented her sense of herself too. She had this capable, competitive, and intelligent side which aroused envy, but the other side went unnoticed, especially within her family.

Her omnipotence in the secondary Adam side of herself was significant—she recounted various incidents where, if it hadn't been for her presence or quick thinking, a disaster might have happened; such as a near car accident in which she was certain that, if anyone else had been driving, she and the others in the car would have been killed. I related this to the work and spoke about her need to drive as it felt so dangerous.

The next phase of the work was marked by a gradual emergence of anger and an ability to tolerate seeing her father in a more negative light. Her need to boast lessened, and she began to touch on areas that she had avoided in earlier sessions, especially the experience of being bullied. A lot of her emerging anger was directed at the people involved in this, but also at her father in relation to his treatment of her. She also described how difficult she had found relationships with women to be, especially at work. This elicited an opportunity to bring my femaleness into the room and she said that she viewed me as neither male nor female, but nonetheless she did feel comfortable with me. During this time I felt she hung onto my every word and seemed to interpret anything I might say as something she needed to do or carry out. She also began to speak of me to others, saying "My analyst says this" and so on. I felt very uncomfortable about this.

The next phase of work began after I had to cancel a session. In previous sessions Elisa had often spoken about her never having to take time off work, even when she was ill, and her contempt of anyone who did. After she suggested that she was fine about the missed session, I reminded her of her view and she became distressed. It emerged that she felt I either didn't care about her and very easily felt I could cancel, or that I must be seriously ill. Towards the end of this session she told me about her visits to see a horse which was in a field close to her childhood home. This horse was very important to her, and as a teenager she used to talk to it, and she "knew" that he understood her by the look in his eyes. She felt that he was always there for her and she could pour her heart out to him.

I felt that I had let her down considerably. In trying to work through this, it transpired that she could no longer see me as being neither male nor female—I had crossed the boundary into either being the neglectful mother/female (by not caring), or the perfectionist, abusive father/male (by deliberately choosing to hurt her), both of whom she felt she had to subjugate her needs to. In order to keep me as the good object that could possibly care for her, she had to create another transference role for me—her horse. One who would not do, or say, anything that might cause a disturbance in her.

In many ways, this experience of being like the horse was not new. I realised that in my being neither male nor female, she had been relating to me as the horse for a long time. It was when I did or said something that challenged, disappointed, or hurt her that I was seen as male or female. I had seemingly been treading a very fine line as the horse, but a line which she had begun to see as an essential and important part of her life.

Her self-image, weight, and sense of femininity had all been constant threads throughout the work with Elisa. She spoke often about how ugly, fat, and unattractive she felt, and about how she had developed bulimia as a teenager. She also spoke regularly about her perception that people found her overpowering and that she had outgrown her parents. At a simple level, we began to understand that her weight and body size had offered her a protection from physical abuse and to give that up felt terrifying.

For Elisa her father was frightening and physically abusive. He demanded perfection and was aggressive when it wasn't achieved. There was no coming together in equality between Elisa's father and mother; in fact the coupling that was present was one which engendered denigration and fear. There could be no thought of this coupling as having produced something loved and good.

Elisa's self-view, as a product of this coupling (a relationship based on power and control), was one of ugliness and abhorrence. In her mind, in the eyes of her father she was a disappointment as she wasn't male and, as she experienced her mother as not taking her into her mind or protecting her, she felt shameful and abhorrent.

The family dynamic consisted of a secondary Adam father figure who owned creativity, subjugated the women in the house, and had a set of rules that all had to abide by. The creation myth in operation would be a religious "in the beginning was the word" one—father's version of reality was the only reality that could be countenanced, and his word was law. Chaos was met with punishment.

Elisa, having been born into this dynamic, was left with the same dilemma Hans Christian Andersen and the boy in *The Emperor's New Clothes* was faced with. Although, instead of being a moment in time, it was a chronic feature of her childhood. Self and reality, or a sacrifice of the mind.

Elisa grew up with a constant need to be perfect—not only did she think that if she managed to be so, she would gain her father's love, but also she would not be punished. In her mind there was a version of herself that she could reach which would be loved, respected, and valued. This featured heavily in the first few months of the work: she constantly brought her achievements and talents in order to gain my approval and make me happy. It greatly confused her when I seemed to not respond to this. In a way, there seemed to be senses of herself which were good, bad, and ugly. Good when she was able to feel she'd fulfilled her father's expectations and rules; bad when she felt she had failed in this, and ugly as her "me", or status of being, was not being received by her mother.

For quite a long time into the work with her, Elisa was not able to tolerate thinking or putting into words anything negative regarding her father. She joined her father in denigrating her mother, not from a position of awareness of how her mother had failed her needs, but from a position of joining in with her father's view of her mother. It was okay to denigrate mother as she wasn't strong enough for her to be afraid of her. My discomfort at Elisa seemingly treating my words as gospel was an indication of this shift from seeing her father as this god figure to seeing me as such.

From this Garden of Eden family dynamic, in which only father had a valid existence, Elisa grew into a considerably confused and unsettled teenager. Her overeating and bulimia might be understood as her desperate wish to feed herself something that enabled some of this chaos to be contained (intuitively knowing that the process requires a penetrating something that needs to be taken in by her), but as it wasn't the penetrative aspect of the maternal function (curiosity) her body quickly rejected it. It might also be thought of as an expression of the reality of her situation—her mother's food was no good and her body expelled it accordingly. Her overeating represented the need and the vomiting became the action that expressed the reality.

It is interesting to note that Elisa's bulimia stopped around the time when she was able to stand up to her father. Suddenly it must have seemed to her that in overeating and feeding herself, something good had been enabled. She was now physically strong and big enough to stop her father. The food was no longer no good, it now benefitted her; but in eating so much, she became fat and hated herself for it.

The only version of events available in the mind of Elisa, initially, was that her father was a good man who was very talented and needed to be obeyed. He was the god in the family who expected all the members to live and achieve according to his wishes. If she failed to meet his expectations, she would be punished as she had not been perfect and it was her fault for failing. Her mother was just another member of the household who was beholden to these rules and who seemed to fail often—hence why she was demeaned by father. Elisa's denigration of her mother was mainly due to the sense that she was not able to follow father's rules and so was not perfect.

This version of events, or story, or family narrative, served to hold Elisa together during her childhood. It was the creation myth from which the family operated and which the family used to orientate themselves within the universe, whilst enabling them to feel they had a structure which held them together. It delineated everybody's position in the family, the hierarchy of power, the ownership of creativity, man's relationship to woman, the nature of the coupling between them, and the relative importance given to each.

Elisa's fascination with the god Janus seemed to indicate an awareness of two potential aspects of herself—one which she was more aware of than the other. It seemed that the story of her father as the god who had to be obeyed and her sense of herself within this structure was available to her; she needed to be perfect to offset punishment and to reach the goal of her father finally loving her.

The other aspect was more hidden and had little or no story of its own. This was her "me"—the pain, hurt, rage, needs, envy, hatred, terror: her passions—which did not have the words for her self to feel she was not abhorrent. She had had enough of an awareness of this aspect of herself to bring a full box of tissues to our first session. She knew that she had many tears, but was also unable to "ordinarily assume" I would be able or willing to reach them, let alone have enough tissues of my own to soak them up.

Her awareness of herself within this family story when she had grown big enough to stand up to her father was of someone who could also be overpowering and bullying. She sensed that she evoked envy and fear in others, while feeling that no one could see another side to her. This fear, that she might become her father, was part of the reason for her to seek help. She did not want to treat any potential children of her own the same way. In order to not become her mother—denigrated, downtrodden, and beaten—she had to become her father. Within this family narrative, these were the only roles available—a god or his subject. Elisa had found a way to become her own god as she had toppled the alpha male from his position, and could now set her own laws. She innately understood the perils of being in this position as she could overpower, overwhelm, dictate, bully, and punish, whilst also knowing that others would hate, envy, and fear her.

This position wasn't without costs, one being her weight—she had to constantly feed herself to keep big enough to not be toppled herself—and another was the unsettled awareness somewhere of another aspect of herself, one that needed a full box of tissues to soak up her tears, one that wobbled on the stairs, one that needed to pour her heart out to her horse, and one which felt deeply hurt, confused, and frightened when I cancelled a session.

From this perspective, it is understandable that she was unable to see me as male or female—both positions would be incredibly problematic. If I were male (in her mind) I would undoubtedly end up taking a position of a god, set my own rules, expect her to be perfect, and punish her when she was not. If I were female, I would become someone ineffective, unable to stand up to father, and having no function. In making me the horse she was very creatively making me something that she could use in a different way. She removed me from the father–mother dynamic and placed me into something she felt was safer to her. Perhaps without this option, we might have been engaged in "analysis interminable" due to the binary oscillating transference. My role became to expand the function of the horse she was accustomed to into a more active one; from the horse who was listening and taking in her words and projections, to a more curious and active presence who could put different words to her experience. In this way, slowly over time, her family narrative was replaced with a living narration of her "me".

She had a sense of her pain being taken in by someone, and so she didn't feel so shameful, ugly, or abhorrent; she became aware of her anger and rage towards her father and mother and they began to be seen in more real terms. She began to not need to feed herself so much as she didn't need to protect herself from him. It was only within the original family narrative or creation myth that all these things were necessary. Her personal creation myth had shifted. She no longer needed to have a story in which a god was powerfully in control and who owned creation. Her relationship with her parents became realistic (not idealised and denigrated)—she saw them for who they were, positive and negative. And, before we ended the work, she was able to see me as a woman.

CHAPTER 25

To myth or not to myth

The whole of a person, both in mind and body, is divided into Adam and Eve from conception. The two psychologies and ways of being need to work together to enable a person to function—again, in both mind and body. In the womb, this wholeness works well, and the Adam and Eve aspects are in a dynamic and equal tension with each other. Post-birth, when trauma has been too great or the environmental provision has been too poor, this dynamic, equal tension is disrupted. If this persists, the balance between Adam and Eve becomes skewed towards Adam. When Adam and Eve are working well together, the person or creature can find an ease of being in the universe. Their needs are being adequately met and trauma can be survived.

Symbolisation can take place from both Adam and Eve, and represents a third position arrived at after an experience which enables some space for thought to take place. It only becomes possible *after* a process has occurred in which a lowering of tension happens. The first symbolisation that the infant becomes aware of is that from Eve in the maternal function; this is the mother's capacity to create an image, idea, word, or thought in her mind in relation to the infant. This symbolisation is an inner awareness of a state of being which belongs to both mother and infant, and is dependent upon her own experience of having had an adequate Eve interaction herself. Both Bion and Winnicott describe this exchange in the container–contained and primary maternal preoccupation experience. Both understood the importance of this, especially in relation to the ongoing emotional and mental well-being of the infant.

If the maternal function has been inadequate or the trauma (perceived or real) too great, then this lowering of tension is only felt after the tumult has been jettisoned or projected. The Eve symbolisation needed is either absent or traumatic in itself; instead of lowering the tension and furnishing the void with Eve words which give a sense of healthy fullness, the infant is left empty and closed off, or becomes full of heightened tumult and toxicity. Adam (who projects) is then felt to be the god that has diminished tension and pain. He, and his processes, become the focus from which the infant orientates himself, as it is felt to be these processes which have solved his pain, rather than the introjective ones. If this continues, the defences, taboos, rules, and religions that are the consequences of this ultimately allow Adam to feel superior, and also mirror the situation in his mind. Instead of feeling diminished by Eve's capacity to create babies, feed them, and enable them to feel safe, S-Adam can now own creativity himself. He can use his symbolisation (a word situated from the external perspective) to name things and create thoughts that can influence the internal child aspect of himself as well as future children he may have too.

This can be seen in many societies which operate according to an alpha-male system. The chimpanzee alpha male controls the society—he gets the best food, he keeps the females for himself, and he hits the females with sticks. He growls and makes a lot of noise to reinforce his position. He is the powerful, godlike figure who all others need to listen to and obey. Symbolisation here is the rudimentary language exhibited by grunts, growls, and shrieks, as well as the concurrent image in the minds of both the alpha male and other members of the society which is associated with the grunt or growl. A shriek from the alpha male has the impact of stopping or changing the behaviour of the other members of the group. He is powerful in that his words represent the beginning of time for this society, as the time he spent with his mother, who fed him, kept him safe, and nurtured him has been destroyed in his mind or forgotten. Any member of the group who might go against this word is punished physically.

This whole system becomes a group who are operating from a creation myth put in place by the alpha male; any other way of being is prevented by the immediacy of the system. The alpha male's word is law and all dilemmas are solved via it. Young chimps learn to play according to their gender: the young males seemingly copying the alpha male by using sticks to beat the females, and the young females carry the sticks as if they were a baby. This shows how much of this society is learned through generations of watching and being subject to the conditions of an alpha male. Symbolisation in these settings becomes focused on control, competition, and power, and the symbolisation that takes precedence is that of Adam.

When ancient human societies have evolved in similar conditions—food being scarce and conditions harsh—it is easy to see how symbolisation might become the preserve of an alpha-male–like figure who would use it to reinforce his position. Laws, taboos, and religions are created which justify, vindicate, and preserve his position. The society then watches and learns and this creation myth becomes established. The inherent guilt and original sin that this then leads to become part of the unconscious and serve to reinforce its structure due to the difficulty in coming to terms with the original sin of having psychologically murdered Eve.

Due to the impoverishment of Eve in these situations, her need for expression becomes stunted and overpowered. She is relegated to the unconscious and has to wait whilst endlessly and compulsively repeating her traumas, until they might find symbolisation of their own.

This symbolisation is of a completely different order to that used by the alpha male or secondary Adam.

Adam words come from the external environment which is felt to be where the projections (the "me") from Adam reside. Thus, the contents of the "me" are felt to be only manageable in an external environment via a paternal process or law (the formation of a superego, the rigid boundaries of taboos, the sense of goodness coming from the following of religious or societal law, and so on), as they have not undergone an adequate maternal function. In this situation external structures dominate the manner of being, but the emptiness that is felt inside due to the lack of Eve words which give fullness constantly demands attention. Perhaps after many thousands of years of Adam dominating the symbolic realm in society, the consequence is a population riddled with drug, food, and alcohol problems.

Eve words come from an inner awareness, and are the symbolic outcome of the maternal function. When this works well, it leaves the infant feeling known and full of a sense of who he is. The tumults and tensions have been reduced, not by an external force, but by a body who has taken them in and has managed to not only survive but also to create a third aspect to it. It is important that the infant knows that this word, or thought, or image, belongs to both the mother and the infant. In this way, he knows that the tumult is something that the mother is intimately aware of, that she has been able to feel it and then stand apart from it to begin to formulate it into a survivable and tolerable feeling. Bion was aware of these two different sources of words or thought—his "no memory and desire" was trying to diminish a certain type of thought that he felt got in the way of being able to be fully with a patient. When Adam and Eve are felt to be equal in both the mind and society, a person has both types of word available to them. They are then able to access a symbolic realm appropriate for the occasion. Containing, nurturing, admonishing, reining in, and so on. When it comes from secondary Adam and Eve working in apparent isolation, it is none of these things—it can only punish, control, demean, or be ineffective.

What sets us apart from possibly all other animals isn't the ability to symbolise (many primates can too): it is the extent to which we have taken symbolisation—the sheer complexity of the language we use and how much we have forsaken the un-symbolised and Eve-symbolised realms. Each advance in symbolisation (from no words, to words, to written) has involved a corresponding impact on our psyches. The power of naming is represented across the world in creation myths—it is given a status of magic, of a sense of time beginning at that point, and also generally of being a male preserve. It is still present in christenings, baptisms, law making, and the labelling impact of diagnoses. This type of word comes from secondary Adam, and comes about from an alpha-male Adam, who in the history of mankind was also the creator of religion.

In this environment, words from Eve become effectively wordless, banished to the unconscious and having to fight for representation and expression. An impact of this is the evolution of myth.

As previously stated, I see myth as serving a holding or containing purpose, a representation of what is known about the universe and the way of life, as well as providing answers to the unknown or mysterious forces of nature too. Added to this also has to be the justification or vindication of a particular way of life or state of mind. Myth serves all of these functions, and I see that myth could have arisen out of the situation described above.

When most words that have a presence in society are those from S-Adam then the words from Eve go unrepresented in the mind. Even though they are not conscious, they still exert an influence and this influence might be seen in two ways. The first is the incessant need for expression that every experience (especially traumatic ones) wields. The second influence is the need for a structure to provide some sort of containing function. In a world where S-Adam is dominant and Eve, and her words, have been relegated to the unconscious, then the normal container–contained dynamic function is not available. A structure needs to be found which might serve as a substitute for this.

I feel that myth provides all of this. A place where the words are consciously describing a situation that satisfies S-Adam (gods, male power, and female subservience are all described copiously in myths); a story which tends to justify and vindicate the particular system in place; a story which can evolve or move according to knowledge, but also answers the mysteries of the unknown; a story which has meanings that are hidden or serve as allegories which gives Eve a voice, and a story which itself becomes a containing structure as that function has been stripped away from Eve.

The further human kind moves away from nature, the more these external containing structures are needed. They hold the person together in relation to the "who". This who needs a frame or structure which serves as a narrative which provides all that the moving away from nature and the destruction of Eve entails.

When writing evolved, and spoken words and thoughts could be written, suddenly eternal life was possible. Myths could be written down and the author who originally composed them could have his own creation myth, structure of life, religion, god, supremacy, hierarchical construct, and understanding of the world set in stone for ever. From the immediacy of a live metaphor, they became dead ones that were handed down from ancient fathers whose word needed to be heeded. The transition from no words to words had impacted the psyche in that it facilitated the birth of the paternal function and then resulted in the unconscious wish for S-Adam to own creation for himself. When the spoken word then transitioned to become the written word, the psyche was impacted again. The dynamic container of an oral myth became the stultified and rigid container of the written myth.

The horse has bolted, so to speak; Adam symbolisation is here to stay and the many positives it has given us are obvious. However, there are also consequences, and the biggest consequence of all is the subjugation of Eve and nature. The argument that I have put forward here is that it is the position Eve finds herself in (pushed to the unconscious) that brings about the need for myth and other creative representations. So, am I saying that all myth and creativity (scientific as well as artistic) is bad? No. I am saying that myth, when it is alive, dynamic, and is able to grow according to need, is an essential part of life. Myth which is dead and serves as a tool for S-Adam to justify his position comes with an enormous cost—it really does bring with it suffering, sin, pain, and, as Langdon-Davies says (1938, pp. 89–98), the cloistering of the entire female sex.

Perhaps science has always been the frontier of bringing Eve out of her prison in that it is built upon discovery, curiosity, not knowing, and putting to one side the stagnant creation myths of the day—like with Mendeleev. This is an Eve—tolerating the unknown, being curious, discovering things—rather than an Adam domain. Science, in its purest form, belongs to Eve. Mark Twain knew this, as his book *The Diaries of Adam and Eve* (1904–05) attests. He depicts Eve as being the scientist who experiments, is constantly curious, and discovers. It is she who wants to know the insides of things and knows the right words (names) to apply to them. She doesn't have to think about it, she knows—it comes from a place deep inside her. Adam ruminates and delays and cannot easily think of a name, but the name he eventually arrives at is divorced from nature. Eve is in nature, whilst Adam is more apart from nature. Adam is initially frustrated with Eve, thinking her constant curiosity to be wearisome and threatening, when he wishes to just build. He then gains the insight or realisation that he would rather be outside Eden and with her, her delight, and curiosity with the world, than in Eden alone. Interestingly, Twain also depicts Eve hiding the birth of Cain and Abel from Adam, as if he knew that Adam would not be able to countenance the knowledge of Eve having given birth. The final entry in the Adam section of the diary is "wheresoever she was; there was Eden" (p. 109).

Stagnant myths (straight-line myths in the context of this book) and religions serve to keep S-Adam in a position of priority and importance, not only in external situations, but also within the mind. The challenge to this, over history, has been science in all its forms (astronomy and Galileo; the anatomists; Darwin and *The Origin of Species*, and so on), unorthodox literature, myth, and art, and most of all woman. The most innovative and effective of all forms of creativity is that which can access the Eve within, to draw on something that is a result of curiosity, nature, and the reservoir of innate knowledge of nature that Eve possesses. Curiosity, in the sense I am using it here, is that which is interested in the inside of something—wishes to be inside and actively positions itself inside. Not in a way that bestows gratification on either the curious object or the object of curiosity, but in a way which is a wish to become aware of an inner state of being. This function firmly belongs to Eve. If Adam is curious, it is a curiosity that is more about cause and effect. Eve wishes to see inside—Adam wishes to find out what might happen when he does something. The biggest advances in science have been when the scientists have allowed the Eve aspects of their minds to have a presence.

Freud used myth as a helpful elucidation of many of his thoughts and theories—famously the Oedipus myth led to his Oedipus complex. R. A. Segal (1999) explores the differences between Freud and Jung in their approach and thoughts about myth, noting that "Rather than a defence against the naked expression of the unconscious, as for Freud, myth, for Jung is the naked expression of the unconscious" (p. 83). Thus for both Freud and Jung, mythic thinking is dream thinking, but they differ on the nature of what that entails. For Freud, myths, like dreams, represent a mode of expression within which a compromise between the unconscious and conscious world has been attained. The existence of defences against becoming aware of the unconscious render both the dream and the myth to be obscure, and a hidden meaning is needed to be found. Jung, on the other hand, felt that both dreams and myths *were* the unconscious.

If they both agreed that dreams and myths symbolise the unconscious in one way or other, then perhaps they are disagreeing on the mode of symbolisation. For Jung, he feels that dreams and myths represent something that emanates directly from what is unconscious and, in the context of this book, he is suggesting that it is communication directly from Eve herself. Freud suggests that it is a compromise between something that is unexpressed and the everyday defences that exist to prevent awareness of this something. Thus, the nature of the dream and the myth become dominated by Adam symbolism, and Eve needs to be discovered—the manifest and latent contents. Perhaps the mistake they both made was to consider it an either/or question. From the understanding arrived at from considering the mind to be both Adam and Eve, the nature of dreams and myth will differ depending upon which form of symbolisation is dominant. In an Adam-dominated conscious mind, the defences against an awareness of Eve will strip away symbolisation from her; thus, dreams and myth will have a latent and manifest content. When a mind is working in a dynamic and mostly equal tension between Adam and Eve, then the dream and myth content would be mixed. Eve symbolisation would be manifest alongside that from Adam.

In working through my hermeneutic loop in this book, I have arrived at a different place to the one I started from.

This process, although perhaps not as rigorous as some might like, has been incredibly important to me. It has been a highly personal endeavour, one which has been necessary and exacting. The awareness of the importance of myth has been an important revelation to me. It is not just an awareness on a cognitive, understanding level—it is a deep, fundamental awareness. In order to emerge from our parents' care, we need a working myth, or structure, by which we can orientate ourselves in the universe. Not only in the sense of how we might conceive of ourselves and others, but also about how we *are* conceived in the natural order of the universe. Until this myth has been constructed, often in our unconscious, we are tied to our parents.

As we have seen, Géza Róheim (1971, pp. 122–132) argues that humans are born too soon and so are more dependent upon their mothers than other animals. He sees culture, including myth, to have arisen from this experience—culture being a sublimation of infantile attachments, losses, and fears. The process of being able to emerge from this dependency therefore involves the formation of something that would serve as a substitute for the mother's care. This has been the subject of much theorising—Klein's introjection of the good object; Winnicott's facilitating maternal environment and transitional objects; Bion's container–contained; and much more. What I have discovered is that myth, in particular the creation myth, is a very important part of this emergence.

Myth is the product of the coming together of Adam and Eve. It is Adam's action and mobility coupled with Eve's awareness of states of being—pain, love, need, vulnerability, and so on—and her need to have these states expressed. The myth is a structure which combines the two in a way which enables both to have life. Adam's action is a big feature of all myth and Eve's pain is also present, often without actually being said. The whole story itself provides the structure which serves as a maternal substitute. If the gender dynamic within society or the family is not balanced enough, or the experience of maternal care has not been good enough, then the myth that is in place when the child has moved away from mother will be Adam biased. It will be an unconscious belief in a magical creation myth which may well elevate Adam to a godlike status. Eve will need to be denigrated and controlled. Gratification takes over from the real experience of being with another and the joy that that can elicit.

Working with each patient to discover their own personal myth involves not only giving a narration or words to the Eve within them, but ultimately it involves enabling a new myth to be written. Their Eve has been heard and been with—this allows a magical creation myth to evolve into a different myth, based more in nature and reality.

Money-Kyrle's three facts of life fits this well too (1968, p. 693). He felt that it is a lifelong endeavour to come to a fundamental awareness of the fact that we are all made from the sexual coupling of our parents, the fact that we need each other, and the fact that we are going to die. That is, we are all created by the coming together of an egg and a sperm, we are all in need of others to exchange aspects of our experience with (undergo the penetrative processes), we are all part of nature and the universe, and we are not special in that we will return to a particulate state like everything else. Chris Mawson, in his book *Psychoanalysis and Anxiety: From Knowing to Being* (2019), writes about this:

> A truthful picture of the couple—first as represented by the conjunction of mouth and nipple, then infant and breast, infant and mother and so on, as foundational for the parental couple itself, is anathema to the omnipotence supporting narcissism … The stories told by the self to the self in order to avert such a catastrophe … can be considered instances of what Bion was exploring … in which every conceivable theory or model is allowed to be considered, except the one closest to the truth. (p. 170)

The myth we create in order to enter adulthood is one which examines each of these facts. What we come up with is our own personal creation myth. If that is an oral one, in the sense that I have discussed in previous chapters, then it can be flexible, evolve, and take account of differing experiences. However, if it is a written one, it is very difficult for it to develop or evolve over time.

As psychoanalysts, we have a duty to discover what myth we ourselves might be operating from. Perhaps, in a way, an analyst who is operating from an Adam-biased myth would consider any patient whose myth does not have an Adam bias as psychotic. Maybe (from the point of view of these analysts) neurosis can be defined as those disturbances which arise from difficulties within an Adam-biased myth, while psychosis can be defined as a disturbance from not having an Adam-biased myth in operation. Again, maybe an analyst can only effectively work with patients with whom they share a similar creation myth.

Perhaps severe disturbance exists as the structures endemic in society are Adam-biased—and for those who have been traumatised, are at the bottom of the hierarchy, and have been parentally failed, these myths do not suffice. This suggests that those working with severe disturbance would only be effective if they are orientating themselves to others, nature, and the world from a creation myth which is not Adam biased.

In understanding that creation myths are essential and that no one can enter adulthood without one, the next awareness must be how these creation myths can differ. From oral to written, from being a straight line to being a hermeneutic loop, from being Adam or Eve biased to being one which brings the two together as an equal couple; from being a narrative to becoming a narration. In understanding the roots of the differences between these myths, significant therapeutic development becomes possible.

CHAPTER 26

Final thoughts

In working through my hermeneutic loop in this book, I have arrived at a different place to the one I started from, but as T. S. Eliot suggests, it is also the same place, known in a different way:

> We shall not cease from exploration
> And the end of all our exploring
> Will be to arrive where we started
> And know the place for the first time.
> Through the unknown, unremembered gate
> When the last of earth left to discover
> Is that which was the beginning;
> At the source of the longest river
> The voice of the hidden waterfall
> And the children in the apple-tree
>
> Not known, because not looked for
> But heard, half-heard, in the stillness
> Between two waves of the sea.
> Quick now, here, now, always—
> A condition of complete simplicity
> (Costing not less than everything)
> And all shall be well and
> All manner of thing shall be well

When the tongues of flames are in-folded
Into the crowned knot of fire
And the fire and the rose are one.

From "Little Gidding" (2004, pp. 197–198)

From my memory of being taken to the derelict buildings of my childhood, and the wish to rebuild something, accompanied by a painful shame in the awareness of having such a wish, I feel like I have arrived at my beginning. I have reconfigured and rebuilt my collapsed creation myth and, in writing about the process of this, I have also realised that shame is no longer such a paralysing presence.

I believe that this memory has been so vivid and persistent as it represented my sense of something being profoundly broken. If you like, it is the space between having a functioning Adam-biased myth and a myth which answers well enough Money-Kyrle's facts of life and the vicissitudes of penetration. I did not bring these buildings down due to destructiveness, envy, or aggression; they were collapsed because of generational family pains and difficulties which left all members struggling to find a structure which could offer the security and sense of being that was needed. The derelict buildings also represented an awareness at some level of how inadequate an Adam-biased myth is. In a way, if I tried to rebuild something according to an Adam-biased myth, then it would need to be a bigger house than before, which would inevitably collapse again, and need to be built up again as a palace, which would inevitably collapse and so on.

I have understood my shame to be about the Eve part of me that hadn't been received well enough to provide a living narration. The derelict buildings represented in stark terms the truth that I didn't have a working creation myth and I believe this existential situation is always felt to be a deeply shameful position. Due to this shame, I became unable to acknowledge my wish to rebuild as then everyone would know that I didn't have a structure already in place (that is, I didn't have a creation myth, therefore I hadn't had a good enough parental experience and therefore there must be something abhorrent about me that had prevented it). It is only in being able to engage in a living narration with someone that the essential creation myths, buildings, and structures can be built.

This book, alongside my analysis, has enabled me to arrive at my own creation myth. It is not definitive or absolute and undoubtedly will undergo further revisions, but nonetheless, it is a structure from which I can be curious, adventurous, and robust. It is firmly based in the natural order of things and what goes on in between. It is built from an awareness of both Adam and Eve, and how they need to come together in equality. It is by no means a palace, rather a *bwthyn fach* (a small cottage) which is able to contain my Eve history, my family dynamics, my awareness of life and death, and, most importantly, gives me a secure sense of who I am.

Another question that the writing of this book has brought to the fore of my mind is, "What exactly do I believe in?" It is easily apparent to those readers that have persisted to the end of this book that I have arrived at a disbelief in a transcendent god. Unlike Augustine, I cannot believe in a deity who is thought to have created or ordered life and the universe, leaving man in a "special position". For me, the truly awe-inspiring and bewildering mystery of the universe lies in that first interaction between speck and other-speck, which then went on to be part of life. This is where the perhaps unanswerable and unknowable mystery lies, and therefore, if I believe in anything, I believe in the power that exists in that interaction. This is the wonder by which a speck full of tumult can meet another speck and have that tumult reduced, the wonder of the interaction between sperm and egg, between Adam and Eve, between child and parent, and between patient and analyst. I see that power existing in all particles and life, and perhaps in many ways the battle between Augustine and Pelagius was truly a battle between a wish to be above nature and this interaction, and a deep awareness of being in nature and an understanding of the power of this interaction. For me, this—if there is a deity—is the site of its presence and expression. The universe itself, with all particles interacting to create a myriad of entities, provides the very structure from which an infant can emerge in safety. The periodic table, a structure which holds the universe, becomes the creation myth which can provide meaning, existence, interaction, and containment, as well as space for the unknown too.

The dispute between Augustine and Pelagius was really the perpetual disagreement between Adam and Eve about who is felt to own creativity, symbolisation, and ultimately to manage pain. Both feel there is a deity or mysterious power that is the source of all things—Augustine places this source in the external, thereby prioritising Adam symbolisation and management of pain. The inevitable outcome of this position is an unconscious or original sin which can only be managed by a more powerful external father.

Pelagius places it in the internal, thereby recognising Eve and her capacity to ameliorate pain. The outcome of this situation is a sense of inner goodness. The prioritisation of Adam, his symbolism, creativity, and pain management inevitably leads to the formation of a transcendent god, taboo, and laws which prevent awareness of Eve, and great suffering for those at the bottom of the hierarchical structures which are always present.

This question about where god might reside becomes: where is it better to manage pain, chaos, or tumult? Where is the source of creation? And, which word has power? In being placed either internally or externally, the assumed content of the internal and the unconscious also shifts. With an Adam-based creation myth in operation, the internal and the unconscious become full of the demons, monsters, and hell that is the end of the straight-line process in place. This also becomes equated with Eve as she has been left unrepresented in the mind. With a more natural-based creation myth in operation the nature of chaos or tumult is neither good nor bad; it actually consists of an imperative inherent within each of us to intimately connect with another in order to create form from formlessness. It is the awareness of an existential anxiety that comes from the two sources of a felt formlessness, and the need to find another to connect with to alleviate it.

If pain is felt to be managed in the external location, Adam can own all of these powers; he manages pain by projection and creating hierarchies; he owns creation for himself and his word is law. However, instead of becoming full of a sense of who he is, he is left empty, and has to fill himself with substitutes. In the internal location, pain is managed by a circular exchange process; bodies are used to contain and render the tumult more tolerable; the creative process becomes the product of this interaction and the word generated is felt to be substantive.

Creation myths throughout time have oscillated between locating the answers to the questions about ownership of creation, symbolisation, and pain management either inside or outside. This is shown by the myths which emphasise either a female or male deity as being the source of all. For the last 4,000 years or so, the answers to these questions, in the myths available, have settled on the external, male source. In the universal acceptance of this beginning, much damage is perpetuated, and any psychoanalytic theory which is arrived at from this given must be thought of as fundamentally flawed.

In placing pleasure, sexuality, desire, destructiveness, aggression, envy, and greed as being the original and orientating factors in life, analytic theory is unconsciously removing the human condition from nature. The creation myth it perpetuates is an Adam-based one and Eve is relegated (at best) to the unconscious. This situation, in effect, is the trapping of mankind into the characterisation present within a story created by an alpha male and becomes deeply misogynistic and damaging to Eve everywhere.

In reality, the beginning is the interaction between speck and other-speck, and the forces at play inherent in this interaction are eternal. The first experience that initiates any object-seeking behaviour is pain, tumult, and chaos, leading to an action to seek another for it to be alleviated (not a seeking of pleasure). This can only be achieved by a maternal function which brings order and form to the chaos. It is in the attempted management of this chaos and pain that pleasure and gratification can become overly cathected or imbued with a power they don't really have.

In order not to become trapped as a character in the story created by Adam, therefore, pain and its management through a penetrative maternal function need to take a primary position in any theory; while those processes of sexuality, destructiveness, and pleasure need to be seen as secondary. This allows a nature-based creation myth to be in place and an equality between Adam and Eve to exist.

In returning to a beginning and allowing first thoughts, I feel I can begin to "know the place for the first time". Eliot's poem becomes a description of Adam's journey towards ownership of the earth along with a corresponding disconnect with the beginning and Eve. The children of the Garden of Eden who existed before God was created cannot be known, because the Adam-dominated adult never looks for them, leaving a world full of suffering, misogyny, racism, habitat destruction and climate crisis. To be able to find them, stillness and simplicity are needed, which, as Eliot says, "cost(s) not less than everything". The foregoing of Adam, for Adam, does feel like it costs the world, as it takes away his material ownership of it and Eve, but until he is foregone, the cost to the rest of the world *is* everything.

References

Adams, H. (1995). *The Education of Henry Adams*. J. Gooder (Ed.). London: Penguin.

Allen, J. P. (2014). *Middle Egyptian: An Introduction to the Language and Culture of Hieroglyphs*. Cambridge: Cambridge University Press.

Bell, M. (2020). Private communication.

Bion, W. R. (1962). *Learning from Experience*. In: C. Mawson (Ed.), *The Complete Works of W. R. Bion, Vol. 4* (pp. 261–365). London: Routledge, 2014.

Bion, W. R. (1967). *Second Thoughts: Selected Papers on Psychoanalysis*. London: Karnac, 2007.

Bion, W. R. (1968–69). Further cogitations. In: C. Mawson (Ed.), *The Complete Works of W. R. Bion, Vol. 15* (pp. 61–88). London: Routledge, 2014.

Bion, W. R. (1970). *Attention and Interpretation*. In: C. Mawson (Ed.), *The Complete Works of W. R. Bion, Vol. 6* (pp. 221–330). London: Routledge, 2014.

Bion, W. R. (1975). *Memoir of a Dream*. In: C. Mawson (Ed.), *The Complete Works of W. R. Bion, Vol. 12* (pp. 11–201). London: Routledge, 2014.

Bion, W. R. (1977a). *Bion in New York and Sao Paulo: New York*. In: C. Mawson (Ed.), *The Complete Works of W. R. Bion, Vol. 8* (pp. 235–311). London: Routledge, 2014.

Bion, W. R. (1977b). New and improved. In: C. Mawson (Ed.), *The Complete Works of W. R. Bion, Vol. 15* (pp. 47–58). London: Routledge, 2014.

Bion, W. R. (1979). *The Dawn of Oblivion*. In: *A Memoir of the Future* (pp. 427–578). London: Karnac, 1991.

Bion, W. R. (1991). *Cogitations*. In: C. Mawson (Ed.), *The Complete Works of W. R. Bion, Vol. 11*. London: Routledge, 2014.

Bott Spillius, E., Milton, J., Garvey, P., Couve, C., & Steiner, D. (Eds.) (2011). *The New Dictionary of Kleinian Thought*. Hove, UK: Routledge.

Browning, R. (1957). *The Poetical Works of Robert Browning*. London: Oxford University Press.

Caputo, J. D. (2018). *Hermeneutics: Facts and Interpretations in the Age of Information*. London: Penguin.

Cartwright, S. (1852). Diseases and peculiarities of the Negro race. *Southern Quarterly Review, 22*(43): 49–63.

Cather, W. (1913). *O Pioneers!*. Boston, MA: Houghton Mifflin.

de Waal, F. D. M. (2006). Bonobo sex and society. *Scientific American Special Editions, 16*(3): https://scientificamerican.com/article/bonobo-sex-and-society-2006-06/ [last accessed November 25, 2020].

Eliade, M. (1976). *Myths, Rites, Symbols*. 2 vols. W. C. Beane & W. G. Doty (Eds.). New York: Harper Colophon.

Eliot, T. S. (2004). *The Complete Poems and Plays*. London: Faber & Faber.

Ferenczi, S. (1949). Confusion of tongues between the adult and the child. *The International Journal of Psycho-Analysis, 30*: 225–230.

Frank, D. C., & Frank, J. (Eds.) (2005). *The Stories of Hans Christian Andersen: A New Translation from the Danish*. Durham, NC: Duke University Press.

Freud, S. (1912e). Recommendations to Physicians Practising Psycho-Analysis. *S. E., 12*: 109–120. London : Hogarth.

Freud, S. (1912–13). *Totem and Taboo. S. E., 13*: 1–162. London: Hogarth.

Freud, S. (1920g). *Beyond the Pleasure Principle. S. E., 18*: 7–64. London: Hogarth.

Freud, S. (1923b). *The Ego and the Id. S. E., 19*: 3–66. London: Hogarth.

Freud, S. (1930a). *Civilization and Its Discontents. S. E., 21*: 59–145. London: Hogarth.

Freud, S. (1939a). *Moses and Monotheism. S. E., 23*: 3–137. London: Hogarth.

Freud, S. (1940a). *An Outline of Psycho-analysis. S. E. 23*: 141–208. London: Hogarth.

Gibson, J. C. L. (1981). *The Daily Study Bible: Genesis, Vol. I*. Edinburgh: Saint Andrew.

Good News Study Bible, The. 2nd edition edn. Swindon, UK: The Bible Societies, 1994.

Greenblatt, S. (2017). *The Rise and Fall of Adam and Eve: The Story that Created Us*. London: Penguin.

Hadas, P. (1976). *The Passion of Lilith*. St. Louis, MO: Cauldron.

Hamilton, V. (1992). *In the Beginning: Creation Stories from Around the World*. London: Pavilion.

Harris, R. (2015). The hermeneutic loop: framework for the hero's journey. https://yourheroicjourney.com/the-hermeneutic-foundation-of-the-heros-journey-2/ [last accessed November 9, 2020].

Hart, G. (1990). *Egyptian Myths: The Legendary Past*. London: British Museum.

Hoagland, T. (2019). Among the intellectuals. *The New Yorker*, September 2, 2019. https://newyorker.com/magazine/2019/09/02/among-the-intellectuals [last accessed November 25, 2020].

Hurwitz, S. (1992). *Lilith—The First Eve: Historical and Psychological Aspects of the Dark Feminine* (English edition). Einsiedeln, Switzerland: Daimon, 2009.

Ionesco, E. (1971). *Present Past, Past Present: A Personal Memoir*. Boston, MA: Da Capo.

Jacobs, J., & Broydé, I. (1906). ZOHAR (called also in the earlier literature Midrash ha-Zohar and Midrash de-Rabbi Shim'on ben Yohai). *Jewish Encyclopedia*. http://jewishencyclopedia.com/articles/15278-zohar [last accessed November 25, 2020].

Keats, J. B. (1899). *The Complete Poetical Works and Letters of John Keats*. Cambridge: Houghton Mifflin.

Klein, M. (1946). Notes on some schizoid mechanisms. In: *Envy and Gratitude and Other Works, 1946–1963* (pp. 1–24). London: Vintage, 1997.

Klein, M. (1957). Envy and gratitude. In: *Envy and Gratitude and Other Works, 1946–1963* (pp. 176–235). London: Vintage, 1997.

Klein, M. (1958). On the development of mental functioning. In: *Envy and Gratitude and Other Works, 1946–1963* (pp. 236–246). London: Vintage, 1997.

Lang, A. (1901). *Magic and Religion*. London: Longmans, Green.

Langdon-Davies, J. (1938). *A Short History of Women: A Revealing Record of Customs and Practices Governing the Position of Women from the Earliest Times Down to the Present Day*. London: Watts.

Lewis, C. S. (1942). *A Preface to Paradise Lost*. London: Oxford University Press.

Mathis, A. (2016, April 17). Which subjects are underrepresented in contemporary fiction? *The New York Times*, https://nytimes.com/2016/04/17/books/review/which-subjects-are-underrepresented-in-contemporary-fiction.html [last accessed November 25, 2020].

Mawson, C. (2014). Editor's introduction. In: *The Complete Works of W. R. Bion, Vol. 4* (pp. 249–257). London: Routledge.

Mawson, C. (2019). *Psychoanalysis and Anxiety: From Knowing to Being*. Abingdon, UK: Routledge.

Money-Kryle, R. E. (1968). Cognitive development. *International Journal of Psychoanalysis, 49*: 691–698.

Morrison, T. (1993). Interview on PBS. https://youtube.com/watch?v=lsiETgcYM7s [last accessed November 25, 2020].

Newell, J. P. (1999). *The Book of Creation: The Practice of Celtic Spirituality*. Norwich, UK: Canterbury.

Orzel, C. (2020). How Were Atoms Created? *Forbes*. https://forbes.com/sites/chadorzel/2020/05/12/how-were-atoms-created/?sh=20ea24f31a50 [last accessed November 24, 2020].

Phillpotts, E. (1918). *A Shadow Passes*. London: Cecil Palmer & Hayward.

Plato (360 BCE). *The Symposium and Other Dialogues*. M. Joyce (Trans.). London: Dent, 1964.

Regulski, I. (2016). The origins and early development of writing in Egypt. *Oxford Handbooks Online*. https://doi.org/10.1093/oxfordhb/9780199935413.013.61 [last accessed November 25, 2020].

Róheim, G. (1971). *The Origin and Function of Culture*. New York: Anchor.

Rosenfeld, H. (1965). On the psychopathology of narcissism. In: *Psychotic States* (pp. 169–179). London: Hogarth.

Rosenfeld, H. (2002). Afterthought: changing theories and changing techniques in psychoanalysis. In: D. Tuckett (Ed.), *Impasse and Interpretation: Therapeutic and Anti-therapeutic Factors in the Psychoanalytic Treatment of Psychotic, Borderline, and Neurotic Patients*. Hove, UK: Brunner-Routledge.

Rovelli, C. (2016). *Seven Brief Lessons on Physics*. London: Penguin.

Rushdie, S. (2008). *Midnight's Children*. London: Vintage.

Sacks, O. (2001). *Uncle Tungsten: Memories of a Chemical Boyhood*. London: Picador.

Savery, D. S. (2018). *Echoism: The Silenced Response to Narcissism*. London: Routledge.

Schiller, F. (1795). *On the Aesthetic Education of Man*. K. Tribe (Trans.). London: Penguin, 2016.

Schopf, J. W., Kitajima, K., Spicuzza, M. J., Kudryavtsev, A. B., & Valley, J. W. (2018). SIMS analyses of the oldest known assemblage of microfossils. *Proceedings of the National Academy of Sciences of the United States of America, 115*(1): 53–58.

Segal, H. (1950). Some aspects of the analysis of a schizophrenic. In: *The Work of Hanna Segal*. New York: Jason Aronson, 1981.

Segal, R. A. (1999). *Theorizing About Myth*. Amherst, MA: University of Massachusetts Press.

Seth, A. (2017). Your brain hallucinates your conscious reality. *TED2017*, https://ted.com/talks/anil_seth_your_brain_hallucinates_your_conscious_reality/transcript [last accessed November 13, 2020].

Shorter Oxford English Dictionary, The (2002). 2 vols. Oxford: Oxford University Press.

Stark, F. (1977). *Letters.. Vol. 4, Bridge of the Levant 1940–43*. L. Moorehead (Ed.). Salisbury, UK: Michael Russell.

Thoreau, H. D. (1882). *Early Spring in Massachusetts*. Boston, MA: Houghton Mifflin.

Twain, M. (1927). *More Maxims of Mark*. M. Johnson (Ed.). Private Printing.

Twain, M. (1904–05). *The Diaries of Adam and Eve*. San Francisco, CA: Fair Oaks, 1997.

Tyson, N. D. (2012, March 5). Neil DeGrasse Tyson on the most astounding fact in the universe (video). *The Washington Post*. https://washingtonpost.com/blogs/blogpost/post/neil-degrasse-tyson-on-the-most-astounding-fact-in-the-universe-video/2012/03/05/gIQAZwv6sR_blog.html [last accessed November 25, 2020].

Viviano, P. A. (1999). Source criticism. In: S. R. Haynes & S. L. McKenzie (Eds.), *To Each Its Own Meaning: An Introduction to Biblical Criticisms and Their Application* (pp. 35–57). Louisville, KY: Westminster John Knox.

Vital, C. (2015). *The Tree of Life, Volume One: The Palace of Adam Kadmon*. English-Hebrew edition. E. Colle & H. Colle (Trans.). London: Amazon.

Von Franz, M.-L. (1995). *Creation Myths*, revised edition. Boulder, CO: Shambhala.

Williams, M. H. (2019). *Embracing Lilith*. Circulos Tenebris Matrem Arcanas.

Winnicott, D. W. (1965). *The Maturational Processes and the Facilitating Environment*. London: Karnac, 2007.

Winnicott, D. W. (1971). *Playing and Reality*. London: Routledge, 2005.

Winnicott, D. W. (1975). *Through Paediatrics to Psychoanalysis: Collected Papers*. London: Karnac, 1984.

Zulueta, F. de (2006). *From Pain to Violence: The Traumatic Roots of Destructiveness*. Chichester, UK: John Wiley.

Acknowledgements

There are many people who have constantly encouraged, supported, and remained enthusiastic during the process of first thinking about Adam and Eve, and subsequently the eventual writing of this book. These people, to varying extents, have offered their time, attention, and patience during countless hours spent engaged in talking over the ideas, and also the reading of drafts. These very important friends are Tricia Coleman, Jenny Hodder, Janet Land, Liz Winning, and especially Matthew Bell who has read through the entire draft many times and had faith in this book when, at times, I had lost it. I will be eternally grateful.

Jenny Hodder, along with reading through the draft, also very generously created the paintings of Speck and The Garden. She did this with little to work from, except her imagination, and I am both pleased and grateful to include them in this book.

Other people who have been instrumental in offering support and encouragement, especially during my training, are Viqui Rosenberg, Julia Sandelson, and Joscelyn Richards. I wish to thank them, along with my analyst, for helping me through this soul-searching time.

A special thanks goes to Kate Pearce from Phoenix Publishing. I met her in 2019 at a conference and she too has been very generous with her time and encouragement when I just had disparate pieces of writing with little structure holding them together.

My family has been unstintingly supportive, and they too seemed to have a faith in me that I found difficult to have in myself. They have read through drafts and offered not only their perspective on what I had written, but also their expertise to help me finalise the book. I could not have done so without them.

And, of course, I thank Chris Mawson for enabling me to "find" the book he seemed to think I had within me. There are no words that could suffice in describing the depth of my gratitude.

About the author

Jayne Hankinson is a member of the British Psychoanalytic Association and the International Psychoanalytical Association, and has been working in the field of psychoanalysis for almost ten years. Prior to her training she was a psychodynamic counsellor, and has been engaged in either training or post-qualification counselling and psychoanalysis for about twenty years.

During this time she has worked in a variety of counselling agencies, and has also spent two years at an NHS psychotherapy and psychiatric unit. Presently, she has a private psychoanalytic practice, and works as a supervisor, near High Wycombe in Buckinghamshire.

Before she entered into the counselling and psychoanalytic world, she was a secondary school science teacher.

Index